DATE DUE

Alternative
Work Schedules:

Selecting . . .
Implementing . . .
and Evaluating

Alternative Work Schedules:

Selecting . . .
Implementing . . .
and Evaluating

Simcha Ronen

DOW JONES-IRWIN
Homewood, Illinois 60430

This publication is designed to provide accurate and
authoritative information in regard to the subject matter
covered. It is sold with the understanding that the
publisher is not engaged in rendering legal, accounting, or
other professional service. If legal advice or other expert
assistance is required, the services of a competent
professional person should be sought.

*From a Declaration of Principles jointly adopted by a Committee
of the American Bar Association and a Committee of Publishers.*

ISBN 0-87094-511-4

Library of Congress Catalog Card No. 84–70601

Printed in the United States of America

1 2 3 4 5 6 7 8 9 0 K 1 0 9 8 7 6 5 4

Dedicated to
Yaacov, Batsheva, Harold, and Bernice
Who always extend themselves beyond all schedules

Preface

The purpose of this book is threefold. First, it provides policymakers, executives, and students of organizations with the rationale for considering alternative schedules and choosing the one that best suits their needs. This purpose is achieved by reviewing the relevant trends in human resource management and in the available work force. The second purpose is to describe the alternative schedules and their resulting effect on organizational and individual effectiveness and attitudes. Finally, the book provides the necessary resources for developing an action plan for implementing and evaluating a successful alternative schedule.

The three parts of the book reflect these purposes. The two chapters in Part I describe the changes in the work force and the appropriate results on human resource management policy. Part II includes four chapters, each devoted to a different work schedule. Part III describes considerations for implementation procedures that are essential for successful results.

One final personal note is necessary. No book is produced without including some of its writer's biases; this book is no exception. My interest in alternative schedules resulted from my research work and consulting experience. As an applied social scientist, I have devoted my career to searching for innovative improvements in the management of organizations and their employees. Matching individuals' needs and values to the employing organizations' goals is the task I have found most challenging. Various techniques have recently been devised to facilitate this matching process. These techniques include job restructuring, increased teamwork, increased democratization in the workplace, managerial styles that emphasize a goal-setting approach, and the providing of opportunities for growth and development. My own experience is that alternative schedules have successfully addressed many of the issues that the above techniques address, as well.

Moreover, alternative schedules respond to the most challenging management issue of our decade. These schedules treat the employee as a whole person by incorporating his or her needs at work and at home, in keeping with a basic assumption of individual differences. Rarely does a method of solving problems and implementing changes have such potential for simultaneous benefit to the organization, the individual, and even our whole society.

This potential is what attracted me to the study of alternative work schedules. There is persuasive evidence that alternative schedules can address many of the challenges facing us in the contemporary world of work. Properly understood and implemented, alternative work schedules can make the work domain a happier place not only for the employee, but for the employer as well.

Simcha Ronen

Acknowledgments

I would like to thank those people who contributed their expertise and time to assist me in writing this book.

Barney Olmstead of New Ways To Work and Gail Rosenberg of the National Council for Alternative Work Schedules have supplied useful resources. Gerald Schilan and Deborah Watarz provided the valuable material in the legal and contractual chapter and have been a continual source of encouragement and friendship. Sophia Primps and Rose Lee Kravitz contributed their talent and time and helped to produce and update drafts of the various work schedules. Ed Myers provided important and invaluable final touches and skillfully turned incomprehensible sentences into meaningful messages. Miryam Farber diligently produced the various drafts all the way to the final product.

Finally, I wish to thank the Business School at New York University for the supportive climate and helpful services.

S. R.

Contents

PART ONE

HUMAN RESOURCE CONSIDERATIONS

Introduction

In recent years, many people have questioned the logic of maintaining fixed work schedules for all employees. The increased use of alternative work schedules—such as flexitime, compressed work week, part-time work, and job sharing—is evidence of this change in attitude. The purpose of this book, therefore, is to describe these options and to help guide organizations in choosing and implementing an alternative that meets both the employees' and the employer's needs.

Why are fixed work schedules so common? And why have the alternatives arisen only now? A look at the history of fixed schedules reveals not only their origins, but also the rationale for switching to more flexible schedules today.

History

Only since the mid-1800s have Americans known fixed schedules on such a wide scale. Before the modern era, most people were self-employed in various craft occupations or on family-run farms. Individual workers generally determined their own schedules. With the later trend toward working outside the home, workers relinquished this responsibility to their employers. A frequent result was fixed work schedules. The most obvious justification for fixed schedules was that they allowed employers to coordinate the individual workers' efforts. This reasoning is valid even today in many situations—especially those that require interdependence and those that involve assembly line work. However, the movement toward fixed schedules was caused by more than the desire to have an orderly workplace, and the predominant management theories of the time provide further insights as to why the change occurred.

Generally, management saw the employer's role as motivating work for economic betterment. Employers tended to presume that people naturally disliked work and responsibility. These beliefs served as the basis for rigidly controlled organizations. Only by setting up a strictly enforced schedule and paying for labor could an employer get someone to work. The implication was that as long as an employer paid the employees, the employees would work as many hours as they could physically endure. Ironically, these attitudes prevailed (and gave so little credit to human nature) not long after a time when most people had responsibly determined their own work schedules.

The premises of these theories have of course been questioned; therefore, it makes sense to question the applicability of fixed schedules today. There are many factors to consider. Most managers are less suspicious than managers in the past. In addition, most people recognize that many things motivate workers—not all of them connected with economics.

Another reason for studying alternative schedules is their potential for improving the quality of work life. This is a particularly rich topic and will be dealt with in detail in the following chapters. However, one point is relevant here. Since the earliest times, there have been movements to humanize working conditions. A result of one such movement was the decrease in the number of hours worked. A steady decline in hours from about 60 to 40 hours occurred between 1900 and 1940. Since then, there has been no real change in hours worked—which is somewhat surprising, considering the cultural changes and trends that reflect a desire for more leisure time. Moreover, it seems questionable that more time off from work will result from reduction in hours—economic inflation makes that unlikely.

Today's Concerns

One of business's prime concerns today is that increasing costs are eating away at profits. Consequently, it seems unlikely that companies will lower full-time employees' number of hours while paying them the same wage. Even if companies could afford the decreased productivity (in fewer hours), it seems even more unlikely that employees could afford a cut in pay—even for something as cherished as *time*.

Interestingly, and in part as a consequence of the large percentage of families in which both spouses work, there has actually been an increase in the number of hours worked per family over the years. Many observers would contend that this has occurred merely to maintain, and not necessarily improve, their standard of living. (Later we will explore in greater detail the effects that having both spouses employed has on scheduling.)

Considering this rather bleak scenario, it makes sense to focus attention on alternative work schedules as a way of satisfying employees' time needs. Furthermore, these alternatives can be put into effect at relatively low cost and with no loss of production.

Increased interest in scheduling innovations reflects the attention paid by legislators, economists, and psychologists to issues of productivity and quality of work life. Many people believe that alternative work schedules may increase both organizational effectiveness and individual satisfaction. Such schedules have been incorporated into theories currently popular in the literature. For example, researchers have included alternative work schedules in their theory building for quality-of-work-life models,[1] career-development models,[2] and life-cycle stages within the context of the organizational context.[3]

Although such factors as production processes, task interdependence, union contracts, and federal and state legislation may rule out alternative work schedules in some cases, creative managers unbound by traditional management philosophy have found sufficient space for innovation. The most accepted and popularized alternatives include the compressed (or four-day) week, part-time work, job sharing, and the many variations of flexible work hours. Each of these schedules represents variations in one or two dimensions of work scheduling. The first dimension is the *number* of hours worked during a given period—usually a day. The second is the *timing* of these hours of work—that is, when the required number of hours are scheduled within the work period.

The number of hours required is a decision rarely left to the individual employee; instead, either a provision of law or a particular organizational policy dictates it. Timing, on the other hand, is a sufficiently flexible dimension to allow the individual some freedom of choice. Organizational constraints and task characteristics will determine the alternative work scheduling variation feasible within these dimensions.

Before examining these alternatives in detail, we should consider them more generally. The following is an overview of the most popular alternative work schedules.

Compressed Work Week

The compressed work week (CWW) is an alternative work schedule designed to allow employees the standard number of weekly work hours in less than five days. The most common compressed schedule is a 10-hour day, four-day week—which is often designated as the 4/40, although the number of hours worked per day and days per week vary considerably.

The basic concept behind the compressed week is a trade-off between the number of days worked per week and the number of hours worked per day. For the opportunity to work *fewer* days per week, the employee agrees to work more hours per day. However, beyond the designation of hours per week and days per week, there can be many variations in scheduling. For example, if a firm remains open to customers five or six days per week, employees on a compressed week must work staggered schedules; different groups work different days in order to ensure full coverage. One group of employees might work Monday through Thursday, and a second group might report to work Tuesday through Friday. In general, keep in mind that the compressed work week describes the employee's timetable. This will probably differ from the firm's business hours.

The CWW has several clear implications; some affect the employee. The CWW does not offer a choice of schedule, for instance, but it does offer potentially better utilization of leisure time for recreation, personal business, and family life. In addition, the extended workday and possible reduction in the work force present on a given day has the potential for changing such job aspects as the delegation of authority and task responsibility, cooperation, and increased job knowledge. Other implications concern the employer. Having only a portion of the work force available on certain days may influence managers' efforts in maintaining coverage and supervision, delegating authority, and disseminating information.

The concept of the compressed work week first gained acceptance in the United States during the late 1960s and early 1970s. Its use increased rapidly in the early 70s, and this growth leveled off by the middle of that decade. Approximately 2 million American employees are now on some form of CWW. Despite the potential appeal of the CWW, certain environmental factors have limited its rate of adoption. For example, state and federal legislation designed to protect the worker's right to overtime payments have restricted the number of hours an employee can work per day without overtime. (Recent legislation has replaced these laws for civil service employees in order to allow experimentation with alternative work schedules.) Some unions have also been hostile toward the CWW: they view it as a threat to overtime payments. However, others have been more receptive, regarding the system as a step toward further reduction in work hours and an eventual four-day/32-hour work week.

Part-Time Work

Part-time employment cannot be considered a recent innovation in work scheduling, since it has been an accepted and popular alternative work schedule for many years. As of May 1977, part-time workers constituted 22 percent of the nonagricultural work force—that is, 13 million employees worked less than a full-time schedule. However, the influx into the work force of more working mothers, older adults, students, and other groups with special needs has required employers to evaluate the availability and the nature of part-time work.

Part-time employment is regular employment in which the employee works less than the full-time schedule. The schedule is not temporary, intermittent, or casual. Part-time employment is most common among sales, clerical, and labor jobs and in the service industries. It is less common in management and the trades. A recent innovation in the part-time sector is job sharing—two employees fulfilling the duties of one job.

There are four distinct categories of part-time workers, which represent different populations and fill different needs. Two of these are temporary part-time workers and permanent part-time workers. Temporary part-time workers include former full-time workers who have decreased their work hours for a period of time—for example, the working parent who has temporarily decreased work hours to simplify child-rearing responsibilities. Alternatively, one may *enter* the work force on a temporary part-time basis, as often happens with students holding part-time jobs. Permanent part-time workers are those who have chosen part-time work as the optimal arrangement between work and nonwork obligations.

The third category is the voluntary part-time worker, and the fourth is the involuntary part-time worker. Voluntary part-time workers are simply those who prefer to work part-time. In contrast, involuntary part-time workers are those who would prefer full-time work but are unable to find full-time employment appropriate to their skills and education levels. Members of this group are typically young and often members of minority groups.

Of the total part-time work force, 64 percent are regular, voluntary part-time employees. Furthermore, there is competition for permanent part-time positions; these jobs are clearly desirable or necessary for many who wish to work. Despite the competition for such jobs, however, managers often perceive part-time workers as extrinsically economically motivated, less than fully committed to their jobs, and lacking in career-mindedness. This perception is reflected in the lack of benefits and the paucity of professional or managerial-level jobs available to this sector of the labor force. However, recent legislation requires the Office of Personnel Management to make part-time jobs available at all levels of federal government. These changes and pressure from many professionals (especially women) for part-time opportunities should help to improve attitudes.

Flexitime

Flexible working hours (flexitime) is an alternative work schedule that grants employees certain freedom in choosing their times of arrival and departure. The organization usually defines the degree of variation possible. The simplest variation of the system allows the employees to determine starting and finishing times within a certain time range set by the employer, provided the employee works the contracted daily attendance hours. Conditions governing the degree of flexibility may include the total number of hours the company operates during the day; the hours an employee is required to be present; and the level of interdependence between jobs, between departments, and with suppliers and customers.

However, employee choices are restricted. They may choose among variations in the times to be present at work and in the distribution of working hours, but they may *not* vary the total number of working hours required by the employment contract. This condition remains unaltered and is mandated by the organization. Furthermore, flexitime does not alter current management policies regarding vacations or sick leave allowances.

Allowing the employee to create a better fit between individual needs and the work environment through scheduling affects many other aspects of the work experience. Flexitime can influence an employee's sense of autonomy by increasing his or her participation in decision making and responsibility for maintaining coverage for absent employees. It can also enhance group cohesiveness and orientation toward the organization's objectives, since employees must now cooperate to maintain work processes. In addition to its potential for improving the quality of work life, flexitime can help to accommodate work life and quality of life. Consider how the invention of flexitime in Europe came about: A work environment created a specific organizational need. A serious traffic problem arose in the Ottonbrunn Research and Development plant (part of the German Messerschmitt Bolkow Blohm aerospace company) in 1976. Congestion on the local major highways limited access to the plant. A personnel manager invented the concept of flexible working hours to alleviate this problem.

Because of its rapid rate of adoption, it is difficult to estimate exactly how many employees in organizations are currently using flexitime systems. A rough estimate by the U.S. Department of Labor reported that, as of 1981, close to 10 million employees in the United States used some version of flexible scheduling. About 300,000 of these were public sector employees. An estimated 13 percent of all nongovernment organizations have some type of flexitime program for 50 or more employees, and a national usage rate of 17 percent is projected for the near future.

In short, alternative work schedules are becoming more important as organizations focus on ways to maintain and increase productivity levels and as individuals attempt to cope with economic pressures by returning to or remaining in the labor force. We can say in general that the more scheduling flexibility given to employees and the larger the allowed variance from the organization's traditional schedule, the greater the changes likely in the organization. The outcomes associated with alternative work schedules are positive for both the individual and the organization. One can avoid the few problem areas associated with this change through rigorous planning and thoughtful implementaton. Appropriate organizational change techniques should be used—especially for the training and preparation of first-line supervisors. Often, this particular group is less receptive toward the concept and needs special attention.

In general, *all* levels of employees respond better to a new concept if they have had the opportunity to take part in the planning stages and to contribute their own ideas. They may provide insights otherwise overlooked at higher levels of management. In the same context, it is important to design *each* installation of an alternative schedule around the demands of the immediate work environment. This may mean different designs within an organization, or even within a department.

Having concluded this overview, we should now explore in detail the past, present, and future of alternative work schedules. The following chapters provide executives, consultants, labor leaders, and students of organizational behavior with information concerning the different schedules. The final chapters serve as a guide for implementing them.

Notes

1. Ronen, 1981; Rosow, 1979.
2. Van Maanen and Schein, 1977.
3. Cohen and Gadon, 1978.

CHAPTER ONE

Changes in the Work Force

Employee Discontent

A number of scholars have recently noted changes in composition of the American work force and consequent changing attitudes toward work.[1] In general, the demand for improved quality of work life (QWL) is a function of various values, including the following:

Declining confidence in institutions (whether government, military, church, business, or labor).

Greater tendency to question authority.

Less loyalty to work organizations.

Less willingness for workers to subordinate their personal lives to their jobs.

Less dedication to work.

More inclination to look for alternatives to the large, traditional, hierarchical organizations.

Greater importance assigned to leisure activities.

Less willingness to accept routine jobs.

Increased expectations by employees for a greater voice in decisions affecting their work lives.[2]

Quality of Work Life

The movement to improve the quality of work life in America reflects how much society has recognized the signs of employee discontent (such as alienation and stress) and changes in values (such as the recognition of individual differences). The term *quality of work life* includes the gamut of approaches, prescriptions, and solutions for improving the total work environment for both individuals and the organization. It considers the organization to be a sociotechnical system that integrates individuals and groups with the technology of goods and services offered. Thus quality of work life refers to changes in both the sociology and the technology of the workplace.[3] This suggests that the traditional adversary relationship between employer and employee needs reevaluation: Quality of work life for employees and organizational effectiveness may not be mutually exclusive goals after all.

A few elements will optimize employee well-being by humanizing work: (1) job security, (2) equitable compensation, (3) development and use of each person's unique abilities, (4) the opportunity to participate in decision making, and (5) increased autonomy over the job and its environment.

Changing Expectations

In his view of employees' changing value systems, Yankelovich refers to the "new breed" in America. He claims that although employees often start a job willing to work hard and be productive, if the job fails to meet their expectations—if it doesn't give them the incentives they need—then they lose interest. The preoccupation with self (the hallmark of the new breed) places the burden of providing incentives for hard work more on the employer than it did under the old value system. A job's capacity to meet expectations and provide incentives is tantamount to the employee's quality of life. Exposure to more challenging and interesting work and the opportunity to exercise control and autonomy through increase participation in decision-making processes are considered rights rather than privileges. Employees achieve fulfillment through the search for *personal* meaning; that is, the pursuit of a lifestyle that combines a job, leisure time, and the interaction between them, all in a way pleasing to the individual. Fulfillment is not dependent on an identification with an organization or national institution. (See Figure 1–1.)

Perhaps the most significant aspect of this trend is the willingness to trade certain levels of extrinsic rewards for intrinsic ones. This is consistent with the concept of centrality of work life as expressed by many employees. The primary potential source of fulfillment in an individual's life—especially for those in high job levels—is the work domain. For example, in making their choice of occupation,

Figure 1–1

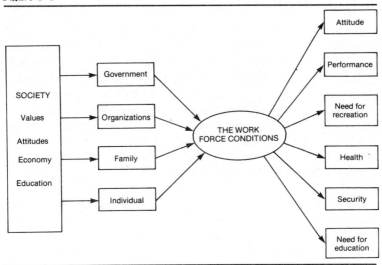

many employees have been willing to trade marginal income levels for more intrinsically satisfying work.

One criterion for the economic success of a society is the availability of goods. An implied criterion, however, is the availability of alternatives—the opportunity for the individual to choose between similar or equivalent goods. In terms of day-to-day economic transactions, we assume the ability to choose. The value of choice has been an important economic assumption in American society and is highly promoted on all levels. Witness the protection of competition between producers of goods evidenced by legislation against monopolies and the millions of dollars spent each year on product development, marketing, and advertising. In a society whose people take alternatives for granted and in which the choice is integrated into almost every aspect of day-to-day life, it seems inconsistent that employees usually have so little choice available in their work situations.

The various socialization processes individuals experience create a conflict within the formal work organization. Socialization during childhood and adolescence has prepared people for self-determination, autonomy, privacy, mastery over their environment, use of initiative, and an independent identity. The work domain, however, thwarts these expectations with negative consequences for the em-

ployee and the organization. Response to employee pressure on industry for increased control and autonomy over their work process and
environment is only now allowing employees to express some of
these values in the workplace. This emphasis on choice in the work
place, along with employee disenchantment with extrinsic rewards
in both work and nonwork domains, have focused the individual's
attention squarely on the organization as a source of additional intrinsic rewards. Generally, people perceive these rewards as heightened
autonomy and self-determination—that is, the availability of choice.
Individual differences (needs, biological cycles, and factors from the
nonwork domain) all interact with work-related factors to produce
varying results for each employee.

Allowing employees to create a better fit between their individual
needs and the work environment through scheduling affects many
other aspects of the work experience. Alternative work schedules
have the potential of influencing the degree of autonomy the employee
experiences. This may also enhance group cohesiveness and orientation toward the organization's objectives, since employees often find
cooperation necessary to maintain work processes.

Furthermore, in addition to their potential for improving the
quality of work life, alternative schedules can help to improve the
fit between the employee's work and nonwork domains.

Changes in the Work Force Composition

One reason employers notice changes in employee needs, values,
and expectations is that the composition of the work force has
changed. There is no longer a virtually unlimited number of qualified
young people eager and willing to work long, hard hours merely
for a "decent" wage. The following sections detail the areas in which
the most dramatic changes have been found.

In comparison with earlier decades, the work force of the 1980s
is younger, more mobile, more educated, and more predominantly
female. However, the high expectations of youth, reinforced by higher
education levels, may not be met because of job shortages, especially
for higher-level jobs. The competition for jobs, caused not only by
a slumping economy but aggravated by the clustering of baby-boom
entrants into the work force, will require a major readjustment for
employees as well as for the organizations employing them.

The *mobility* of Americans has increased dramatically in the
past decade. For example, a recent statistic indicates that 36 million
Americans relocate each year, which means an enormous turnover
in the work force. The *unemployment* rate has remained at a high

level for the past several years, fluctuating between 6 and 8 percent. More individuals experience midcareer crises and change; people are putting off marriage and child rearing. Longer vacations, free time for schooling, and recreational activities are therefore desirable because of the relatively high value placed on leisure time.

For women, the economic pressure and/or personal desire to work outside the home often conflict with responsibilities toward husband and family. Women must equalize these pressures in order to achieve some degree of fit btween work and nonwork domains. Although the increasing numbers of women entering the work force have required organizations and families to provide a more supportive environment for the working mother, a fully supportive network remains a long way off. Furthermore, inflation and the longer life span may increase the number of older workers, who have their own set of needs and expectations.

American businesses are exploring every possible means of dealing with all these problems. One partial solution that prompts considerable hope is the concept of alternative work schedules. We will therefore examine the possible effectiveness of alternative work schedules in helping businesses to tap three currently underused segments of the labor pool: women, students, and the elderly.

Women

Today, 56 percent of the female population works for pay, as opposed to 31 percent in 1940. The work force is composed of 41 percent women, compared with 29 in 1940. This increased presence of women implies that women's traditional role is changing. Whether to comply with regulations or to confront economic realities, many firms have had to adjust their hiring, promotion, and salary and wage policies to deal with the increased presence of women in the work force. However, not yet fully realized are the implications stemming from the expansion of women's role of mother and homemaker to include wage earner. Typically, women have been putting off marriage and childbearing until their late 20s and early 30s. As a result, it is common for a woman to have approximately 10 years of work experience behind her when she has her first child. Considering the time and expense involved in training, it makes sense for organizations to retain that seasoned employee.

There are several factors pertinent to a discussion of working women. One factor, interestingly described by Owen, is the "time bind."[4] Owen contends that although hours worked per week have been decreasing since the industrial revolution, there has been a more recent leveling off to an average work week of about 43 hours. Moreover, the total number of hours per family per week has been rising, due primarily to the increase in the number of women in the work force. An increase in the family's income might logically be expected to lead to the "good life," but families are finding instead that the realities of both spouses working do not necessarily meet their expectations. This lifestyle leads to little or no increase in free time, thus making it difficult to reap the benefits of their labor. Furthermore, as Owen states, higher standards of living have brought a more complicated life. Much of a family's free time is spent on "household production activities." There are, in short, more activities competing for our time, and this competition results in a time bind. Working women feel the burden of the time bind most acutely. In fact, working women have less free time than do working men or full-time homemakers. It is within this context that alternative work schedules can be most helpful.

Many women are trying to "have it all"—that is, family and career. Some are succeeding. However, not everyone has the necessary drive and stamina. Coupled with conflicting goals and/or needs (a more satisfying lifestyle, a family, more material goods), the traditional work schedules can create an extremely stressful situation. Flexible working hours and part-time jobs (in particular) provide a working mother with the flexibility that her life demands. If the strain of working, keeping house, and being a mother is too great, but if the woman does not want to fall behind in her career, part-time work might be the answer. The married woman whose spouse's paycheck does not adequately support the family and the single parent who has trouble making ends meet may be compelled to find employment for economic reasons alone. Part-time jobs are particularly appealing to such women because they simplify child care arrangements. Child care often presents a major barrier to seeking employment due to the difficulty and expense of finding reliable sitters. The ideal situation for a mother of school-age children would be a job from 10 A.M. to 3 P.M. There would be little or no need for babysitters during the school year and teenage sitters are available during the summer.

If this schedule were available in more industries, especially at higher levels (it is already a common shift for sales people, bank tellers, and clerical personnel), many qualified and competent women could rejoin the job market. Although unemployment is running at fairly high levels, one can make a case for attracting and retaining skilled, productive employees. Because of currently slow population growth, we may soon be faced with a short supply of younger people. Since 1977, after 17 years of rising numbers, the number of people between the ages of 16 and 24 has been falling. The peak of more than 36 million in that age group was reached in 1980, but this number is expected to fall 10 percent by 1985 and another 7 percent by 1990.[5] More than ever, the organization's best interests will lie in keeping women on the job.

Students/Education

The proportion of students in the work force has increased substantially since 1940.[6] This trend is not as overwhelming as that involving women, but it is significant because it may suggest the beginning of a new movement.

More people than ever before are pursuing higher education. This was particularly true with the introduction of the GI Bill after World War II and the subsequent rapid growth of community colleges. Currently, 50 percent of all high school graduates attend college. The motivation for attending school is to prepare for a better job so as to attain the good life. This life could mean security, money, or a fulfilling job; regardless of the focus, however, each one is theoretically possible with the proper education. To put it another way: Given the relative stability and prosperity of society after World War II, the only perceived obstacle to success was a lack of education. Today, for college graduates dissatisfied with their careers, *postgraduate* work is always possible.[7]

In the past, a student was typically a young person. This is not necessarily so today, since education is an alternative at any age. Finally, due to the technological nature of our society, people may end up back in school to keep up with changes in their fields even if they are not pursuing a career change. For adult students the problem is how to take the time off to get the desired schooling and still support themselves on their current jobs. The problem for young students is similar; rising costs and government budget cuts have reduced the number of students whose parents put them through school. Without the availability of flexible and alternative schedules, many employees would be unable to continue their schooling.

The implication for the organization is significant. If, as we have seen, people perceive education as a way to improve their lot, and if such education is unattainable, then many people will end up feeling stuck in unrewarding jobs. This frustration may affect the organization through such withdrawal behavior as greater absenteeism and tardiness. Furthermore, if college enrollment declines for economic reasons, corporations will not have the same kind of pool from which to choose employees. In addition, they will have fewer job applicants who have the advantage of on-the-job training combined with higher education.

The Aging Population

The baby boom generation is growing older; population growth has slowed; life expectancy is increasing. It follows, then, that senior citizens will represent a greater proportion of our society. This will have repercussions in business and society. It may become desirable (or even necessary) to postpone retirement past the popular age 65, both to alleviate the expected shortage of skilled workers and to ensure some degree of financial security for our older citizens.

Travelers Insurance, for example, has found that 85 percent of its employees older than 55 would like to work at least part time after retirement. The major reason is economic.[8] Pensions simply do not go as far as planned; in light of recent deliberations to *cut back* social security benefits, it is not expected that public monetary support will increase. Yet not all people who wish to continue working past age 65 will be physically able to work a full 40-hour work week. It seems more plausible to imagine many senior citizens working on a part-time basis. By doing this, the organization delays the loss of a valuable asset; and if used in conjunction with part-time younger students (as in job sharing), the program could produce favorable results. The young person could benefit greatly from working with an experienced employee. The company could well end up with more qualified personnel both during the phasing-out process and after the employee retires for good. The gap between experienced personnel and replacement would be filled. As mentioned before, this situation may be acute when the baby boom generation reaches its 60s.[9]

The Young

The average age of employees during the 1970–80 decade decreased from 40 to 34. The baby boom generation is growing older, and the average worker is younger and further removed from the influence of the Depression years. The clustering of the work forces around this age group may mean intense competition for existing jobs. Note also that population growth has slowed, and life expectancy is increasing.

In light of slower population growth, we may be faced in the near future with a shortage of young people entering the job market.

Since 1977 the number of people from age 16 to 24 has been falling after more than 17 years of growth. During the peak year 1980, that age group had more than 36 million people, but this number is expected to fall 10 percent by 1985 and another 7 percent by 1990.[10]

Conclusions

America's work force is indeed diverse. As American Con's Robert Bogart put it: "There is no typical employee."[11] Unfortunately, employers created the standard work schedule under the premise that there was.

We have stressed some changes in the composition of the work force. It is clear that unless employers make adjustments to accommodate people, companies will be unable to attract and retain the best employees. Changing demographics and the maturing baby boom generation "could blunt American industry's drive to improve its competitive edge in world markets."[12] However, organizations that incorporate alternative work schedules into their policies may be better positioned than others in meeting the challenges of tomorrow. Such companies will be able to attract and retain qualified and loyal employees, and this ability is an essential ingredient for success.

Work and Nonwork Domain

Researchers have generally treated people's behavior within an organization as separate from their behavior elsewhere. The implication is that a person's "outside" life does not influence his or her life at work. Researchers justify this approach in part with the belief that work is spatially, temporally, and for the most part socially distinct from those other spheres of life.[13] Besides, according to this assumption, work-related activities take up more time than any other human activity except sleeping.[14]

However, organizational behaviorists have recently started to take a more holistic approach. They see the employee as an entity whose life in general may influence behavior within the organization. The individual's satisfaction with part of his or her life (work, for instance) can affect attitudes toward the rest of it. In defining these subsystems, people frequently make a distinction between the work domain and the nonwork domain. Behaviors in each domain define it. For example, behaviors in the workplace are often described as job performance or membership behaviors. In the nonwork domain, behaviors are described in terms of choice of leisure activity. Yet we cannot consider the nonwork domain relevant to the study of organizational behavior unless it is in some way connected to behavior within the organization. One argument is that the connection exists through the contribution of both domains—work and nonwork—to the quality of life. If each domain contributes independently, however, we have no justification for considering the nonwork domain. Only if the two domains somehow interact can such an investigation become more relevant to organizational behavior.

The centrality of work to life satisfaction helped justify studies of organizational behavior in isolation from other spheres of life.[15] Researchers assumed that work satisfaction affects nonwork satisfaction, thus making the most important contribution to life satisfaction. Katz and Kahn also acknowledged the importance of nonwork spheres in their discussion of "partial inclusion."[16] This theory suggests that people are involved in a particular system only on a partial basis. An individual does not have to belong to an organization totally—either as a physical or psychological being. Such total belonging may not even be desirable. Instead, the organization demands that individuals put aside part of themselves to perform a role considered appropriate by the organization.[17] The individual must participate in the various systems that include him or her as a member. At times this means regarding one activity as more important than another—for instance, working full-time rather than enjoying more leisure or working one job rather than another. What someone chooses to do depends partly on what a particular role demands and partly on what the role gives in return. The role may meet needs or address values. In short, one domain—work or nonwork— has the potential to influence values held in another domain. Furthermore, similar needs may be fulfilled by different sources in different settings. The ability of the various domains to produce different need valences suggests a connectedness between the attitudinal and behavioral outcomes associated with these domains.

Just as researchers have started to believe that the nonwork domain can influence behavior at work, they have also accepted the idea that the nonwork domain may be more satisfying than work to certain individuals. The nonwork domain may be more important to those people whose central life interest is nonwork activities. For those individuals whose central life interest is work, certain aspects of a job are more satisfying than others, and these aspects differ from person to person. Similarly, for nonwork-centered individuals, aspects of the nonwork domain may vary in how they affect nonwork and life satisfaction.[18]

Recent studies have investigated this relationship between the work and nonwork domains and the implications for behaviors, attitudes, and the individual's overall sense of well-being. In his attempt to clarify the meaning of organizational behavior, Weick argues that the domains are connected: "Events inside organizations resemble events outside organizations; sensitivities of the worker inside are continuous with sensitivities of the worker outside. Since people have as much desire to integrate the various portions of their lives as to compartmentalize them, what happens inside affects what happens outside and vice versa."[19] This suggests that priorities in the nonwork domain may influence outcomes in the work domain and vice versa.

Defining the Work and Nonwork Domains

The concept of work is difficult to define because of the numerous and often conflicting values and beliefs associated with it. In the United States, for example, the Protestant work ethic emphasizes work (industry) as the path to virtue, self-improvement, and social status.[20] An alternate view of work is that it is not as much fun as leisure, that any value derived from work comes from extrinsic rewards, and that individuals work only out of economic necessity. These conflicting ideas give rise to the notion of the alienated worker.[21]

Kabanoff takes a more behavioral approach in describing how work has become distinct from other role systems of kinship, religion, politics, and education: "Work refers to the set of prescribed tasks that an individual performs while occupying a position in an organization."[22] In general, work is a *spatially, temporally,* and to an extent, *socially* discrete, well-defined role that we have little trouble in identifying."[23] This task-based approach is useful. It is unambiguous in differentiating between work and nonwork. As implied in the definition, the approach makes the significant contrast between work and leisure. Furthermore, it focuses on membership in an organization as part of the definition, and membership is an important component of organizational behavior associated with outcomes that reflect the relationship between work and nonwork domains.

Defining the nonwork domain presents some problems. The variety of nonwork activities and desirable outcomes experienced by an individual cannot be appropriately combined to form a single contrast to work outcomes. Attitudes and behaviors considered outcomes in the work domain have traditionally been subdivided into various aspects, and it has been recognized that these aspects contribute differentially to overall job satisfaction and life satisfaction.[24] Similarly, there may be facets of the nonwork domain that contribute differentially to nonwork and to life satisfaction. Little has been done, however, to conceptualize facets of nonwork that would be meaningful to the study of organizational behavior. Family,[25] community,[26] and leisure,[27] have been variously used in studies of facets of the nonwork domain, and these nonwork facets may have relevance to work outcomes.

In examining nonwork facets, researchers have written only about the types of relationships between work and leisure. The purpose of this research has been to demonstrate a relationship between work and leisure behaviors or between work and leisure attitudes. These studies take a narrow view of time allocation, however, by excluding other facets of nonwork that may be related to the work domain. Yet an alternative subdivision of the nonwork domain, facilitating our understanding of the individual in the context of organizational behavior, would include two facets: leisure and maintenance activities.[28] This conceptualization is useful for two reasons. First, it is broad enough to provide an appropriate contrast to work. Second, it is all-inclusive; virtually all nonwork activities can be categorized as leisure or maintenance. We can now proceed to define these two facets of nonwork and to discuss their relevance to work outcomes.

Defining leisure provides similar problems to those that arise in defining work. When people think of leisure, they associate it with a sense of freedom, discretionary time, or time left over when work is completed. As a psychological state, leisure is associated with relaxation, pleasure, and freedom. If we consider a psychological definition of leisure, however, it is more difficult to distinguish between domains. People who experience relaxation and pleasure for example, would not find these two domains mutually exclusive. Similarly, the boundaries between leisure and maintenance are not always clear; they vary for each individual. For example, some people might consider cooking a maintenance activity; others might see it as a leisure activity; others might see it as work. A task-based definition of leisure, as with work, will help to avoid these problems. Thus we can define leisure as tasks or activities the individual chooses, as opposed to activities the organization prescribes or personal or family needs and responsibilities require. The important part of the leisure definition is the concept of discretion, which clearly differentiates it from the context of work or maintenance activities.

Unlike this definition of leisure, which excludes maintenance, others have often defined leisure as all activities that are not work. This has been particularly true of investigations of job satisfaction and life satisfaction.[29] However, such definitions require us to classify many pursuits as leisure that are not ordinarily considered as such. For example, sleeping, doing the dishes, buying food, and providing child care may be part of the leisure domain as we have defined it; yet few would argue that these are true leisure activities. Kabanoff describes these pursuits as belonging to the *maintenance* domain:

There appear to be a number of activities that are essential to basic physical maintenance that everyone is constrained to perform. These activities are performed mainly in a person's residential social setting and are best described as maintenance activities. They may be distinguished from leisure activities because of the element of constraint. Of course, there is an overlap or imprecision involved in the distinction. For example, people may eat to live or they may eat to enjoy themselves.[30]

Maintenance activities are thus defined as those associated with the care and upkeep of the self and any dependents; that is, those activities directly associated with meeting basic physiological and security needs.

The Relationship between Work and Nonwork Domains

One hypothesis describing the work-leisure relationship is *segmentation*. According to this hypothesis, people segment their experiences so that attitudes or behaviors in one domain do not influence attitudes or behaviors in the other domain. More simply put, the outcomes associated with each domain are independent of each other.

The segmentation model suggests that individuals segment the experiences occurring in each domain, so that the feelings produced in each are basically unrelated. Dubin suggests that "the social world of urban man is continuously subdivided into areas of activity and interest, with each social segment lived out more or less independently of the rest."[31] Dubin's study on the central life interest of industrial workers is a well-known work supporting the segmentalist view, although its methodology has been criticized because of the forced choice between two mutually exclusive categories.[32] Still, other researchers supported the segmentation hypothesis.[33]

Two other alternative hypotheses have emerged in the literature to describe the relationship between work and leisure.[34] The first, the *spillover* hypothesis (also called *generalization*), suggests that individuals may generalize any sense of alienation from work to an alienation from leisure. This hypothesis was extended further to suggest that individuals who are highly involved in their jobs would seek leisure activities that also require high levels of involvement, activity, or participation. Other researchers supported this hypothesis,[35] and most people are still intuitively attracted to it, especially those who promote the notion of the centrality of work in people's lives.

The second, the *compensatory hypothesis,* suggests an explosive "letting off steam" associated with the deprivations alienated employees feel. Alternatively, compensation could describe a highly job-involved individual seeking leisure in the form of quiet and solitude after a hectic day at work. Research partially supports this hypothesis.[36] Rousseau, who reviewed the literature on the compensatory model, concluded:

Studies supporting the spillover model tend to have a range of jobs varying in content, while those supporting the compensatory model have been based largely on jobs with undesirable features. Thus the relationship of work to nonwork may vary as a function of the type of work the individual experiences. Although for a broad range of jobs the spillover model may hold, jobs characterized by extreme conditions . . . may be associated with compensatory activities off work. Thus, a nonlinear relationship may exist between work and nonwork.[37]

Rousseau thus suggests that job characteristics moderate the work-leisure relationship and that one may observe both generalization and compensation under certain circumstances.[38]

One factor in the compensation model that may help to explain the mixed results is the model's focus on different settings for the compensation to occur, rather than compensation within the setting in which the perceived deprivation is taking place. It seems more likely that, before attempting to compensate elsewhere for needs unmet at work, the individual would try to compensate through other channels at work. For example, an employee who perceives a job as boring and routine may first attempt to alleviate the sense of boredom through increased social interaction at work or may escape the job through various forms of withdrawal behavior. Alleviating on-the-job boredom through off-the-job activities is a less direct course of action, and by implication it is a more difficult relationship to measure empirically.

To summarize these studies presented and the conclusions of other researchers who have conducted reviews on the subject, there is little unequivocal support for any of the three hypotheses.[39] There are several explanations for the inconsistent nature of the findings. First, the work-leisure relationship is moderated by characteristics of the *group* studies (e.g., economic, demographic, sex, age, marital status, occupation). Second *individuals* differ in their approach to work and leisure, depending upon their needs and interests. Further, the same people may vary in the type of relationship they create, depending on their place in the life cycle. The hypotheses discussed, however, may serve as a departure point for evaluating the relationship between the two domains, and they suggest possible stages in an individual's attitude to these domains. The important point is the interdependence of these areas in the totality of the human experience.

Compensation differs from generalization in the way it can be studied because of the nature of the construct. Unlike generalization, the compensation hypothesis is based on need theory. An individual has certain needs; if not met in one domain, they will be met in another. Instead of describing the results in terms of undesirable job characteristics, it may be more appropriate to ascertain which lower-level needs in these jobs were deprived. These extreme conditions certainly facilitate our interpreting the choice of leisure behavior in terms of needs. Under less extreme conditions, however, it is more difficult to interpret behaviors or attitudes as attempts at need fulfillment. And as a motivation theory, need theory tells us that an individual will be motivated to fulfill unmet needs; if those needs are not met in one domain, the individual should be motivated to try to fulfill them in another. If the needs are met in one doman, however, they lose their prepotency and their ability to motivate.

In contrast to compensation, which deals with needs, the generalization hypothesis appears to describe behaviors and (in particular) attitudes. It reflects the similarity in attitude between the domains; more important, it removes the explanation of need theory as a source of motivation for behavior and attitudes manifested in each domain because of the lack of implied contrast between outcomes across domain boundaries. The notion of "spillover" indicates that one domain has precedence over and influences attitudes in the other and consequently, in overall life satisfaction.

The Holistic View

We have described three domains: *work, maintenance,* and *leisure.* Maintenance plus leisure can be considered the total nonwork domain—everything that is not work. Having described these three domains, however, it remains unclear why the maintenance domain is appropriate to the study of organizational behavior.

Maintenance is important to the study of work outcomes because it suggests a similar lack of opportunity for discretion in a different setting or domain. The definition of work—prescribed tasks and required roles—may also apply to the maintenance domain, although the specific tasks and roles themselves are different. After making certain choices about the work and nonwork domains, one takes on a set of roles that require specific behaviors. The lack of opportunity for discretion with respect to behaviors thus becomes a similarity between work and maintenance. The existence of this similarity suggests that the behavioral and attitudinal outcomes associated with these two domains may be related, as depicted in Figure 1–2.

In contrast to work and maintenance, leisure incorporates the opportunity for discretionary behavior. It can be argued, therefore, that when an individual makes choices about the personal resources he or she will allocate to work and maintenance activities, the level of discretion associated with the role expectations in one domain will influence the level of discretion available in the other. The direction of influence will be determined by one's set of priorities between domains. The resulting behaviors and attitudes in each domain will not be independent. Thus, not only may the maintenance and leisure facets of the nonwork domain influence and contribute to the individual's sense of well-being in the nonwork domain, they may affect such work outcomes as job performance and satisfaction and may, in certain cases, influence the importance of work with respect to its contribution to life satisfaction.

Despite the use of task-based definitions for each domain, it is important to note that there may still be confusion between domains. Determining the boundaries may be an important problem. For instance, work is often associated more with occupying a role (membership requirements) than with performing a task. If the spatial, temporal, and/or social borders in such situations are removed, it becomes more difficult to differentiate work from the other two domains. This is consistent with the notion of partial inclusion discussed

Figure 1–2

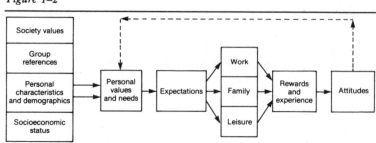

earlier.[40] To the extent that spatial and temporal requirements are relaxed, the individual is less "included" in the work domain. In some cases this may suggest a decrease in the organization's control over the employee as the dimensions or requirements of membership in the organization ease. For the employee, however, domains with vaguely defined borders will have important implications for the type of relationships the individual creates among work, leisure, and maintenance as well as for the relationship with the organization itself.

The literature on part-time employees offers an example of how the choice process can reveal how different individuals values work, and it also reveals the implications for attitudinal outcomes. For example, certain aspects of job satisfaction may have differing levels of importance, depending upon the individual's reason for working. Similarly, within the nonwork domain most people would perceive the opportunity for choice of leisure activities and for allocating time between the leisure and maintenance domains. Suppose a woman with primary child care responsibility believes that the maintenance domain (taking care of children) receives priority over the work domain. At the same time she chooses to or must work. The choices the woman makes about work—choice of career, job, and location, for instance—will require some sort of accommodation with the demands from the maintenance domain.

We can assume that voluntary part-time employees have chosen a part-time schedule because demands from either the leisure domain, the maintenance domain, or both have priority. This implies that nonwork considerations are inputs to the work decisions. Hom conducted a study comparing part-time to full-time employees with respect to job-facet satisfaction. He describes his findings:

Full-time employees included promotional opportunities as an integral part of overall satisfaction with their jobs, but the part-time employees excluded such opportunities. The nature of work satisfaction also was defined differently by the two groups of workers. Full-time workers perceived their work in terms of multiple facets of job satisfaction; part-time workers defined the nature of their work satisfaction solely in terms of co-worker satisfaction.[41]

Hom's findings suggest that full-time employees seek to meet different needs at work than do their part-time counterparts.

If the importance of job satisfaction facets varies in relation to choices about the work schedule, it follows that importance of facets of nonwork satisfaction may systematically vary in relation to such

Table 1-1

Life and Career Stages and the Resulting Attitudes toward Working Hours

Age	Parallel Life Stages	Career Stages	Differential Effects of Life Stages on Men and Women in Regard to Time Availability and Desired Work Hours
18–22	Early-adult transitional period: Leaving family and reduced dependency Peer support becoming critical Marriage or college major transition	Exploration—preparation for work	Part-time work, odd jobs, odd hours (after school, vacations)
22–28	Getting into adult world: Adult and initial occupational roles Marriage and children demanding structures	Establishment stage—mutual recruitment between the organization and the individual, acceptance and entry, leveling off, transfer and/or promotion	Willingness to work long hours, overtime—not weekends or evenings
28–32	Transitional period: Reworking occupational and family changes and increased financial needs	Granting of tenure—evaluation by the organization of the individual, leading to commitment to the individual, release, or sidetracking	a. Men: Long hours, take work home b. Women: Drop out/part time
33–40	Settling down: Stability and order, security and control established Becoming one's own person	Maintenance (mid-career)—self-reexamination in the presence of security; occurrence of midlife crisis	a. Men: (1) If upwardly mobile, long hours, community work, flexibility (2) If plateau in work, regular hours, second job, attention to family b. Women: Back into career, part or full-time, shared jobs, flexible hours desired

40–45	Midlife transition and nurturance of others: Children leaving home to enter adult world. Reevaluation and commitment to lifestyle	Maintenance (late career)—teaching instead of striving, deceleration at work, growing interest in nonwork activities	a. Men: Steady hours, not as long, longer vacations, weekends; education for renewal, either evenings or on sabbatical. b. Women: Longer hours, perhaps flexibility
45–55	Restabilization and establishment: Adaptive, Conforming orientation, Renewed interests	Wish for more enriching personal life; renewal of important relationships; establishment of mentor-mentee relationships	Health problems may begin to emerge requiring reduced hours, increased interest in leisure
55–65	Anticipation of retirement	Decline—preparation for retirement, increasing reliance on wisdom gleaned from experience, self-acceptance	Men and women: Tapering to part time

Source: This table is based on the seven life stages reported by D. J. Levinson, C. Darrow, E. Klein, M. Levinson, and B. McKee, *The Seasons of Man's Life* (New York: Alfred A. Knopf, 1978); the information in E. Schein, *Career Dynamics: Matching Individual and Organizational Needs* (Reading, Mass.: Addison-Wesley, 1978); and the desired work hours from A. R. Cohen, and H. Gadon, *Alternative Work Schedules: Integrating Individual and Organizational Needs* (Reading, Mass.: Addison-Wesley, 1978).

choices and that the components of satisfaction within each domain may be systematically related. Furthermore, there is no reason to limit this process to choice of work schedule; the same process may apply to other choices that reflect the allocation of resources to work and nonwork. The compressed work week and flexible working hours offer ideal alternative solutions for the individual's balance between work and nonwork activities.

Summary

As a final note, it is necessary to emphasize the potential differences in employees preference for working hours based on their life and career stages. These variations are depicted in Table 1–1, which is based on the extensive work of Levinson and his associates, Edgar Schein, Allen Cohen, and Herman Gadon. The important message here is the fact that in addition to interindividual differences in balance between needs in the work and nonwork domains, there are intraindividual differences that cannot be ignored.

Notes

1. Yankelovich, 1979; Katzell, 1979; Rosow, 1979; O'Toole, 1977; Greenberg and Glaser, 1980; Institute for Social Research, 1979; Walton, 1972, 1979.
2. Greenberg and Glaser, 1980, p. 5.
3. Kerr and Rosow, 1979; Davis and Cherns, 1975; Herrick and Maccoby, 1975; Suttle, 1978; Walton, 1972.
4. Owen, 1981.
5. Effects of "baby buts" are shrinking ranks of younger workers.
6. Owen, 1978*a*.
7. Sarason, 1977.
8. Ex-travelers Insurance employees work out problems of retirement, p. 31.
9. Jacobson, 1980.
10. Effects of "baby buts."
11. The workplace is changing . . . but not too fast.
12. Effects of "baby buts."
13. Kabanoff, 1980.
14. Robinson, 1977.
15. e.g., Blauner, 1964; Dubin, 1956.
16. Katz and Kahn, 1978.
17. Katz and Kahn, 1978, p. 46.
18. Dubin, 1956; Kabanoff, 1980; Rice, Near, and Hunt, 1980.

19. Weick, 1979, p. 31.
20. Neff, 1968.
21. Seeman, 1967.
22. Kabanoff, 1980.
23. Ibid., p. 68.
24. e.g., Smith, Kendall, and Hulin, 1969.
25. Iris and Barrett, 1972.
26. Hagedorn and Labovitz, 1968.
27. e.g., Kornhauser, 1965; Meissner, 1971; Kabanoff and O'Brien, 1980.
28. Kabanoff, 1980.
29. see Rice et al., 1980.
30. Kabanoff, 1980.
31. Dubin, 1956.
32. Kabanoff, 1980.
33. Bacon, 1975; Hagedorn and Labovitz, 1968; Harry, 1971; Kabanoff, and O'Brien, 1980.
34. Wilensky, 1960; Kabanoff, 1980; Rice et al., 1980.
35. Iris and Barrett, 1972; Kornhauser, 1965; Meissner, 1971; Orpen, 1978; Rousseau, 1978; and Wilensky, 1960.
36. Dennis, Henriques, and Slaughter, 1956; Iris and Barrett, 1972; Mansfield and Evans, 1975; Tunstall, 1962; and Rousseau, 1978.
37. Rousseau, 1978, p. 513.
38. Rousseau, 1978.
39. Kabanoff, 1980.
40. Katz and Kahn, 1978.
41. Hom, 1979, p. 553.

CHAPTER TWO

Human Resource Management

Introduction

As discussed in the previous chapter, the worker's discontent with the workplace, changing expectations of the organization, and the quest for improved worklife have placed a responsibility on management unparalleled in history. Today the organization must view the management of human resources much as it views the management of financial, technological, or material resources. Just as the organization must be alert for better mechanized and automated systems to stay competitive, so must it also continuously reexamine human resource policies, evaluate new trends, and adopt new programs to increase employee effectiveness and efficiency.

The organization may accomplish these objectives through human resources management, which is the attraction, selection, retention, development, and utilization of human resources in order to achieve both individual and organizational objectives.[1]

Since the purpose of this book is to introduce a tool that can help achieve consonance between individual and organizational objectives, the purpose of this chapter is to explain how the tool may prove useful in carrying out the functions of human resource management.

This tool is, of course, alternative work schedules. These schedules are flexitime, the compressed work week, part-time work, and job sharing arrangements. Although arguments can be made in favor of each alternative (and will be in the following chapters) the general goals are: (1) to retain and attract productive workers, (2) to improve worker productivity and attitude, (3) to decrease personnel costs, and (4) to improve organizational climate.

Before taking a closer look at each of these goals, we should note that it is personnel's responsibility to provide sound, timely information on issues and trends that will help management make better use of the organization's human resources.[2] One aspect of this responsibility is staying abreast of changes and trends in the external environment that will affect the organization. Once the personnel department has pinpointed key innovations that may help the organization meet its needs, the department has a responsibility to experiment with the tool or strategy. In the case of alternative work schedules, we recommend that the department investigate and evaluate experience in other companies before bringing a possible recommendation to management.

A Systems View of Personnel Management

We will view the management of human resources from a systems approach because it synthesizes the internal organization as well as its relationship with the environment. Furthermore, a systems approach considers changes in any of the four previously mentioned resources and allows a more comprehensive evaluation of the effect of the change on the organization.

Most organizations are efficient partly because of their sensitivity and adaptability to the environment in the areas of finances, technology, and materials; however, it is in the area of human resources that the systems approach helps to recognize a harmful oversight. Evaluating the accountability of human resources only in terms of financial gains per hour per employee is a long-outdated policy. Admittedly, it is difficult for an organization financially to estimate and justify the management of human resources. Yet any disregard for human resources is ultimately negligent. Ignoring aspects of how the organization interacts with its external environment, whether in terms of contraints or availabilities, may also be detrimental to the organization's competitive ability or effectiveness.

Consider the topic of human resources management from a systems point of view, including input, work process, and output. The inputs into the system are the people who are either actual or potential employees of the organization. The larger the pool of applicants from which the organization may draw to fill its personnel needs, the better equipped the organization will be to meet its goals and objectives. Alternative work schedules provide a means by which organizations can either retain trained, productive employees or recruit new, productive workers. For example, consider the professional woman who must choose between career and family. A flexitime, part-time, or job-sharing arrangement can give her the option of combining career and family, thereby eliminating her need to make a choice between the two. Even more important, an alternative work schedule gives the organization the advantage of retaining an experienced, dedicated employees. Consider an older worker who is almost 65 and healthy and wants to continue working. An alternative work schedule can give this worker the option of phasing into retirement while remaining productive member of the organization. The older worker could even assume some training responsibilities for the person who will eventually assume his or her duties.

In addition to retaining trained, experienced, dedicated employees, alternative work schedules also broaden the pool from which organizations may recruit workers. The organization gains a reputation for flexibility in terms of work days and hours; more applicants consequently seek employment with that organization.

Yuchtman and Seashore have offered a concept that emphasizes the system resource approach to organizational effectiveness.[3] According to this concept, the organization can utilize its environment as a bargaining position to the extent that the organization can acquire resources. Applied to human resources, this comprehensive approach implies that if the organization wants to make maximum use of its human resources, it must make effective use of those resources within the organization as well as those resources available in the environment—that is, outside the organization. The Yuchtman and Seashore concept also implies that for the organization to optimize its human resources, it must "mobilize and control" employees according to both long- and short-term organizational needs. Furthermore, they indicate that the organization achieves effective mobilizing and controlling of human resources by improving its bargaining ability. This approach, due to its dynamic characteristic, considers long-range availability of resources and the application of innovations that will continually maintain its bargaining attribute and thus its competitive power. This conceptualization supports the notion that alternative work schedules can improve the organization's bargaining ability by making maximum use of current employees and the broad pool of talented workers whose other needs or obligations prevent them from working the typical eight-hour, five-day work week. Alternative work schedules can enhance organizational effectiveness by more effectively utilizing the human resources both within and outside the organization through the options of flexitime, part-time, and job-sharing arrangements.

It is precisely the organization's needs to be competitive and to bargain effectively for human resources that have spurred progressive organizations to adopt policies and techniques that can help them satisfy those needs. Some policies have been directed toward employees, and others have been aimed at potential environmental resources. The alternative work schedule is an innovation that can enhance organizational effectiveness in terms of the Yuchtman and Seashore conceptualization.[4] It applies to present employees as well as to potential human resources.

Improved Performance

The American decline in productivity is not merely a slogan for the 1970s and 1980s; it is a reality. Figures released by the U.S. Department of Labor in June 1978 showed that 25 of 66 major industrial groups studied actually produced less in 1977 than in 1976.[5] As a whole, the increase in productivity within the manufacturing sector slowed to only a 2.2 percent in 1977, compared with 6.8 percent in 1976. Economists attribute the decreased productivity to a combination of factors: lagging outlays in research and development, decreased capital investment for the purchase of more productive machines, and the upsurge in costly environmental and safety regulations.[6] One might also point to worker alienation and sagging morale as contributing to the decline in worker productivity.

C. Jackson Grayson, Jr., of the American Productivity Center, does not agree that Americans have lost the work ethic. Grayson believes "that autocratic, bureaucratic organizations in business and public service have suppressed the desires and ability of the individual to feel that he or she is contributing. People do not mind contributing to the success of an enterprise, so long as they feel they have a hand in helping to shape it and are rewarded."[7]

Although the alternative work schedule is not the whole solution to America's productivity problem, it certainly is a tool American business may use to ameliorate the problem. If we assume that worker fatigue and lack of autonomy and control of the work environment have caused the decline in productivity, then we can see how alternative work schedules can enhance organizational effectiveness. Particularly those workers at tedious or hectic jobs may be unable to tolerate the boredom or pressures of a 40-hour work week. Permanent part-time employment may be exactly what these individuals need and desire. Similarly, replacing one unproductive worker with two productive, permanent part-timers may result in stepped-up productivity for the organization. Those two part-timers might well come from within the ranks of the presently employed and might be found either by their own or the organization's initiative. They might even be today's unproductive 40-hour worker.

Lack of autonomy and control in the workplace is a critical issue and deserves elaboration. Consider first why an individual chooses to work in one organization rather than another. In general, the views of such social scientists as MacGregor, Herzberg, Argyris, Likert, Mouton, and Maslow, may be summarized as follows: Individuals are growing and developing organisms, not "fixed" individuals. Consequently, employers should:

> View the contribution in terms of their whole person, not only as the fulfillment of a certain job description.
>
> Accept the preposition of individual differences.
>
> Emphasize cooperation among people rather than competitiveness.
>
> Understand the value employees attach to different rewards and job experiences.
>
> Ensure that employees perceive a positive relationship between the efforts they invest and their resulting level of performance.
>
> Enable individual employees to participate in decisions concerning their work goals and processes.
>
> Facilitate a high level of autonomy to each employee over his or her time.

The applied behavioral sciences stress the belief that individuals' needs and motivations are a prime concern. Furthermore, there is an acceptance of the individual's value as a thinking, feeling organism. Without this consideration and without taking individual differences into account, the organization falls short of its purpose as a societal entity. Behavioral scientists assume an innate human potential for independence, creativity, productivity, and the capability for contributing to the organization's objectives. This assumption stresses not only that people have these potentials, but that they will actualize them under the proper conditions. Coupling the humanistic approach with economic concerns, human potential can be effective in reaching organizational goals. Furthermore, an optimum utilization of this potential actually results in increased productivity and profit for the firm. The individual's needs and the organization's needs are consonant, not opposed to each other.

In a society in which workers enter and leave an organization at will, management has to take the individual's values and expectations as seriously as it does those of the organization. Management must understand the needs and values that motivate employee behavior and must determine the choice of activities in which the individual invests his or her efforts. If the organization can do so, it is on its way to increasing the employee's motivation, deepening the employee's identity with the organization, and increasing the employee's involvement with the job.

Popular psychology, the civil rights movement, and other phenomena have increased our desire for autonomy and self-esteem. A movement toward self-awareness and sensitization to our fellow human beings has only reinforced the basic ethical belief in the individual's value. Any disregard for these needs by management can be counterproductive. Rather than creating an alienating environment in the work organization by disregarding these needs and value systems, managers should understand their implication and provide supportive conditions.

Management must comprehend that the changes of values in the workforce and the need for more hospitable environments for independent, self-determined people do not necessarily contradict organizational goals. On the contrary, fulfilling such needs and work goals can heighten employee commitment to the organization and increase involvement in the job, resulting in greater employee effectiveness.

Worker needs for growth and development coincide with improvement of the work force. Providing conditions for growth and reinforcing it may improve the effectiveness of the organization and simultaneously improve the individual's work life. We all search for meaningful experiences for growth, development, and a sense of worthiness and self-esteem. We may find it in the workplace or may look for it elsewhere, seeking work only as a means to make certain ends possible outside the workplace.

The imaginative organization will make efforts to make its environment the place where individuals can gain the recognition and affirmation they seek. Management must recognize that if it disregards worker needs, values, expectations, and individual differences, it will fail to produce the team or group necessary for the organization's goals.

Giving the individual responsibility for determining the number of hours, days of the week, and months of the year he or she works can add a dimension of autonomy to the workplace and give the worker a sense of control over the work environment. Letting the employee set a day and arrival time shifts accountability from punctuality to performance. By allowing the individual to choose working hours, alternate schedules carry with them still another inherent message: management recognizes individuality.

Alternative work schedules can increase employee responsibility, autonomy, and potential for personal growth. The employee is now responsible for working as many hours each week as agreed upon with the management. The employee has autonomy to make decisions based on personal needs and does not have to submit to a rigid structure. This increased autonomy can satisfy the need for self-actualization because employees can alter the work schedule to accommodate the work process and consider the load while coordinating other activities important to growth, such as hobbies, sports, education, and family activities. The presence of these intrinsically motivating factors in the jobs may create greater job satisfaction and improved performance.

Organizations must change if industry intends to create conditions that encourage high performance in today's new breed society. For the sake of successful competition, organizations should find ways to adapt to social change and to individual needs for self-esteem, flexibility, and autonomy. Although organizations are generally conservative regarding human resources, the price of resisting change may be too high for most organizations. Innovations are no longer optional; they are necessary.

Increased Personnel Costs

The cost of recruiting, selecting, and training a police officer may be as high as $12,000 even before the officer first walks the beat. In a large technical sales organization, the cost of a new salesperson (including company car and expense account) can reach $20,000 before the company realizes any tangible return on its investment. Just the training budgets of many large corporations are comparable to those of medium-size universities.[8] Continuing inflation boosts both direct and indirect payroll costs, and fringe benefits run as high as 35 percent of payroll costs.[9] In fact, when we consider both direct and indirect costs, the human resources element constitutes between 40 and 70 percent of total costs in most businesses.[10] Workers' compensation claims must be included in our examination, as well as turnover costs. The bottom line of this cursory view is clear: Ineffective management of human resources is intolerable.

It's no surprise that the single largest drawback to alternative work schedules is the increased personnel costs associated with them. Typically, alternative work schedules result in increased payrolls, additional paperwork, and added costs in fringe benefits. There is no disputing the reality of these three costs, but it remains true that the benefits derived from alternative work schedules may better than offset them.

Evidence now indicates that organizations can present positive bottom-line results to prove the advantages of alternative work schedules. These benefits largely result from decreased turnover, decreased recruiting and training costs, reduced lateness, and reduced absenteeism.

Alternative work schedules offer workers the option of staying in the work force and combining work with family, recreation, charity work, or leisure. They eliminate the need for either/or decisions. This flexible policy, from the organization's viewpoint, allows keeping valued employees, reducing turnover, and reducing recruitment and training costs.

Lateness and absenteeism have reached epidemic proportions in this country. Alternative work schedules can reduce or even eliminate these problems. Consider, for example, the chronically late worker. Given the option of working from 10 A.M. until 6 P.M., this worker may well reduce his/her lateness record to zero. Similarly, early-risers who prefer to avoid rush-hour traffic would probably be willing to work a 7 A.M. to 3 P.M. shift to avoid the morning and afternoon crowds. The point here is that if the organization's needs are met first, alternative working schedules can give workers the flexibility to combine working and nonworking schedules in a way that best suits their needs. This situation can lead to increased organizational effectiveness and increased job satisfaction.

Organizational Climate

Climate refers to the relatively constant variables in a work environment that are important to the efficient use of human resources. Climate is the personality of an organization as seen by its members.[11] Note that climate is what employees believe it to be—not necessarily what it really is. Furthermore, the climate within an organization is a major determinant of employee behavior.

The variables in studies of organizational climate vary, but most researchers deal with items associated directly with or influencing employees' perceptions of their jobs. These variables include the following:

Level of freedom to decide or participate in decisions concerning aspects of the job process (including style of work, control of time, and sequence of tasks).

Level of autonomy, responsibility, and independence.

Degree of structure imposed by supervisor versus his or her level of consideration and support (leadership style).

Rewards provided by the organization and employee attitude toward these rewards.

Opportunities for growth and development and opportunities to exercise initiative.

Level of communication and discrimination of information.

There is no best or most suitable climate. Instead, management must determine what its goals are and then attempt to create a climate appropriate for both its own and its employees' goals. Much evidence supports the notion that achievement-oriented and employee-centered climates positively correlate with job satisfaction. Going one step further, we may consider organizations that offer employee alternative work schedules to be achievement-oriented and employee-centered. An organization's offer of alternative work schedules implies an appreciation of individual needs and differences, as well as an attempt or even a commitment to support those differences within the constraints of organizational goals. Documented evidence supports the finding that achievement-oriented climates—where emphasis is placed on goal attainment—result in creative behavior and high productivity. The achievement climate also leads to high job satisfaction, positive group attitudes, and high achievement-motivation levels. Other evidence shows that employee-centered climates— open communications, mutual support, and decentralized decision making—generally lead to increased employee performance, reduced turnover, lower manufacturing cost, and reduced training time.[12] When we compare these and other findings, the most favorable climate for both production and satisfaction is one emphasizing both employee achievement and employee consideration, and these are precisely the emphases of alternative work schedules. Such a climate represents an exchange between employees and employer by which both work together to satisfy mutual objectives in the long run.[13]

If climate is a perceptual concept, it is also a powerful one for attracting and keeping employees. Workers will want to find jobs and keep working in organizations that provide achievement-oriented and employee-centered climates. Such climates show the employee that this organization respects individual needs, values, and expectations, and it recognizes the individual's need for autonomy and control over his or her work environment. Alternative work schedules can be a key indicator of a climate that encourages both the individual's and the organization's effectiveness.

Summary

The focus of this chapter has been the recognition that certain work conditions benefit both the employee and the organization. Under such conditions, *individual goals and organizational goals may coincide.* However, this progressive work environment requires a managerial philosophy that can provide the appropriate organizational climate. Changes in societal values have created an emphasis on individual development and have led to a recognition of the problems facing us as we cope with increasing pressures. These factors have led to a perception that the person is a unique entity and that organizations and society must consider his or her special needs. From there, we described the concept of quality of work life and some of the components that can help to improve the individual's work domain. We then introduced work schedules as an innovation that incorporates acceptance and accommodation of individual differences into the work environment. These have the *potential* to influence individual and organizational outcomes. For example, work schedules can improve organizational effectiveness, employee motivation, recognition of individual differences, and the focus on the employee's personal development.

Employees are satisfied with their work to the extent that working conditions fulfill their values and needs. We believe that employees for whom alternative schedules provide desirable conditions will experience greater job satisfaction. Moreover, alternative schedules may help to improve membership behavior, such as turnover and attendance. These forms of behavior are closely related to attitudes. As job attitudes improve, membership will probably improve also.

Figure 2–1 is a comprehensive model representing the interaction between the environmental influences (on the organization and the individual) and the potential outcomes resulting from the implementation of alternative work schedules. Organizational factors include aspects of climate and technology; individual factors include value systems, family commitments, socioeconomic status, and leisure and recreational activities. Environmental influences represent inputs into

Figure 2–1
Antecedents and Consequences of Alternative Work Schedules

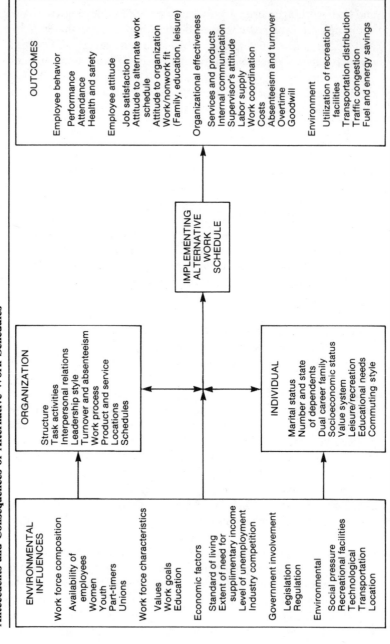

the organization and the individual's situation. Outcomes are listed for *both* the individual and the organization as a result of the work process. We may therefore consider implementation of alternative work schedules as a moderator or catalyst in the process by which the organization and the individual achieve their desired goals together.

The following chapters report the results from various available studies on the different alternative schedules. The analysis of the variables described follow Figure 2–1, although in most cases we present only parts of these variables. We have tried, however, to summarize the outcomes of each schedule in terms of the criteria variables delineated in Figure 2–1.

Notes

1. E.g., Burrack and Smith, 1982; Beach, 1980; Sayles and Straus, 1977.
2. Cascio and Awad, 1981.
3. Yuchtman (Yaar) and Seashore, 1967.
4. Cascio and Awad, 1981.
5. "Vanishing Vigor," 1978.
6. Loeb, 1978.
7. Campbell, 1971.
8. Patten, 1977.
9. Cheek, 1973.
10. Steers and Porter, 1979.
11. Steers, 1977.
12. Steers and Porter, 1979.
13. Ibid.

THE ALTERNATIVE SCHEDULES

CHAPTER THREE

The Compressed Work Week

Definitions, Variations, and Examples

Definitions

The compressed work week (CWW) is an alternative work schedule in which the full-time employee completes the prescribed number of weekly work hours in fewer than five full days. The most common compressed schedule is a four-day week, 10-hour day, often designated the "4/40." A 38-hour week, designated as "4/38," would mean a four-day week, 9½-hour day, and so on. The many variations of CWW range from a 3/36 (often seen in computer operation centers) to a 4½/40 (which allows the employee free Friday afternoons in exchange for a slightly longer workday Monday through Thursday).

We should keep in mind that the CWW describes the employee's timetable, which may differ from the firm's open-for-business schedule. For the employee the CWW does not offer a choice of schedule but offers the potential for better use of leisure time for recreation, personal business, and family life. For the employer the compressed week has the effect of extending the workday. It also reduces the total work force reporting on a given day (provided the firm does not reduce the number of days open to correspond with the compressed schedule). Reducing the work force present on a given day has the potential for (1) changing such job aspects as authority and task responsibility delegation, (2) allowing for job enlargement, and (3) increasing job knowledge for employees.

The CWW concept first gained acceptance in the United States during the late 1960s and early 1970s. Its use grew rapidly in the early 1970s, and this growth leveled off by the middle of that decade. As of 1976 approximately 1.3 million workers (2.1 percent of full-time, nonfarm wage and salary earners) used some form of compressed schedules. This number represented a slight decrease from 1975, when 2.2 percent of the full-time salary earners used the compressed work week.[1] According to Hedges, those who worked *more* than five days per week on a regular basis amounted to 16 percent of full-time workers.[2]

A survey of more than 800 firms yielded interesting data on the types of organizations using the schedule:

The "pioneers" of the CWW are small (usually nonunion, nonurban) manufacturing firms and service retail companies.

There has recently been a trend toward more urban-centered organizations—particularly hospitals, insurance companies, and municipal agencies, such as police departments.

There is rapid growth in the service and retail areas. By now 35–40 percent of those firms on CWW are in nonmanufacturing areas.

The specific areas in which compressed schedules have been found are data processing departments, hospital nursing staffs, law enforcement agencies, and assembly line operations.[3]

In addition to this data, the Hedges study revealed the following:

Employees who worked less than five days per week tended to be several years younger than other employees.

Employees on the four-day work week were twice as likely to hold a second job as were full-time employees.[4]

Finally, a survey of 155 firms on various forms of the compressed work week provides us with information about distribution of the various compressed schedules.

Of the 155 firms in the study, 57 percent were on some form of four-day compressed week.

Eighteen percent had three-day schedules.

Eighteen percent were on 4½-day schedules.

In most firms, only certain employees were on the compressed work week. In 40 percent of the samples, fewer than 10 percent were on a CWW. In 30 percent of the cases, 75 percent or more of the employees were on the CWW.[5]

This last statistic raises an interesting point about the compressed work week schedules. Unlike flexitime, in which the schedule is typically made available to all but a few employees, the CWW is often implemented in single departments, such as data processing; the remainder of employees continue on regular five-day schedules. Perhaps employers view the CWW as a more drastic change than flexitime, less feasible for some employees. For example, the extended work day combined with an extra day off may require major adjustments in the employee's relationship between work and family life. Since the compressed week is an inflexible schedule, it represents an "all or nothing" proposition to the employee, as compared with flexitime, wherein the amount of change (within defined limits) is up to the employee. Contributing to this reservation about CWW is the concern about feasibility, given departmental interdependencies, task requirements, availability to customers, and maintenance of supervisory control.

Given these reservations, it appears that firms' patterns of adoption have differed from their uses of flexitime. As Finkle indicated, implementation of the CWW is more often found in certain departments within a firm and in certain industries.[6] The reservations expressed here may account for its slower rate of adoption compared with flexitime, which by now is much more widespread in the United States. (Chapter 7 will discuss further specifics of implementing CWW.)

Despite the potential appeal of CWW, certain environmental factors have limited its rate of adoption. For example, state and federal legislation designed to protect the worker's right to overtime payments have limited the number of hours an employee can work per day without overtime. (Recent legislation has relaxed these laws for Civil Service employees in order to allow experimentation with alternative work schedules.) Some unions have also been extremely protective of the hard-won shorter work day of 7½ to 8 hours per day and its associated overtime rights; they view CWW as a threat to these rights. Joseph Cointin, a regional official of the Machinists Union in St. Louis, sums up this feeling as he argues for a four-day, 32-hour week at 40 hours of pay:

This business of working 10-hour days strikes at the heart of what our unions have accomplished for us over the years, and the shift to four 10-

hour days in a work week that is taking place in many sections of the country can only wreak havoc in the universal 8-hour day that unions so long fought for.[7]

Other union leaders have taken the opposite view, however, regarding the compressed work week as a step toward a four-day, 32-hour week and a further reduction in work hours.

Variations

The basic concept behind the compressed week is a trade-off between the number of days worked per week and the number of hours worked per day. For the opportunity to work *fewer days* per week, the employee agrees to work *more hours* per day. Beyond the total number of hours worked per week and the number of days the employee reports to work, however, there are many variations in scheduling. In practice, the compressed work week varies in its impact on employees, depending upon the variation of the system assigned. Some of the considerations influencing the type of compressed schedule devised include the following:

Availability to Customers

If the task is one associated with high start-up or shutdown costs, as is typical of a manufacturing environment, or if it is a continuous process that rarely or never shuts down, then managers must carefully plan and control scheduling to maintain full coverage and to maximize potential cost savings from the schedule. This is consistent with the idea that CWW refers to the employee's timetable, which may differ from the company's schedule.

Rotating versus Fixed Schedules

Where services to customers or continuous plant operations take precedence, the firm must decide whether employees will be assigned to permanent or rotating shifts. Rotating shifts are often necessary because the compressed schedule is not an evenly divisible portion of the work week. For example, a four-day shift within a six-day work week, where each shift fully staffs the operation, requires some form of rotation. An additional complication is the scheduling of day and night shifts—especially if these are rotated.

Interdependence of Functions

If each employee can perform his or her task independently of the others, more flexibility in scheduling is possible. On the other hand, high interdependence requires carefully planned and coordinated scheduling to avoid interruptions in the work flow. Some overlap between shifts may be desirable to provide a smooth interaction.

Employee Choice

Should it decide to let employees choose their schedules, management must allocate choice by some system, such as seniority or taking turns, and must clearly define the criteria for system use. Possibilities include merit (e.g., measured productivity), seniority, and creating a well-balanced team of workers. Variations can range from simple systems in which all employees work the same schedule to extremely complex systems with much variation in hours worked.

We should emphasize that *the greater the level of complexity in the CWW schedule, the greater the impact the schedule will have on job design and task requirements.* If the organization decides to implement a complex system, it must determine the level of change in job design required and must be prepared to plan for such change. We will discuss this aspect of implementation at length later in the chapter.

Examples

To give the reader an idea of some of the variations possible, we present the schedules devised by four companies implementing the compressed work week. The first three have been adapted from Swerdloff;[8] the fourth is the result of interviews we have conducted in a large insurance company.

4/40—Monday and Friday Off

Management in one firm decided that the firm must remain open five days per week, although employees would report to work only four days out of the five. Employees were divided into two groups: One group worked on Monday through Thursday; the other worked Tuesday through Friday.

This system is simple to administer, and there is little problem with assigning employees to the two schedules. The disadvantage of the system is that on Mondays and Fridays only half of the work force is present, which could become a staffing problem in a service-oriented staff. Other considerations for management are task interdependency and departmental interdependency. If employees must work closely together within or between departments, having the total work force available only three days per week might cause difficulties. The firm must weigh the simplicity of this compressed

week schedule against its feasibility for the departments and employees involved.

4/40—Monday, Wednesday, or Friday Off

Another firm minimized the problem of staff availability by creating three equal shifts instead of two. The creation of three shifts
made the assignment of days off more complicated. Three days (Monday, Wednesday, and Friday) were allocated as shift off days. To
most employees a Wednesday day off is less desirable than a Monday
or Friday; consequently, the shifts rotated so that days off alternated.
Thus one shift would be off on Monday one week, Wednesday the
next, and Friday the next. Weekends were always off for all of the
shifts. However, this rotation of shifts created a four-day weekend
every third week and a two-day weekend on either side of the Wednesday off. The result of this schedule was that a full two thirds of
employees were present on Monday, Wednesday, and Friday, instead
of half on Mondays and Fridays. The disadvantage was that all
employees were present only two days per week, Tuesdays and Thurs-
days. This system may require additional planning for meetings requiring the presence of all employees.

Variations of the 3/36

A data processing unit in a large firm changed its schedule from
a five-day week to a three-day week. Data processing is a continuous,
24-hour-per-day operation in which most of the work involves monitoring equipment. Because this type of *passive* activity places fewer
physical demands on the employee and because of the continuous,
24-hour nature of the operation, many computer centers have experimented with the 3/36 schedule. A 12-hour shift would be impractical
in a job requiring constant activity or physical labor, but it becomes
feasible in an environment of this type.

This particular firm instituted an actual working shift of 11 hours
and 55 minutes, including one 25-minute break. In addition, employees took a 35-minute lunch break, which was not included in the
working time. All employees were permanently assigned to a day
shift or a night shift, although days off were rotated within each
shift. The schedules were arranged so that no employee worked more
than two consecutive days or nights. The assigned hours for day
shift employees were from 7:30 to 8:00 P.M. on the day shift and
from 7:30 P.M. to 8:00 A.M. on the night shift, allowing a half hour
when both shifts were present for a smooth transition.

An assumption about a schedule of this type, where there is little or no overlap between shifts, is that the shifts are interdependent of each other and in fact that each employee functions more or less autonomously. From this, one would predict that each employee has a counterpart in the opposite shift on those jobs requiring constant attentions. The half-hour overlap serves in this case to maintain continuity of processing. Once having been informed by the prior shift of the status of the particular responsibility area, the employee assumes responsibility for task assignment.

The 4–5/9

A major insurance company uses another variation of the compressed work week.[9] As in the previous example, the data processing department developed a system called the 4–5/9, allowing additional days off from work in exchange for slightly longer work days. More flexible than the 4/40 system and less extreme than the 3/36, a 4–5/9 schedule calls for employees to work five days one week, four days the next, then take a three-day weekend, and work five days the following week. Thus, within a two-week period, the employee works a total of nine days. The 10th day, or day off, is referred to as a "bi-day" by employees.

At Equitable the standard hours worked per five-day week is 36¼ (or 7¼ hours per day). The company requires 72½ hours over a two-week period. In order to work the 72½ hours in nine days, managers extended the working day from 7¼ to 8 hours per day. Since 8 hours per day means a total of only 72 hours, employees must make up the additional ½ hour on their honor.

Within the two-week accounting period, there are four possible schedules under this system, and employees are permanently assigned to one of these schedules. M_1 employees have the first Monday in the accounting period as their bi-day. Other schedules are M_2, F_1, and F_2. Management specifies that, although the assignments are permanent, the employees have some input into the decision over which schedule they will work. Management also occasionally makes exceptions and reschedules.

To maintain smooth operational functioning and full services to users, the department stipulated the following with regard to use of the system.

1. No more than 25 percent of the work force can be absent on any one day.
2. The employee may choose whether or not to participate in the system.

3. All departmental meetings are scheduled for Tuesday, Wednesday, and Thursday. Employees reported liking this system. The middle three days of the week were busy, but Monday and Friday tended to be quiet days good for concentrating on paperwork and contacts outside the company.
4. If the supervisor asks the employee to work on a bi-day for a special reason, the employee can take the missed bi-day during the middle of the week. The employee must take the bi-day during the two week accounting period, however, or else forfeit it.

Within the data processing department, all types of personnel participated in the program—programmers, secretaries, project managers, and technicians—and it was equally successful at all levels. Implemented in January 1974, the system includes some 1,500 people at present. Although the firm has conducted no formal evaluation of the system in terms of changes resulting from the 4–5/9 system, employees are reported to be almost unanimously in favor of it.

A more objective measure of the system's success is the daily feedback (report card) provided to the department on the status of such data processing quality control measures as turnaround time, system downtime, and response time. These criteria have been maintained or improved. One manager pointed out that the data processing department is under considerable pressure to maintain its level of service because users (other departments) who do not necessarily use the 4–5/9 system will complain immediately and loudly if they perceive a drop in service. This tension serves as an impetus to maintain high service standards.

This schedule was relatively easy to implement because of the short work week (36½ hours). Since the preimplementation schedule let employees work only 7¼ hours, they could work one hour longer or more per day without encountering such legal restrictions as overtime or dinner pay. (At this firm employees receive money for dinner after they have worked 9 hours in one day; they receive overtime after 40 hours of work in one week.)

Field Results and Surveys

Field Results

To summarize the actual effects of the compressed work week on the organization and its members, we have compiled and reviewed the findings from the relevant published studies in the area conducted during the past decade.[10] These 14 studies investigated the outcomes associated with CWW in organizations that had implemented the schedule (or, in two cases, were planning to implement it).[11]

We have summarized the results from each study and have categorized trends in the positive direction, negative direction, or no change. The total number for each category of outcomes represents the number of studies reporting results. (In several studies we investigated more than one organization.) In addition to our review of results, we present findings from a similar review of studies for additional viewpoints and interpretations.[12]

Organizational Effectiveness

The results describing organizational effectiveness (see Table 3–1) included measurements of productivity and service to customers, problems of fatigue associated with the schedule, and absenteeism.

We collected this data using objective measures of effectiveness, such as company records, employee reports, and supervisory reports of employees' perceptions.

Productivity and Service to Customers. Findings grouped under productivity and service indicated either improvements in specific areas or no change associated with implementing CWW. Although the evidence partially supports the claim of improvements in this area, the diversity of criteria used for measuring effectiveness makes it difficult to generalize about results. Furthermore, that employees prefer the CWW to the old schedule and wish to continue using it may influence the predominantly positive employee reports. There

Table 3–1

Organizational Effectiveness

	Positive	Negative	No Change	Total
Productivity/Service*	4	0	3	7
Fatigue	0	5	0	5
Absenteeism	3	0	2	5

Note: Summary of study results reporting changes in organizational effectiveness. Numbers in each category refer to the findings of studies; some studies investigated more than one organization.
* Preimplementation surveys omitted.

Source: Adapted from S. Ronen and S. B. Primps, The Compressed Work Week as Organizational Change: Behavioral and Attitudinal Outcomes. *Academy of Management Review*, 1981, 6, p. 70.)

also appears to be some evidence that the CWW may increase productivity, but we need more research in this area before we can draw conclusions.

In his review, Nollen emphasizes that we can expect productivity improvements in settings with high start-up and shutdown costs and where there are chances to increase utilization of capital equipment.[13] His conclusions are consistent with the nature of the CWW as an innovation: Under most CWW schedules we cannot expect major changes in job responsibilities, as there is little or no flexibility or employee choice involved.

Fatigue.   Of the 14 studies we reviewed, 5 reported that the CWW affected fatigue level, and all reported that fatigue had increased. This is consistent with what one would expect, based on the longer working hours each day and the subjective nature of the data. Further support comes from one study that found employees in jobs that made low physical demands tending to hold more favorable attitudes toward the CWW. Some evidence also indicates that older workers find fatigue more of a problem than do younger workers. (We will discuss this issue later in this chapter.) The important issue for the organization is whether or not increased fatigue reduces employee effectiveness. No one has yet effectively addressed this issue.

Absenteeism.   Five studies measured changes in absenteeism. Two reported no change, and three reported a decrease. Nollen also reported that although absenteeism often decreases, the improvements tend to diminish over time.[14] Researchers have argued that there should be a decrease in absenteeism for two reasons. First, the extra day off per week should allow employees to attend to personal business that they might otherwise do on work time. Second, if the employer docks the employee for absences, a day's absence from work represents a greater loss to the employee in terms of both pay and work accomplished. Although the trend is positive, there appear to be mitigating factors influencing the relationship over time. One such negative factor may be accumulated fatigue. Another possible problem is that the novelty of the new system wears off in time, and employees return to their original, preimplementation criteria for deciding whether or not to come to work. In some environments (especially union), employees may feel peer pressure to maintain a certain level of absenteeism in order to avoid the imposition of stricter attendance standards.

CWW and the Employee

In attempting to determine the impact of the CWW on the employee, we investigated employee attitudes toward the schedule and changes in attitudes toward the job associated with implementation of the CWW. These are indirect measures if one assumes that attitudes are the *result* of CWW effects on the employee. The CWW can affect job attitudes by enhancing or facilitating production under certain circumstances. More specifically, increases in responsibility, autonomy, and job knowledge resulting from implementing the schedule may be associated with more positive attitudes toward the job itself.

Also associated with attitudes is the CWW impact on the employee's nonwork domain. Outcomes associated with home and family life, leisure, and recreational activities will clearly affect attitudes. These summarized results are presented in Table 3-2.

Attitudes toward the CWW and the Job. Regarding attitudes toward the CWW, employees were consistently favorable. However, one study found that although employees were positive in their responses, supervisors felt a *personal* dissatisfaction with the compressed week. The researchers explained their finding by hypothesizing that supervisors felt unable to take advantage of the new schedules. To them effective supervision required their presence at all times.

Regarding job satisfaction, relationships appear to be more complex. Five of the nine studies investigating changes in job satisfaction found an improvement; two reported decreases; two reported no changes.

Table 3-2

CWW and the Employee

	Positive	Negative	No Change	Total
Attitudes toward CWW	10	1	0	11
Attitudes toward job	5	2	2	9
Home/personal life	4	1	1	6
Leisure/recreation	6	0	0	6

Note: Summary of study results reporting changes in attitudes and the nonwork domain of the employee. Numbers in each category refer to the findings of studies; some studies investigated more than one organization.

Source: Adapted from S. Ronen and S. B. Primps, The Compressed Work Week as Organizational Change: Behavioral and Attitudinal Outcomes. Academy of Management Review, 1981, 6, pp. 66–67.

Certain studies found differences in job satisfaction associated with different facets or *components* of satisfaction. Extrinsic components include those aspects of the jobs not *directly* associated with performance itself, such as pay, promotion, interpersonal relations, and feelings about the company. Intrinsic facets include those aspects of the job directly related to its performance, such as autonomy, responsibility, and enjoyment of the task itself.

Two studies found an improvement in job satisfaction associated with extrinsic facets and no improvement associated with intrinsic facets. In another study, a specific extrinsic facet—attitudes toward the company—improved in association with implementing the CWW.

With respect to intrinsic components, one study found that job satisfaction improved when the CWW resulted in additional responsibility and requirements for job knowledge. However, whether the CWW can significantly alter these aspects and result in job enrichment remains in doubt. On the other hand, positive attitudes toward the CWW also stemmed from the fact that employees still considered their jobs boring; they seemed to view the CWW as a means of escaping the work environment.

In another study job satisfaction was related to pressure to work overtime and fatigue associated with the CWW. Job satisfaction tended to decrease as overtime and fatigue increased. Other variables positively related to satisfaction with the CWW and job satisfaction included jobs with low physical demands, opportunity for additional responsibility, dissatisfaction with pay, and dissatisfaction with the company.

Further examining the confusing array of relationships described or implied between the CWW and job attitudes produces one possible explanation. Various facets of job satisfaction and any prior experience with the schedules influence initial attitudes toward the CWW. After implementation and after employees experience its full effects on the job and work environments, the CWW may be a factor in changing job attitudes.

This process is circular. Whereas some evidence suggests that certain types of employees may be more receptive to the CWW because of their negative work environment, the ways in which the CWW changes a job may help to improve the work situation and, as a result, improve attitudes toward the jobs.

In his review of changes in job satisfaction associated with the CWW, Nollen was somewhat more negative.[15] He emphasizes that because the CWW does not alter the relationship between employees and their work, any increase in job satisfaction comes from the schedule's ability to rearrange leisure, not from any increased attractiveness of the job itself.

The reason for improved satisfaction with the work schedule is traceable to the longer weekend it provides. Most workers perceived compressed workweeks to be a benefit to the firm rather than a benefit from the firm. It seems that compressed workweeks are regarded in part as an escape from a negative work situation.

Relationship of Sex and Age to Attitudes toward the CWW. In the studies investigating attitudes toward the CWW and jobs, employees expressed favorable attitudes in varying degrees, although at least two variables moderate the relationship—sex and age. Eight studies measured differences in attitudes between males and females, and nine studies reported differences based on age.

Of the eight studies investigating sex as a mediating variable, two found that men were more favorable than women; the remainder indicated no difference. One study reported that women seemed to expect disruptions in home and family life, whereas men viewed the system in terms of the three-day weekend and the additional leisure available.

There appears to be some weak evidence for male preferences, but the evidence leads us to conclude that there are no significant sex differences in attitudes toward the schedule. Apparently any difference based on sex result from different orientation toward rearranged time.

The other major demographic variable explored with respect to CWW attitudes and job satisfaction was age. Of the nine studies measuring age, five reported that younger employees felt more favorable than did older employees; the remainder reported no differences. It seems that fatigue may influence the age/attitude relationship. Older workers are on average more easily fatigued and may therefore find it more difficult to cope with the longer day.

Attitudes of Supervisors. One study found that although employees were very favorable, supervisors felt a personal dissatisfaction with the compressed work week. Only one firm reported this as a problem, yet it is worth mentioning because lack of supervisor support can hamper the success of the schedule. Under certain circumstances supervisors apparently felt unable to take advantage of the new schedule. For them, effective supervision meant being present five days per week, regardless of the 4/40 schedule. Furthermore, some supervisors believed that it was an additional burden to provide for cover-

age on days when some of the work force was out. Those schedules
in which less than the full work force is present each day would
probably require more of an adjustment from first-line supervisors
in order to maintain coverage and to ensure that employees are
fully occupied in the supervisor's absence.

Impact on Home and Personal Life.   Of six studies investigating
this area, four reported a positive effect on home and personal life.
Variables measured included marriage, personal business, family life,
housework, and shopping. One study reported no significant differences in parental or marital satisfaction between the 4/40 and 5/
40 workers. However, studies found significant differences based on
the life cycle (or stage) of the employee, implying a changing relationship between age and CWW attitudes. Another study reported that
women feared disruption in their family life under a compressed
week.

Leisure and Recreation.   Six studies surveyed employees on
changes in leisure and recreation since the implementation of the
compressed week, and all six reported positive results. Most employees believed that the new system provided more leisure time or better
arranged leisure. According to one study, however, males adopted
more of a leisure orientation to the new schedule, and females tended
to view the system in terms of its impact on the family.

One study hypothesized that employees perceive the compressed
week favorably if they see leisure in terms of days rather than hours.
In other words, the compressed week deprives the employee of leisure
hours but adds a day of leisure each week. A complicating factor
is the employee's orientation towards the *use* of leisure—whether
he or she uses it to fulfill family responsibilities or recreation. As
mentioned above, there is some evidence of differences between males
and females here, but more research is required to investigate employee preferences for leisure as the basis for choosing a schedule.

In their study of the leisure patterns of employees who work
four-day compressed schedules, Seltzer and Wilson found that males
and those with incomes above the median used more of their time
for self-development.[16] According to the authors, one who has more
money will devote leisure time to self-development activities instead
of having to moonlight, consistent with the cultural expectation that
men should work hard in order to increase their earning capacity.
On the other hand, women were already considered to be moonlighting because most of them still had primary responsibility for the

job of homemaking.[17] The categories of leisure activities that increased the most in association with a four-day work week were "home-centered relaxation"—which included resting, relaxation, loafing, watching TV, and spending time with family—and "activities at home," including work at home, spending time with family, and hobbies.[18]

Management Surveys

In addition to the studies describing the outcomes associated with the CWW, we have summarized three surveys of management in companies using the CWW. These surveys focus mainly on the compressed week's impact on the effective organizational functioning and, to a lesser extent, on the schedule's impact on the employees. Table 3–3 presents the results from these surveys.

We have differentiated these management surveys from the other study results because they represent the report of one manager (typically a director of personnel or vice president of human resources) describing the schedule's impact on the company. This is different from the studies that survey a firm's employees and managers on their personal experiences. In the case of the studies, we have aggregated to provide a comprehensive view of the organization. In the case of the surveys, the report from a personnel manager may be based on internally conducted surveys of employees or on the manager's personal opinion. Thus we have chosen to report this data separately because of the difference in sources of information. We should also add that although these managers may be making certain assumptions that the schedule's impact on the employee, they may be in a better position to report the schedule's terms of productivity and effectiveness on the firm itself. This may of course vary from firm to firm.

Participating in the Surveys

The survey by Wheeler, Gorman, and Tarnowieski, under the auspices of the AMA, included data from executives in 143 companies on the effects of the compressed week.[19] Of these, 60 percent of the firms were on the 4/40 schedule, and 12 percent were on a 4/38. The remaining firms varied between a three-day week and a 4½-day-week schedule, and a variety of hours were worked per week. The majority of firms were small, nonunion, and nonurban. The second survey, by the Bureau of National Affairs (BNA), was smaller, having surveyed 99 companies on the compressed schedule. Of these, 23 percent were unionized, and 48 percent were on a 4/40 schedule.

Table 3-3

Reports from Executives in Firms Using CWW (Each Executive Representing a Single Organization)

Criteria	American Management Association Survey*	Bureau of National Affairs Surveys†	American Management Association Survey‡
Participants in the survey:	143 companies surveyed	81 companies surveyed	156 companies responded
	Days worked:	Days worked:	Days worked:
	5%—3 days/week	75%—4 days/week	18%—3 days/week
	88%—4 days/week	The remainder—unspecified	2%—3½ days/week
	7%—4½ days/week		57%—4 days/week
			18%—4½ days/week
	Hours worked:		5%—4 days one week
	64%—40 hrs/week		5 days the next
	12%—48 hrs/week		
	The remainder vary in hours worked/week.		
		23% unionized	52%—less than 1,000 employees
	Most companies small, non-urban, nonunionized		48%—more than 1,000 employees
Impact on company:			
Production	62% reported increase	35% reported increased production	39% reported better productivity
	3% reported decrease		14% reported worse productivity
Costs	11% experienced increase		36% reported decreased unit labor costs
	38% experienced decrease		8% reported higher unit labor costs
			40% reported decreased overtime costs
			11% reported higher overtime costs
Profits	51% reported an increase		
	4% reported a decrease		

	*	†	‡
Scheduling	26% reported scheduling more difficult		28% reported work scheduling better 25% reported work scheduling worse
Customer relations	18% reported improvements 3% report deteriorated		10% reported improvements 18% reported worse effects
Employee relations	69% reported improvements 31% report no change		
Absenteeism	13% report decrease 2% report increase	54% cite improved absenteeism and/or morale	71% reported improved absenteeism 2% reported worse absenteeism
Impact on employee: Fatigue	29% felt fatigue increased	—	9% reported less fatigue 53% reported worse fatigue
Morale	22% reported increased morale	54% cite improved morale and/or absenteeism	90% reported improved morale 1% reported worse morale
Transportation	—		54% reported better commuting 12% reported worse commuting
Satisfaction W/CWW: Overall company satisfaction with the CWW and its effects	80% felt business results improve	79% reports satisfaction W/CWW	

* K. Wheeler, R. Gorman, and D. Tarnowieski, *Four-Day Week: An AMA Research Report* (New York: American Management Association, 1972).
† Bureau of National Affairs, *ASPA–BNA Survey: The Changing Workweek* (Washington, D.C.: Bureau of National Affairs, 1972).
‡ S. D. Nollen and V. H. Martin, *Alternative Work Schedules, Part 3: The Compressed Workweek* (New York: American Management Association, 1978).

The third survey was conducted by Nollen and Martin; it was also published by the AMA under the auspices of the American Management Association.[20] This survey was based on a mail survey of 2,889 organizations conducted in 1977 on alternative work schedules in general. There were 156 responses from users of compressed work week schedules.[21] Of these, almost 60 percent were on a four-day work week, 18 percent were on some form of three-day week, and 18 percent were on a 4½-day work week.

Impact on Company

The AMA study was detailed in surveying the compressed week's impact on the firm, as reported by a single top executive.[22] Reports of production costs, profits, customer relations, employee relations, and absenteeism were positive or indicated no change. Scheduling was the only area showing significant drawbacks.

The BNA took a different approach in its survey. It queried executives about their reasons for liking the new system. Thirty-five percent cited increased production; 54 percent cited improved absenteeism and/or morale as their chief reason for satisfaction. Thus these two factors represent major reasons for satisfaction for 89 percent of the sample. However, one must be cautious in interpreting this data because of the methodology used to obtain it. The method of asking a reason for satisfaction does not give the respondent an opportunity to report negative attitudes. Thus 89 percent represents the number of times people reported these factors as a reason, *not* the percentage of those satisfied.

In the later AMA study, a substantial portion of the managers reported better productivity (39 percent), and only 14 percent reported worse productivity.[23] Both unit labor costs and overtime costs appeared to be favorably affected from the reports of almost 40 percent of respondents. Work scheduling was more controversial; almost equal percentages of managers reported scheduling improvement and worsening. With respect to changes in membership, absenteeism was reported improved by 71 percent of the sample.

Impact on Employee

Executives in each survey were asked to describe changes in morale and any problems with fatigue resulting from the compressed week. It would of course be inappropriate for these respondents to offer opinions on the impact on employee home life and leisure. The early AMA study reported that a significant number of executives believed their employees were more tired, but a similar number also reported increased morale as an advantage of the compressed week. The AMA second study results were similar. For the BNA, we must repeat the statistic already cited—54 percent believed that improvement in morale and/or turnover was a major benefit of the compressed week. In the second AMA study, more than half of the managers reported improvement in commuting.

Satisfaction with the Compressed Week

There was no overall question on satisfaction in either AMA survey. However, 80 percent of the 1972 group believed that business results had improved. From the BNA survey, 79 percent were satisfied with the schedule, and 14 percent indicated that it was "too soon to tell."

In general, the survey results are consistent with the employee studies. If anything, the surveys tend to be more positive in describing impact on the company. Furthermore, management may believe that because executives are reporting as noninvolved observers, their opinions should be weighted more heavily. If this is the case, we should seriously consider the positive results they report.

Implications for the Employer

Organizational Effectiveness

The data from both the studies and the management surveys are unclear because of the measure of both production and service used as indicators of organizational effectiveness. From the small amount of objective data and the reports from employees, we can conclude that the compressed week results in little or no change in productivity and that changes that did occur reflected improvements. However, the fact that employee reports on performance are positive while objective reports and managements surveys are less conclusive may imply a response generalization of positive attitudes to performance toward the schedule. In other words, since employees like the schedule and wish it to continue, they may tend to report favorably about outcomes associated with it. Positive reports from supervisors and managers may be less prone to positive response generalization, and they lend support to the claim of improved productivity.

To summarize, there is some support for an increase in organizational effectiveness—more specifically, productivity and service—associated with the CWW. However, there is little theoretical justification for major improvements in effectiveness, since the CWW is not associated with the types of organizational and job-related changes often associated with flexitime. We would expect any productivity changes observed to be in such areas as reduced start-up and shutdown costs and better use of plant and equipment.[24] Despite this assumption, however, two of the studies linked the CWW with some degree of increased job knowledge and responsibility for employees, which was a consequence of employee need to cover for absent co-workers. These aspects are criteria for improved effectiveness themselves or facilitators of improved effectiveness.

One important issue that remains to be addressed is the role of fatigue in employee performance. Several studies associated the CWW with higher levels of fatigue. Furthermore, there was some evidence of a relation between age of the worker and fatigue. We would therefore predict that over a period of time, fatigue would harm performance, especially for employees of certain ages.

There are several other measurements of organizational effectiveness which implementing the CWW may affect, although there are few study results to verify our predictions. For example, the organization should experience decreased start-up costs if it reduces the number of work days.[25] This would particularly apply to a manufacturing company using heavy machinery or equipment. If the organization decides to maintain a five-day work week, however, the expanded number of hours worked per day means better utilization of plant and equipment through increased usage each day. Of course, it also requires some sort of rotating schedules or separate shifts for employees, and it may also mean an expanded work force to handle the additional work hours. Better utilization of equipment means higher energy and maintenance costs. Few organizations have really attempted to evaluate the CWW's full impact on such costs.

Another complication in determining the CWW's impact on the organization is the various measures of performance differentially affected by the schedule. For example, job upgrading or enrichment may be associated with the improvements in effectiveness in some situations, and fatigue may cause reduced effectiveness. (Other factors, discussed later in this chapter, may influence performance as well.) The organization must determine its priorities, its reasons for implementing the schedules, and its expectations for the outcome. It must then measure the schedule's impact on effectiveness according to these criteria.

Membership
A schedule in which employees have time off during normal business hours should encourage them to conduct personal business

on their own time. The CWW should lead to decreased use of personal leave time. Regarding sick leave, the CWW's impact is less clear. On the one hand, a missed day of work is a larger percentage of the total work week, thus more costly in time lost away from the job. An employee concerned with work accomplishment or one who is docked for absences may be less willing to call in sick unless absolutely necessary. On the other hand, any problems of cumulative fatigue may lead to increased sick leave use.

Our analysis of the data indicates that most studies did not differentiate between personal leave use and sick leave. However, the combined results along with the management surveys did provide evidence of decreased absenteeism, which is consistent with our hypothesis that the CWW allows more time for personal affairs.

An organization that decides to implement the CWW should establish baseline measure for both types of absenteeism and then keep track of changes in rates of absenteeism after implementation. We have discussed the fact that many employees felt more fatigued as a result of the longer work day, but the study results did not link reports of fatigue to changes in organizational effectiveness. We predict that increased absenteeism would be one manifestation of the fatigue problem, which would have consequences for effectiveness and performance. It is therefore important for the organization to monitor carefully any changes in absenteeism.

Regarding tardiness, there is no reason to predict any changes associated with the schedule, and none has been reported. We expect little or no change in tardiness, since the schedule, unlike flexitime, remains a rigid one with no flexibility in arrival or departure time.

Management Style (First-Line Supervisors)

Another issue that deserves attention is management or supervisory style. To what degree does successful implementation of the CWW require a change of style? The slight evidence of supervisor's resistance to the schedule implies an adjustment process for this group. Employee reports of changes in intrinsic job aspects provide further support. If employees perceive increases in autonomy or responsibility, we might well assume that supervisors are willingly or unwillingly delegating more than they did before implementing the schedule. We would predict that in situations requiring task restructuring and increased delegation of responsibility, supervisors may be more resistant to change. Feelings of loss of control and of an increased workload may aggravate negative perceptions. In this area the implementation process can itself determine the success of an alternative work schedule for supervisors.

Organization Climate and Job Satisfaction

The compressed work week apparently affects employee attitudes toward the job (often favorably), toward the work environment, and toward the organization itself. One could infer that employees reacting favorably toward the new schedule (which provided them with an additional day off) generalized this positive attitude by expressing a higher level of job satisfaction. We should note, however, that improved job attitudes did not stay constant over time, but tended to return to their preimplementation level. This lends support to Nollen's conclusion that changes in attitudes were associated with the schedule, and with the job itself.[26]

Implications for the Employee

Demographic Differences among Employees

The results from the studies indicated that demographic characteristics account for some differences in employee attitudes toward the CWW. However, more satisfactory explanations of employee preferences emerged when we considered those demographic variables within the context of the employees' life cycle or lifestyle. For example, women with families tended to be more negative about the schedule. These women were likely to use their rearranged leisure time for home and family-related responsibilities, whereas men were more likely to pursue leisure and recreational outlets. Women with families were more likely to view the longer work day as a hindrance to the fulfillment of responsibilities, such as adequate day care or providing an evening meal. At this stage of their life cycle, women seemed to view the extra hours per day as more valuable than the extra day of leisure per week. To generalize, we can say that such preferences express how employees conceive of their time off the jobs. The employees' conception of time off is a trade-off between leisure days per week and leisure hours per day. A preference for the latter would result in dissatisfaction with a compressed work week. On the other hand, employees who expressed positive attitudes toward the schedules were those willing to sacrifice hours each evening during the work week for a full free day or a longer weekend. The implication is that personal characteristics and life style determine an employee's attitudes.

Age was the major variable accounting for different employee attitudes toward the CWW. Evidence suggests that younger workers like the schedule more than do older workers, and their leisure orientation may account for some of these differences. Differences based on age may also be a function of fatigue. Perhaps older workers find the longer work day more of problem than do younger ones. Little evidence from our research supported this notion, however.

Work Performance

We have already discussed implications of work performance in terms of organizational effectiveness. Some of these same aspects of change in work performance have implications for the employee as well. For example, there is some evidence that the CWW is associated with a degree of job enrichment. Employees who originally felt less satisfied with intrinsic aspects of their jobs may view the CWW positively if it is associated with changes in the work process. Changes in the task itself are likely to stem from needs for coverage, coordination, and planning where employees report to work four day out of the five (or more) the firm is open. Any job enrichment associated with the schedule—increased autonomy, responsibility, and job knowledge—may have positive implications for employees, as reflected in their attitudes towards the job itself. Furthermore, some employees may view the CWW as a compensation for unpleasant aspects of their jobs, such as boring or repetitive work. If employees view the rearranged leisure associated with the schedules as a benefit (depending upon their life-cycle stage), they may be more willing to endure work that is not intrinsically rewarding.

Nonwork Domain

Perhaps the most significant area affecting employees is that of home and personal life. The extra hours of work per day can have a major impact on an employee's families. For example, time available for the spouse and for children diminishes during the work week; the dinner hour is pushed back; or the children may be unsupervised for a few hours each day until one or both parents get home from work. On the positive side, employees who are parents may now have an extra full day to spend on family-related and leisure activities. The benefits and disadvantages of such a schedule depend on many variables, including whether or not the employee is a single parent, whether or not and when the spouse is employed, age and number of children, transportation needs of family members, commuting distance of the employee, and outside help available.

The family's needs will in turn influence employee satisfaction with the schedules. However, employees may also consider personal needs and outlets, such as hobbies and recreational or educational opportunities, as major factors in their preference for the schedule.

Another important benefit is that if the firm is on a four- (or even three-) day schedule, employees have one less day per week to commute. Aside from savings in cost of commuting, employees avoid the negative aspects of the trip. Few find the commute itself pleasant.

We must emphasize that the CWW means a trade-off between the number of hours worked per day and the number of days worked per week. The employees' nonwork needs and demands heavily influence their receptiveness to the schedule and attitudes toward it.

Summary

Because the CWW exchanges one fixed schedule for another, the resulting changes stem from the additional free day per week (assuming a 4/40) and the longer work day. Changes in job content and other work-related variables are secondary, since there is no element of additional employee choice involved (as there is in other types of schedules, such as flexitime). Consequently, there is little theoretical basis for predicting outcomes associated with performance, although we would predict that positive attitudes toward the schedule may generalize to certain extrinsic job facets, such as attitudes toward the company. The theory applicable to the CWW and its outcomes is that associated with the interaction between the employee's work and nonwork domains. The CWW's most profound effects may be those involving the employee's nonwork domain, its influence varying with the employees's life stage, marital status, age, and so forth. There is substantial evidence that on the job the CWW can improve organizational effectiveness in reduced start-up costs and overtime, although performance outcomes remain uncertain.

Notes

1. Nollen and Martin, 1978.
2. Hedges, 1975.
3. Finkle, 1979.
4. Hedges, 1975.
5. Nollen and Martin, 1978.
6. Finkle, 1979.
7. "Two Views of the Four-Day Work Week, 1971, p. 57; Hellreigel, 1972.
8. Swerdloff, 1975.
9. We wish to thank Mr. John Johnson of the Data Processing Department and Mr. Joseph DeGennaro of the Human Resources Department of Equitable Life for their assistance in providing this information.

10. Ronen and Primps, 1981.

11. Calvasina and Boxx, 1975; Dickenson and Wijting, 1975; Dunham and Hawk, 1977; Foster, Latack, and Reindle, 1979; Fottler, 1977; Goodale and Aagard, 1975; Hodge and Tellier, 1975; Ivancevich, 1974; Ivancevich and Lyon, 1977; Mahoney, Newman, and Frost, 1975; Maklan, 1977; Nord and Costigan, 1973; Poor and Steele, 1970; Tellier, 1974.

12. Nollen, 1979*a*.

13. Ibid., p. 9.

14. Ibid.

15. Ibid.

16. Seltzer and Wilson, 1978.

17. Ibid.

18. Ibid.

19. Wheeler, Gorman, and Tarnowieski, 1972.

20. Nollen and Martin, 1978.

21. Ibid.

22. Wheeler, Gorman, and Tarnowieski, 1972.

23. Nollen and Martin, 1978.

24. Nollen, 1979*b*.

25. Nollen and Martin, 1978.

26. Nollen, 1979*b*.

CHAPTER FOUR

Flexible Working Hours

Definitions, Variations, and Examples

Flexitime is an innovation that uses the work schedule to address issues of individual needs and organizational effectiveness. It assumes that employees have individual needs and therefore allows them to vary work schedules accordingly within certain ranges and dimensions. Employees may vary hours at work and distribution of those hours, but not the total hours worked over a given period.

Allowing employees to adapt their work schedules can affect many other aspects of the work experience. Flexitime can influence employee's autonomy through increased participation in decision making and through responsibility for maintaining coverage. Flexitime can also enhance group cohesiveness and group orientation toward the organization's objectives, as employees must cooperate to maintain work processes. In addition to improving the quality of work life, flexitime can help improve the fit between work and personal domains.

Flexitime was invented in 1967 to alleviate traffic problems for employees of a German aerospace company. People soon recognized other benefits in the system, and the concept spread quickly throughout West Germany and the rest of Western Europe.

Today approximately 30 percent of the West German labor force and 40 percent of the Swiss labor force use some form of flexitime. France, Austria, England, the Scandinavian countries, and (to a lesser extent) Ireland, Italy, Spain, Portugal, and the Benelux countries have adopted the system on a widespread basis. Even the Soviet

Union has granted official approval for the adoption of flexitime in industry.

Between 1970 and 1973 use of flexitime grew rapidly throughout Western Europe. A few factors common to most of these countries help to explain this phenomenon.

1. In the early 1970s, the unemployment level in much of Western Europe was extremely low. A shortage of labor and the desire of employers to attract and retain workers provided a major impetus in adopting alternative work patterns.
2. The compressed work week did not offer a viable alternative to flexitime in Europe, since weekly working hours there extend beyond 40 hours per week. Compressing more than 40 hours into four days would result in extremely long work days when combined with commuting times.
3. Legislation in Europe was less restrictive toward flexitime than in the United States.
4. Although the original adoption of flexitime resulted from practical organizational European needs, industries' commitment to individualization and self-determination contributed to its acceptance.

In the United States, the adoption of flexitime has not been as rapid, since it has had to compete with other alternative schedules, such as the compressed work week. In addition, legal and contractual considerations have limited the flexibility possible for large groups of employees—in particular, for government workers and union members. Furthermore, high unemployment compared with that of the Western European countries and other economic factors have given companies little incentive to compete for valued employees with flexitime.

Within the past four to five years, however, much of this has changed. The concern for employee productivity and quality of life has encouraged many firms to consider flexitime.[1] Projections from one survey indicated the following use levels of flexible work schedules for the United States as of 1977:

Of private sector organizations employing 50 or more people, 12.8 percent used flexitime.

Of all employees 5.8 percent were on flexitime.

Between 2.5 and 3.5 million employees were on flexitime, excluding those who were self-employed and professionals, managers, and salespeople who typically control their working hours anyway.

Government agencies in 42 states are using some form of flexible work schedule arrangement.[2]

The authors of this survey added that the use of flexitime perhaps doubled from 1974 to 1977. However, the system appears to be more popular or feasible in some industries than in others. Nollen and Martin projected the following usage patterns among selected industries:

In manufacturing, 10.3 percent.

In transportation, communication, and utilities, 17.1 percent.

In wholesale and retail trade, 14.4 percent.

In finance and insurance, 19.3 percent.

In service industries, 14.4 percent.[3]

To comprehend better the aspects of flexitime that affect its acceptability and rate of implementation, we should define the possible variations of the system and their implications for the organization.

Basic Definitions

The main objective of flexitime is to create an alternative to traditional fixed work schedules by granting employees a certain freedom to choose their arrival and departure times. The organization usually defines the degree of variation possible. (See Figure 4–1.) The simplest variation allows the employee to determine starting and finishing times within a certain time range set by the employer, provided that the employee works the contracted daily attendance hours. Conditions governing the degree of flexibility may include these factors:

Total number of hours the company is operative during the day.

Hours an employee must be present.

Level of interdependence between jobs, between departments, and with suppliers and customers outside the organization.

We should emphasize here that employee choice is restricted to variations in times present at work and to the distribution of working hours. There is no choice in the number of working hours; this is mandated by the organization. Furthermore, flexitime does not alter current management policies regarding vacations or sick leave allowances.

Important definitions associated with flexitime include the following:

Figure 4–1

Two Examples of Flexitime Schedules

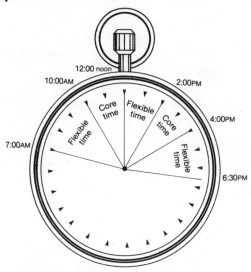

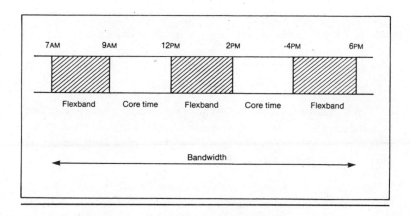

Core Time. Core time refers to the daily mandatory attendance hours during which all employees must be present on the job. This block of time, established by the organization, does not apply to those who are ill, on vacation, or away on company business. The primary purpose for having core hours is to establish times during which normal channels of communication are known to be open.

They also provide minimum coverage hours for working with customers, dealing with the public, and scheduling deliveries from suppliers.

Instead of using a core period through the middle of the day, the organization can provide greater flexibility by splitting the core time into a morning period and an afternoon period, thus creating a flexible lunchtime. Using two core times allows an employee to extend the lunch break to a few hours or to limit it to a minimum amount of time (usually half an hour). Employees can go home for lunch, attend to family chores, go shopping, or pursue recreational activities.

Flexbands.   Flexbands are the periods during which the employee may be present or absent, provided the employee meets the firm's requirements for total hours on the job. Flexbands occur at the beginning and end of the day (or if there are two core periods, on either side of the lunch period).

Lunch Break.   Flexitime systems allow variations in the type of midday breaks other than the traditional nonflexible lunch hour. These include the staggered lunch, semiflexible, and flexible lunch breaks.

Staggered Lunch Break.   Different groups of employees stagger their lunch periods to provide station or office coverage throughout the day and to reduce cafeteria congestion. Either the organization preassigns lunch times, or members of a work team decide on them. These assignments are usually permanent.

Semiflexible Lunch Break.   The organization defines a shutdown period during which all employees must stop work; the period usually lasts about a half hour. Flexbands are established both before and after this required lunch break.

Flexible Lunch Break.   A flexible lunch break requires that the organization define a midday flexband between two core periods. Employees can choose both the duration and timing of their break, as long as it falls between the minimum (usually a half hour) and maximum of the lunch flexband (about two hours in most organizations). Employees like this system because it allows them to schedule the time and duration of the lunch break. (See Figure 4–2.)

Bandwidth.   The bandwidth (or day-span) refers to the number of hours the company is open, from the beginning of the morning

Figure 4–2*

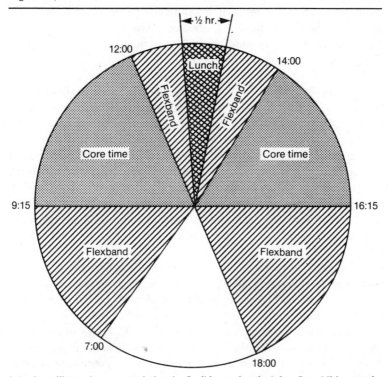

* A chart illustrating one variation in flexible work schedules. In addition to the two flexbands at the beginning and close of the day, there is a flexband on either side of the required half-hour lunch.

Source: Simcha Ronen, *Flexible Working Hours: An Innovation in the Quality of Work Life* (New York: McGraw-Hill, 1981), p. 42.

flexband to the end of the evening flexband. The length of the band-width is an important factor contributing to the system's level of flexibility. (We will discuss considerations governing the length of the bandwidth later.)

Contracted Attendance Hours. The variations in working sched-ules and the extent of the system's flexibility do not affect the basic total contracted attendance hours; the individual employment con-tract or relevant collective agreement stipulates this term. Employees can choose their preferred schedule within the options provided, as long as they complete the contracted number of hours. The idea of a contract implies a negotiation between the employer and the employee with some level of input from the employee. However, this is not the case in most organizations. The contracted attendance hours are accepted as conditions of employment in return for a wage or salary.

Settlement Period.   The period during which the employee must work the contracted hours is the settlement period. For example, if the settlement period is one week, the employee may vary the number of hours worked per day as long as these hours add up to the required number by the end of the week. If the settlement period is one day, there can be no variation in the length of the work day; the only flexibility possible is in the scheduling of hours. Depending on legal, contractual, and organizational constraints, the settlement period may vary from one working day (in which an employee has to work eight hours) to a week, a full month, or even longer.

Banking (Carryover).   One provision of the flexitime allows an employee to carry over debit or credit hours from one settlement period to another. For example, if the settlement period is one week and the contracted number of hours for this period is 40, the organization may allow its employees to work only 35 hours in one week and to compensate for the debit of 5 hours during the next week by working 45 hours. The worker makes up five debit hours during the flexband periods. Credit balances occur when an employee works more than the contracted hours and has no debit hours to make up. It should be noted that credit balances are not compensated as overtime but are additional hours worked during one settlement period in exchange for hours taken off in subsequent periods. In most systems employees must take their credit hours during the flexbands, since presence during the core periods is required.

In a system with little or no core time and banking, the employee may be able to work some version of a 4 or 4½-day work week.

Overtime.   The various possibilities of work scheduling require a clear and precise description of conditions that constitute overtime. Traditionally, *overtime* is defined as the time worked beyond the *regular* starting and finishing time, at the request of a supervisor. However, the definitions of overtime in a flexitime situation may take various forms, depending on the particular system in use. Overtime hours and associated compensation can be included in a flexitime system, but management and the employees should clarify and agree fully on the conditions associated with it.

Conditions used to define overtime situations in flexitime organizations have included the following:

1. Initiation and authorization of overtime by supervisors.
2. Predefined hours during the day charged as overtime either for an individual or for a work group as a whole. The supervisor usually negotiates with the individual or the group to determine what these hours will be.
3. A system to define overtime hours according to involuntary deviations from average starting or quitting times.

We should emphasize that these conditions must be clearly defined to employees before the overtime situation arises.

Time Recording. A time-recording system is necessary to provide an accurate record of the employee's hours worked for the employee and the employer within a specified period of time. Management has the responsibility of ensuring that the employee has worked the contracted number of hours and that the law governing the minimum and maximum number of working hours and other aspects of wage and hour regulations are enforced. For the employee the time recording system should provide a handy reference to the status of hours worked within the settlement period. We should emphasize, however, that the time recording system serves as a source of information for planning and scheduling, not as a means of monitoring employees and policing their activities.

The choice of time-recording device depends chiefly on schedule complexity. Some flexitime systems may be so simple as to require only a log-in sheet for morning arrivals. For example, in a system having no banking or carryover and having an inflexible lunch, starting time would determine quitting time. An arrival at 9:15 A.M. would dictate a departure at 5:15 P.M., given a seven-hour workday and one-hour lunch. A complex, electromechanical time-recording system would be unnecessary. On the other hand, consider the following situation wherein much greater flexibility is allowed:

Arrival:	9:03 A.M.
Lunch begins:	12:22 P.M.
Lunch ends:	1:50 P.M.
Departure:	5:42 P.M.

How much time has the employee worked on this particular day? The flexible lunch hour and variations in the length of the work day make calculation more complex and time-consuming. Here a time-recording device seems necessary. It frees the employee from time-consuming calculations and reduces the possibility of error.[4] The device also provides a basis for information in settling disputes over credit or debit balances. This protects the employee as well as the employer.

There are four alternatives to evaluate carefully when choosing a time-recording system:

1. A manual time-recording system usually includes a daily or weekly log sheet on which each employee records his or her starting and stopping times. An accounting system then compiles this information by settlement period and by group or department. Manual recording systems vary in terms of who does the recording. For example, the supervisor may log all employee activities or may delegate this responsibility to the employees themselves.

2. The simplest form of mechanical recording is the time clock and clock cards, which employees use to punch in. The chief advantage of the time clock system is that it provides a mechanical means of logging time while minimizing capital expenditures. The chief disadvantage is that many employees resent having to clock in— especially in those organizations lacking a history of timing devices.

3. The concept of time recording using a meter has been the most popular and successful of nonmanual recording systems in companies implementing flexitime. The meter system provides a cumulative record of the amount of time worked within a settlement period. Furthermore, it is popular with employees because a cumulative record avoids the invasion of privacy associated with a time clock, which registers starting and stopping times.

4. Computerized attendance recording systems represent the state of the art in time recording. In a typical system employees have their own personalized plastic badges, similar to credit cards, which they insert into a data terminal designed to read the coding on the badge. Telephones have also been used as data terminals to record arrivals and departures. The computer logs the time worked, and this information is periodically provided to management and employees in the form of a computer printout.

Variations and Examples

In considering the possible variations of flexitime, we shall categorize the alternatives within the context of legal and contractual regulations requiring overtime payments. These are a major limiting factor in flexitime systems design. Paradoxically, the requirement of overtime differentials for excess hours worked, which is considered an achievement by unions, is the chief obstacle to flexitime implementation in many cases. These constraints on overtime are based on requirements for wage premiums to certain employees who work in excess of defined work periods. They can be categorized into three broad areas:

1. Overtime premiums for work in excess of a stated number of *hours per day* (e.g., federal employees up to G.S. 10).
2. Overtime premiums for work in excess of stated *hours per week* (e.g., employees in private firms covered by the Fair Labor Standards Act).
3. No overtime premium for extra hours worked (e.g., management or exempt personnel).

Other constraints include shift differentials and Saturday, Sunday, and holiday premiums.

These differences limit the application of the flexible working hours system in several ways. The first group, the "eight-hour employees," can be permitted variations in flexible working hours (FWH) within one working day. The second group, the "40-hour employees," may benefit from variations that allow carryover of either debit or credit hours from one day to another, provided that 40 hours or the specified contracted hours are completed by the end of the work week.

The criteria for how much flexibility to build into the system include the requirements for advanced notice from employees regarding their planned schedule, the number and length of core periods per day, the length of the flexbands, and the existence and amount of banking allowed. Variations in flexibility according to these criteria include the following types of flexitimes:

Flexitour

Under a flexitour employees can determine their starting and quitting time within certain limitations. The decisions may be made individually or in groups. After employees have chosen among the alternatives, that schedule becomes fixed for a preassigned period. The flexitour itself usually refers to the amount of time for which the schedule applies. The duration of the flexitour often corresponds to the settlement period, although some organizations have used one month or three month flexitours as well. Within the flexitour model are two common variations.

Group Flexitour

The group flexitour variation applies to groups of employees constituting a department or an integral office unit. All members of this group must arrive and depart at the same time, based on the predetermined flexitour. The department head is generally responsible for ensuring that these arrangements are in accordance with overall production requirements.

Individual Flexitour

In the individual flexitour variation, each employee chooses his or her schedule for the next accounting or preassigned period. Teams of employees may have to coordinate their chosen alternative to accommodate interrelated work processes. The employees must themselves consider the state of interdependence of working conditions and must arrive at the final schedule through negotiation and mutual consideration. (In the public sector, the Office of Personnel Management [the Civil Service Commission] terms this variation *individual tour.*) In most cases, the final arrangement requires approval by the supervisor involved in the particular work situation.

Flexible Day

The flexible day, also called gliding time by some people, allows each employee to choose a daily arrival hour within the flexible band the organization specifies. The employee does not have to receive supervisory approval ahead of time and is free to choose the starting hour of each separate day as long as he or she works no more than eight hours. There are a few subvariations within this alternative.

Fixed Lunch Break

With the fixed lunch break, the flexible day allows an employee to choose a starting time within a flexband. The lunch break is fixed and there is a single core time that starts at the end of the morning flexband. If the organization designates a specific time and length of the lunch break, the starting hour the employee chooses for a particular day will determine the time he or she finishes the workday.

Variable Lunch Break

In order to accommodate individual needs and desires further, some organizations or departments provide two core time periods each day, allowing a third flexband in the middle of the day. The third flexband allows the employee to decide the time of the lunch break, as well as the duration, within certain limitations. Usually, the organization prescribes a minimum required lunch period. For example, the organization may define a midday flexband of two hours and require a minimum of a half-hour lunch break.

Flexible Week

Under present U.S. laws, many private-sector employees entitled to overtime payments for any number of hours worked over 40 in one week receive it as a premium on their wage or salary. This provision allows a certain level of flexibility *between* days. An employee working extra hours on one day can work fewer hours on another (that same week) as compensation. Thus starting time no longer necessarily defines finishing time. The possibility of debit or credit hours carried over from one day to another provides a much higher level of flexibility and self-determination for the working individual. Like the eight-hour variations, the level of flexibility within the week can differ from one department to another within the same organization. The levels of flexibility within the week are the same as those for the single day (with the exception of the carryover option). Listed from least flexible to most flexible, these options include: one core period daily with a fixed lunch, lunch break with a midday flexband, two core periods, and no core time.

The organization designates the number of carryover hours from one day to another, and this must be consistent with aspects of the flexitime system, such as the width of the flexbands and the range of the bandwidth.

Flexible Settlement Period

Flexible settlement period allows carryover of credit and debit hours from one week to another (usually from 5 to 15 hours can be banked). If it does not violate legal or contractual regulations (as in Europe), banking of hours within a preassigned limit from one month to another is permissible and even recommended. We have summarized each of these variations in terms of level of flexibility in Table 4–1.

Organizations not bound by legal or contractual considerations, with an established climate of trust and responsibility, have more flexibility. Three possible variations are day-off compressed week, weekend redefined, and flexiyear schedule.

Table 4–1

Level of Flexibility for Each Variation

	Flexitour		Flexible Day			
	Group Flexitour	Individual Flexitour	Fixed Lunch	Variable Lunch	Flexible Week	Flexible Settlement Period
Individual discretion	None	Limited	Yes	Yes	Yes	Yes
Core periods	Yes	Yes	One	Two	One or two	One or two
Flexbands	None	None	Two	Three	Two or three	Two or three
Carryover (daily)	None	None	None	None	Yes	Yes
Banking	None	None	None	None	None	Yes

Day-Off Compressed Week

The organization may allow the employee a half day or even a full day off to use accumulated credit hours. The organization allows the employee to be absent during core time. The implication of absence during core times is that the employee may voluntarily schedule a compressed work week. (The advantages and disadvantages of the compressed week were discussed fully in Chapter 3.)

An organization that allows core time off may choose to limit the particular day an employee may opt to be absent by assigning core days. Typical core days are Tuesday, Wednesday, and Thursday; employees *must* be present during core hours of these days. Another way of restricting core time off is to limit the number of absences during core time periods within a settlement period. If, for example, there are 2 core time periods per day or 10 per week, employees might be absent for 2 out of the 10 core periods. This would mean that employees could take two half days or one full day during the settlement period.

Weekend Redefined

A most flexible system allows employees to choose an alternative to the weekend, even to the extent of scheduling it during the middle of the week. Just as an organization may expand its bandwidth, depending on local regulations, to include many hours each day (e.g., 6:00 A.M. to 8:00 P.M.), it may expand the discretionary time available to employees beyond the five days of Monday through

Friday each week. In this case, employees could choose to schedule their working days between any of the six or seven days the facility is open. Employees may decide to schedule their weekend during the middle of the week or to schedule it contiguous to one of the traditional weekend days. Because recreational facilities are often crowded on a Saturday, it might be appealing for the employees to schedule their weekends for Sunday and Monday.

Flexiyear Schedules

Flexiyear scheduling represents the ultimate level of flexibility while still recognizing the organization's needs. Under a flexiyear system, the firm and the employee negotiate the number of hours worked within a year. The organization and the employee can also agree upon the way in which these hours will be worked, or else they can determine hours on a daily or weekly basis.[5] For instance, an employee who contracts to work 1,500 hours for the year may decide to work 30 hours per week for 50 weeks or 37.5 hours per week for 40 weeks.

Swedish, French, and German organizations have experimented with the flexiyear concept; it is gaining some level of acceptance in these countries. In Germany, for instance, the chief group of employees who have utilized the flexiyear schedule are part-time employees in the retail industry.

Having defined the possible variations associated with flexitime, let us now examine how American firms have implemented flexitime and how these programs have affected organizations and employees.

Field Results

We will present a summary and review of findings from approximately 12 private sector and 25 public sector organizations. More detailed results can be found elsewhere. We will compare these findings with those of other researchers who have conducted literature reviews and surveys on the impact of flexitime. This should present the most complete picture possible. We will also discuss explanations and a theoretical basis for these findings.

We did not standardize the experiments we conducted in each organization, but instead determined the criteria for evaluation separately in each case. Even those firms reporting the same dependent variables used varying criteria for their measurement. With this in mind, we are reporting three broad categories of information. To indicate trends we have grouped the measurements taken from these studies on flexitime into three major categories:

Table 4–2 and 4–3—Organizational Effectiveness and Membership.

Table 4–4—Attitudes.

Table 4–5—Time Management.

The results for each organization are reported as direction of change, positive, negative, no change, or inconclusive.

Findings were considered inconclusive when the majority of respondents reported no change or when the percent of employees reporting an improvement varied by 10 percent or less from employees reporting a decrease. In contrast, increases were reported when one third or more of the respondents were positive, and negative responses were minimal. We have been unable to report the amount of change for each organization in this type of summary because of the many different methodologies and degrees of rigor employed in the organizations investigated. The breakdown of results from each agency, including amount of change, is presented in detail elsewhere.[6]

Both objective data and subjective results are reported in these studies. In some cases the information source is strictly attitudinal, such as those results describing attitudes toward the schedule and changed attitudes toward the job and employing organization. In other categories, such as organization effectiveness and membership behavior, the types of results reported include both objective and subjective data. In each table we have differentiated the results between these two types; within this we also present the results from the private and the public sectors.

Organizational Effectiveness and Membership

Table 4–2 presents the summary of all measures relating to effectiveness and membership for both the private and public sectors. Criteria for effectiveness and membership included performance, work climate, costs, absenteeism, and tardiness.

Performance

Under Performance, we have summarized all related measures, including such criteria as quality of work, quantity produced, accuracy, efficiency, ability to meet schedules, increases in interdepartmental or interorganizational communications, facility in contacting customers, and usage of WATS telephone lines.

Note that in both the objective and subjective data and across the public and private sectors, there is only *one* report from an organization of a decrease in productivity. With respect to the objec-

Table 4–2

Organizational Effectiveness and Membership

	Objective Data		Subjective Data	
	Private Sector	Public Sector	Private Sector	Public Sector
Performance	N = 9 4 positive 5 no change	N = 11 9 positive 2 inconclusive	N = 27 19 positive 7 no change 1 negative	N = 17 14 positive 1 no change 2 inconclusive
Work Climate	N = 2 2 positive	N = 1 1 positive	N = 35 16 positive 17 no change 2 negative	N = 17 12 positive 4 no change 1 inconclusive
Costs	N = 3 3 positive	N = 9 6 positive 2 negative 1 no change	N = 2 1 positive 1 no change	N = 4 1 negative 1 no change 2 inconclusive
Absenteeism	N = 11 7 positive 4 no change	N = 11 7 positive 1 negative 2 no change 1 inconclusive	N = 9 4 positive 5 no change	N = 6 6 positive
Tardiness	N = 4 4 positive	N = 9 9 positive	N = 4 2 positive 2 no change	N = 5 5 positive

N = Number of measures reported by organizations.

tive data, the public sector was more positive than was the private sector, which experienced an almost equal distribution of positive and no-change results. Subjective data was consistently positive— although, as with the objective data, more private sector firms reported no-change findings than did public sector firms.

Results reported in other research is consistent with our findings that flexitime tends to be associated with improvements or maintenance of productivity levels. Nollen and Martin report on a survey of 196 managers, each representing a U.S. organization using flexitime.[7] Table 4–3 presents a summary of their results, in which we have categorized their findings to correspond generally with our descriptions of results. Types of performance reports included actual productivity, external communications, work coverage and scheduling, and relationships with those outside the organization (such as

Table 4–3

Nature of Effects	Changes Caused by FWH (percent of all users)		
	Better	No Change	Worse
Performance:			
Productivity	48	48	4
External communications	14	65	21
Work coverage	30	32	38
Work scheduling	21	44	35
Relationship with customers	22	70	8
Relationships with supplies	5	91	4
Work climate:			
Internal communications	6	56	38
Difficulty of management job	5	45	50
Costs:			
Unit labor cost of production	21	73	6
Overtime costs	44	54	2
Personnel administration costs	5	82	13
Recruiting	65	34	1
Training	5	90	5
Utilities costs	4	70	26
Support services costs (security, cafeteria, etc.)	2	80	18
Membership:			
Absenteeism	73	25	2
Tardiness	84	12	4
Turnover	53	46	1
Attitudes:			
Employee morale	97	3	0
Time management employee scheduling	27	35	38
Transportation:			
Employee commuting	77	18	5

N = 196 in the United States, 1977.
Note: Each organization is represented by one reporting executive.

Source: Adapted from Stanley Nollen and V. H. Martin, *Alternative Work Schedules, Part 1: Flexitime* (New York: American Management Association, 1978), p. 18.

customers and suppliers). Regarding productivity, about half of the organizations reported improvements; half reported no change.

Results were more equivocal for work scheduling and work coverage. Those firms reporting changes for the better, no change, and changes for the worse were almost evenly distributed. The areas of coverage and work scheduling are aspects of task performance that flexitime may significantly influence. Firms must maintain coverage and provide adequate scheduling, even though many employees are unavailable during part of each day. Depending upon the nature and demands of the task, the willingness of employees to cooperate, and employee attitudes, implementing flexitime may either facilitate or hinder scheduling and coverage. (We discuss the necessary criteria for maintaining coverage and scheduling needs in Chapter 10.) Flexitime appears to affect very little, or to improve, relationships with groups outside the organization—specifically suppliers and customers.

In a different review of flexitime results, Nollen came to these conclusions about how flexitime affects productivity:

Based on roughly 40 case studies and surveys, containing over 55 separate estimates, a conservative conclusion is that flexitime yields increased productivity for a third to a half of the firms that use it; roughly half the employees on flexitime give self-reports of increased productivity. The magnitude of the productivity increase is in the range of 10 to 15 percent on the average. Possible reasons for these gains are increased effective labor input (fewer paid absences and less idle time while at work), better organization of work (fewer interruptions with meetings and calls concentrated in core hours), increased morale and job satisfaction, better management practices and supervisory style, and better accommodation to workers' biological clocks.[8]

From our review[9] and Nollen's,[10] which cover virtually all the available studies conducted to date, there appears to be substantial evidence for a slight increase in productivity associated with implementing flexitime. However, we hasten to add that changes in productivity may differ depending upon the criteria used. The criteria investigated in the studies conducted thus far differ widely, as we have indicated in presenting these results. Lumping these criteria together and calling them productivity therefore represents a generalization whose trend does not necessarily reflect accurately all of the components of that generalization. The major sources of improved productivity, one would assume, are those criteria associated with improved use of time, organization resources, and human resources. Further research clearly seems necessary to determine systematically the specific criteria that contribute to changes in productivity and to the magnitude of any such changes.

Work Climate

In both the public and private sector, the preponderance of data associated with work climate is subjective. This is consistent with the nature of the variable itself, which measures such perceptions as access to, and relations with, supervisors and co-workers; control over work hours; and quiet time when distractions and noise levels are reduced. The results indicate that employees consistently associate flexitime with improvements or no change in work climate.

One further change in work environment reported by four private sector organizations was the impact of flexitime on aspects of cooperation, communication, and coordination. In all four reports, a high percentage (although not necessarily a majority of those surveyed) believed that the overall effect had been an improvement. From Nollen and Martin's results, we grouped internal communications and difficulty with the task of management.[11] Apparently, such variables as work-unit size, task requirements, management style, and the extent of necessary change moderate the impact of flexitime on these areas of communication and cooperation. The organization's facilitating such change will be an important means for turning components of work climate from positive to negative.

The positive results from both studies indicate that providing employees with some control over work and time scheduling allows them to schedule greatly needed quiet time. This opportunity to work without interruptions can make those employees willing to take advantage of the opportunity more effective.

One report from supervisors in the private sector indicated that employees were better able to manage their own workload. Supervisors in two firms reported an increased need for, and improvement in, planning and scheduling. Apparently, supervisors and managers must supplement or replace monitoring as a form of employee control, depending upon the level of flexibility allowed. Planning and scheduling are among the most effective means available to the supervisor in helping decrease the reliance on monitoring. However, this also implies that inadequate preparation for implementation, consideration of new work flows, and changing work process or scheduling demands may produce less successful implementation of flexitime and less positive evaluations from management.

Costs
The Cost category reflects all aspects of flexitime's impact on the organization that increased or decreased the costs organizations reported. These include night differential expenses, plant operations, power consumption, maintenance, and overtime. In both the private and the public sector, there was evidence that flexitime can be associated with significant reductions in overtime expenditures.

Nollen and Martin's data on costs provide additional information.[12] From Table 4–3 we can see that significant percentages of users reported improvements in overtime and recruiting costs. Approximately one quarter of users reported increases in utilities costs, and slightly less reported increased costs in support services. Overall, however, it appears from this data that the impact of flexitime is not associated with significant cost increases, and that it may in fact produce savings for the organization.

There is a notable lack of data on costs. We still have no information on the actual financial impact of flexitime. Organizations attempting to implement a flexible schedule should record pre- and postimplementation data on expenses in order to assess the program's real costs. Costs to be considered include energy consumption, machine usage and downtime, and support services and savings in such areas as overtime and employee absenteeism or turnover. Managers should weigh start-up costs against any anticipated savings in order to sell the flexitime concept to cost-conscious management.

Absenteeism

Absenteeism includes all forms of absence that organizations report—sick leave, short-term leave, and personal leave. We have made no attempts to subcategorize absenteeism further, since the types of leave granted (with and without pay) and sick leave policy varied among organizations.

The aspect of leave usage that flexitime would seem likely to affect most significantly is short-term leave usage—in particular, absences of one day or less. When we extract these from the private sector data, the results are impressive. Of a total of six objective and subjective measures five were positive. The sixth report, based on objective data, indicated no absence. In order to evaluate the effects of flexitime on membership behavior, it is important to make this distinction.

From the reports on both the private and public sector, there is evidence that flexitime can reduce short-term leave and sick leave usage. These findings agree with those of Nollen and Martin, which found that the executives in approximately three quarters of firms experienced reductions in absenteeism (see Table 4–3).[13] In his review, Nollen reports that absenteeism declined in half to three quarters of the firms that used it.[14] The magnitude of change varied from a small amount to almost 50 percent. (Additional support has recently been published.[15]) These favorable results confirm the notion that flexitime alleviates the need to call in sick when employees have personal business to attend to or want an extra hour of sleep.

Tardiness

The impact of flexitime on tardiness is consistently positive for both objective and subjective measures and in both the public and private sectors, as long as organizations allow discretion on a daily basis. Those organizations that did not allow daily flexibility did not experience the benefits of reduced tardiness.

In general, however, we found that significantly reduced tardiness is one of the most consistently reported benefits of flexible scheduling. Nollen and Martin and Nollen supported these findings.[16] It is interesting that none of the organizations allowing discretion reported any problems with employee arrival after core time had begun. Perhaps this reflects employees arrival patterns. In almost all organizations surveyed, 80–90 percent of employees tend to arrive during the early portion of the morning flexband.[17]

Turnover

Although we had little data on changes in turnover associated with flexitime, other studies did report such results. In the Nollen and Martin survey, slightly more than half of flexitime users reported decreased turnover, and Nollen's review indicated that turnover declined in a third to half of the cases.[18] It seems obvious that flexitime can have an impact on reducing withdrawal from the organization as long as employees perceive flexitime as an important benefit unobtainable elsewhere.

Attitudes

Since an attitude is a form of personal evaluation or perception of an object or situation, the concept of objective measures is inappropriate in analyzing attitudes. All of our data in this regard are subjective; they represent self-evaluations. Still, such information is valuable, since attitudes often predict behavior. For example, an employee with unfavorable attitudes toward the organization is more likely to be absent frequently, to be tardy, and ultimately to leave the organization.

Table 4–4 presents a summary of survey data reporting changes in employee attitudes resulting from flexitime. We have grouped these attitudes into two general categories: (1) changes in *attitudes toward the job* expressed as morale or job satisfaction and (2) *attitude toward the flexitime program itself.* We differentiate between job

Table 4–4

Attitudes

| | Subjective Data | |
	Private Sector	Public Sector
Job satisfaction	N = 13 10 positive 3 no change	N = 17 17 positive
Attitudes towards flexitime	N = 21 21 positive	N = 15 14 positive 1 inconclusive

satisfaction and attitudes toward flexitime as separate perceptions by employees. Although one might hypothesize that favorable attitudes toward flexitime would improve morale, this may not necessarily be the case.

Morale/Job Satisfaction

Our data show that in both the private and public sector, changes in job satisfaction and morale associated with flexitime are consistently positive. In several organizations employees were virtually unanimous in their reports of more positive attitudes. Nollen and Martin reported that 97 percent of the organizations using flexitime experienced an improvement in morale. According to these researchers, "the increased freedom of choice, autonomy, and also responsibility that flexitime provides pay off in the form of more satisfied workers."[19] Additional support has been published in various scientific periodicals.[20]

Despite these positive results, there is one potential problem area. If some employees are for task-related reasons unable to participate in the program, management should expect that group's morale and job satisfaction to drop. Careful education and explanation can minimize the effects of this discrimination. Managers will have to consider lowered morale a possible negative side effect in the overall evaluation of flexitime.

Attitudes toward Flexitime

All entries in our data indicated overwhelming support for the flexible schedules. Types of questions regarding attitudes towards flexitime included desire to continue the program or make it permanent, problems monitoring the program, satisfaction with the use of flexitime, and feelings about returning to fixed hours.

The only nonpositive response in attitudes came from a group of supervisors who reported no change in satisfaction over time. It is difficult to draw conclusions in this regard. One concern is that the impact on supervisor attitudes depends upon the organization's style of implementation, including the training and help provided as supervisors cope with the schedule's new demands on them. (We will discuss these issues more fully later in this chapter.)

Despite these concerns, these positive results can only mean an improved work environment, including enhanced employee-supervisory relations. If these attitudes prove stable over time, the implications for the work climate are significant.

Time Management

Time management is the ability of employees to schedule and allocate their time in the most efficient and productive manner, both on and off the job. This indicator, like attitude, is measured chiefly through subjective reports, since the employees describe changes in their lifestyle outside of work. It is somewhat difficult for the organization to investigate objectively how flexitime affects its employees' personal lives. Furthermore, the organization is probably less concerned with actual changes in work/nonwork fit—since this is outside the realm or organizational functioning—as long as attitudes are favorable. Table 4–5 describes how flexitime affects some of these aspects of employee life outside the job. The categories we have chosen to present here incorporate time for family, recreation, control over personal life, and transportation.

This first category is broad, including various facets of the employ-

Table 4–5

Time Management	Objective Data		Subjective Data	
	Private Sector	Public Sector	Private Sector	Public Sector
Time management	N/A	N/A	N = 16 11 positive 5 no change	N = 9 9 positive
Transportation	N/A	N = 3 3 positive	N = 13 11 positive 2 no change	N = 12 11 positive 1 inconclusive

ee's personal life as well as home/work fit. Examples of the aspects investigated include ease of arranging child care; time available for family; control over work and personal life (through control over hours); community, educational, and social activities; satisfaction with work/nonwork fit; individual freedom and leisure time; and ability to conduct personal business. The results reflected improvements in all areas reported. Employees from 20 organizations out of the 25 studied reported positive results; others reported no change.

One organization in the public sector found that satisfaction with flexible schedules and their effects on personal time usage were related to how much an employee planned his or her recreational and other personal activities. In other words, if leisure or other activities outside of work matter to the individual, flexitime will probably result in a significant change. This also implies that some employees, for whom outside activities are less important, may need counseling or educational activities to help them make full use of their time, thereby improving their work/nonwork fit and quality of life overall.

Transportation

One would expect significant changes in transportation modes, length of commuting times, and expenses to follow the start of a large-scale, coordinated flexitime program within a metropolitan area. Because most metropolitan areas do *not* have extensive flexible hours programs, any small but consistent changes in a positive direction are meaningful. Factors influencing transportation for employees would include whether the employer was located in a suburban or a central business district, major mode of transportation (car or public transportation), and the work schedule of other nearby organizations.

It was clear from employee reports in most organizations (Table 4–5), that employees were already beginning to realize decreased commuting time and gas use, even though flexitime schedules had been implemented in a very limited basis in their geographic areas of work. Nollen and Martin reported that 77 percent of firms found flexitime an aid to employee commuting.[21] Jaeger and Groushko found that the most common reason cited for implementing flexitime was the easing of transportation difficulties.[22] Other studies have emphasized the relationship between flexitime and reduced stress associated with commuting, since employees can travel at off-peak hours and no longer have to be at work at a specific time.[23] If firms were to adopt flexitime on a widespread basis, especially in large cities, the benefits could become substantial. Employees of one private sector organization noted that an immediate benefit of flexitime was decreased pressure during the commute to arrive on time—even without decrease of actual commuting time.

Conclusions from Field Results

From our results, and from the results obtained in other studies, there appears to be substantial evidence that flexitime has positive consequences for both the organization and the individual. However, there are limitations associated with this research. For example, few of the studies we reviewed used controls or comparison groups or provided any longitudinal perspective. A single survey administered after implementation (post-only design) permit only weak conclusions, as Golembiewski and Proehl have pointed out.[24] Furthermore, the effects of flexitime should be investigated to see how they differ among varying employee levels within organization for union and nonunion employees, and among industry types. Despite limited populations and lack of statistical sophistication, the trends indicated by the studies are so consistent that they cannot be dismissed.

Implications

Implications for the Employer

We have thus far described the general empirical results of flexitime implementation. Using these results, we can investigate the overall implications for the employer and the employee related to organizational and individual effectiveness, quality of work life, and quality of life outside the work domain.

Organizational Effectiveness

The empirical results indicated the level of effectiveness improved through flexitime implementation. Objective data on productivity and subjective data on performance and interpersonal relations support this conclusion. Several aspects of flexitime implementation can contribute to improved effectiveness. We must consider not only direct benefits that allow the organization and the individual to work more effectively and efficiently, but also such indirect benefits as improved work climate and employee attitudes.

Something that improves productivity during and after any major, positively perceived intervention is the process of introducing and implementing the change itself. The increase in productivity brought about by such special attention is called the Hawthorne effect. Research on other interventions, however, indicates that increases resulting from the Hawthorne effect are not longlasting. In our data there is sufficient evidence to suggest that changes in productivity have been sustained long past the implementation period. However, to the extent that productivity increases result from the Hawthorne effect, these positive effects may decline somewhat over the long run.

A genuine organizational change that can result in a sustained increase in productivity is a change in employee attitudes toward their work. Flexitime should encourage employees to complete a task rather than simply to work 7½ hours per day. Employees who know they will receive credit for extra time worked tend to complete a task before the end of the workday.

Because employees arrive at different times during the morning, most firms have experienced quicker start-ups; the random manner of arrival tends to reduce casual banter at the beginning and end of each day. Employees quietly settle down to work as they arrive. Furthermore, since employees are scheduling time according to their bioclocks, they are ready to begin work when they arrive. Empirical results from public and private organizations support this perception. In addition, the flexible bands provide a quiet time for many employees, during which they can accomplish a lot without disruptions from telephones, fellow employees, or customers. Many employees arrive at the earliest possible time or work until late precisely for this reason.

Overtime Usage

Many firms' overtime costs have decreased significantly after introducing flexitime. There are two reasons for this decrease. First, a flexible hours system allows the employee to schedule work time not only around personal needs, but around work demands as well. Studies show that employees will voluntarily schedule work periods to coincide with workload peaks. In such schedules, a better overall matching of work time to workload may reduce the need for overtime and may consequently reduce overtime earnings. This implies that the worker is willing (up to a point) to schedule time to experience the intrinsic and extrinsic satisfaction of completing a task and gaining recognition for it. This situation is consistent with the increased productivity that often results from reorienting employee attitudes to emphasize task completion over membership and attendance. Nevertheless, there are other variables affecting the individual's willingness to schedule time by this criterion. The most notable variable is the possible intrusion of work demands into the employee's personal life. Employees who experience no reinforcement for scheduling their time according to work demands are unlikely to continue doing so, since they will have other more rewarding criteria to use in scheduling.

Second, a firm may also experience reduction in overtime simply because employees are available throughout a longer period during the day. For example, at four o'clock someone gives to the staff a memo that must be typed and sent out by 9:00 A.M. the following morning. Under a nonflexible system, completing the memo that afternoon would require staying overtime. Under the flexible hours system, someone could assign the memo to a secretary who routinely works from 10:00 A.M. until 6:00 P.M., thus eliminating the need for overtime.

Other data indicated that decreases in overtime tended to vary based on the type of work environment. Specifically, one study indicated that overtime decreases were consistently higher in administrative environments than in production environments. One would predict that the tasks in administrative environments may be less interdependent and structured, allowing employees to schedule their time independently of others. On the other hand, the high level of task interdependence and structure required in a production environment may limit the flexibility necessary to realize substantial decreases in overtime.

Service to Customer

A tangible and immediate organizational benefit of introducing flexitime is increased service to customers. Because the bandwidth has increased—in some cases by up to three or four hours—service-oriented organizations can increase their responsiveness and availability to their clients. Moreover, this improvement is achieved without having to introduce extra shifts or to hire part-time personnel.

Service organizations that plan to extend their service hours when they implement flexitime should be sure that personnel adequately cover early and late hours. If the work force is sufficiently large, this coverage may take no extra scheduling. If this is not the case, however, some sort of rotating schedule may be necessary, while maintaining as much flexibility as possible.

Those responsible for implementing flexitime should also note that extending service hours to the full bandwidth eliminates the quiet hours available to employees arriving early or staying late. Employees have consistently reported quiet hours as a major benefit associated with improved work effectiveness. With this in mind, it may be feasible to extend service hours though only part of the bandwidth in order to allow some quiet time at the beginning and end of the day.

Costs

One of the chief considerations when implementing flexitime is the cost of the system. These costs include (1) initial capital investment for training and start-up and (2) permanent changes in overhead costs, which can include both savings and additional expenses. Higher initial investment in the system can mean lower administrative or overhead costs over the long run. We will discuss these two types of costs separately.

Implementation Costs. When an organization decides to investigate the possibility of flexitime, management must consider certain initial costs. For a proper investigation, a team or steering committee should be appointed with the responsibility of gathering appropriate information and creating a proposal for implementing the system. The size of the committee will vary, depending upon the firm's size. The initial study should include these employees' salaries as part of the initial study costs, especially if they devote their time exclusively to this project.

Additional costs may include costs for travel, testing equipment, secretarial help, and use of other organizational resources. There may also be costs for a test site and for a small group of employees selected for the initial pilot study. At this stage most companies prefer to use a manual recording system for recording the hours worked.

Once the committee has completed its investigation, submitted a proposal, and received approval, the company is ready to invest in the time-recording equipment required for flexible working hours, unless of course the company has decided to use a manual self-reporting recording system. In general, the more advanced the recording system, the higher the initial investment costs; but the long-term administrative costs will be lower. A computerized system is the most expensive to implement, but it can reduce existing administrative costs by automating functions currently performed manually. The decision makers must also keep in mind that record-keeping becomes more elaborate, and therefore more expensive, as the number of options and possibilities under flexitime increase. For example: a flexitime system which allows banking requires a more sophisticated record-keeping system than a system without banking.

Even the most sophisticated time recording system may require special handling. For example, an employee may forget to shut off the meter and remove a key when he or she leaves for the day. Absence from the office on company business and other contingencies also require special treatment. Such problems may incur additional costs, depending on how well the FWH system can be integrated into existing procedures.

Overhead Costs.   The extended bandwidth built into flexitime prompts many firms to extend business hours. Depending on the length of the bandwidth, open hours may be extended during the normal working week by as much as 25–50 percent. As a result, FWH will increase the costs maintaining the firm's facilities.

Perhaps the more obvious of these additional costs are increases in heat, light, and power costs, which result from services provided at the extremities of the bandwidth. For example, a building was formerly open between 8:00 A.M. and 6:00 P.M.; having it open from 6:00 P.M. until 8:00 P.M. will add four hours of use per day. A firm may also require additional services, such as security personnel, cafeteria facilities, elevator operators, and switchboard operators. The organization must also consider employee safety when implementing FWH. Maintaining security is more difficult when employees arrive and leave during a much wider period of time, and having employees working alone at the extremities of the bandwidth may add the security problems of unauthorized access to confidential information, possibility of theft, and safety of employees themselves. These possibilities may require enlarging the organization's security staff.

Some firms have realized cost savings by utilizing their plant and equipment more efficiently. Extending the available hours over which the fixed assets of the company are utilized in a productive capacity can increase performance. However, only if employee starting and finishing times span the whole bandwidth can the organization increase the use of capital resources efficiently. This would apply mainly to a production environment. In such cases it may even be possible to eliminate certain types of equipment because of decreased demand during peak usage periods of the day. For example, a Swiss machinery producer with 30,000 employees reduced its annual costs for social installations (canteen, showers, and recreational facilities) by 30 percent because these installations had lower peak usage after the introduction of flexitime.

It is difficult to generalize the net effect of flexitime on organizational costs. Such factors as implementation costs, time-recording costs, and savings and expenses for property, plant, and equipment will vary from organization to organization. Data from the public and private sectors provide some support for overall cost savings, although no organization did a complete evaluation of all costs associated with flexitime. Any organization considering such a major intervention should carefully evaluate implementation costs as well as ongoing expenses and savings accrued. We should also emphasize that even if the system ends up costing the organization money, it will probably still be worthwhile because of the less tangible benefits for both the organization and the individual. In fact, if savings were calculated only on such factors as tardiness, absenteeism, and overtime, it is difficult to believe that the organization would find flexitime a major expense.

Membership Behavior
Many firms have silently tolerated occasional-to-frequent tardiness because of late train arrivals, traffic jams, or other situations affecting the employee's arrival at work. Often, if employees arrive during a certain grace period, they are paid for the lost time without having to charge the time to leave credits, personal time off, or vacation time. This typically amounts to between 12 and 20 minutes of tardiness time per employee every accounting period. Considerable costs may accrue to the firm over a period of time because of hours lost to tardiness. Employees may make up these "lost hours" of output at overtime rates of pay outside the normal work hours.

As our data indicated, tardiness virtually disappears as a problem within the flexitime system, since an employee's day begins when he or she arrives. The only way in which an employee might be late is if he or she arrives at work during the core time instead of during the flexbands.

In addition to significant decreases in tardiness, most firms have experienced decreases in absenteeism after introducing flexitime. Researchers have offered several reasons to explain this trend. First, it seems likely that employees who might have called in sick under an *inflexible* system will sleep later and come in later during the morning under flexitime. Such a procedure would constitute a mark against the employee's personnel record under inflexible hours, but is of no consequence under flexitime. Similarly, employees who would have called in sick or taken a day off for personal or family business can often schedule this business during flexbands and take only the time required.

Organizational Climate

Besides the direct effects of flexitime on organizational effectiveness, there are several less direct, subtler influences on the organization and on the employee. We have grouped these influences together under organizational climate to indicate these intangible, difficult-to-measure demands that help to set employees' general mood at work. These elements affect relationships among employees, those between employees and supervisors, and employee attitudes toward the work.

One way flexitime improves the organizational climate is through the system's democratic aspects. Under a fixed system of working hours, there are usually some groups (mainly white-collar employees or individual, privileged employees) who can be a bit freer in their arrival and departure times. Many management employees feel, for instance, that a perquisite of membership in management is the right to arrive a few minutes late each day. With the introduction of flexitime, such privileges disappear for individuals or groups—or rather, *all* groups have this privilege (assuming that flexitime is implemented for management as well as for nonmanagement).

Communications/Coordination/Planning

Many firms implementing flexitime have experienced a significant improvement in the communications patterns within the organization. Under flexitime, the staggered schedules within a department or work group places a strain on both horizontal and vertical channels. Unless more efficient and extensive patterns of communication develop within the work group, the success of the flexitime system will be jeopardized.

For example, temporary absences caused by differing schedules force managers to give employees sufficient instruction to work for a minimal amount of time independently. For the same reasons, employees must communicate their plans with each other, particularly if their job requires cooperation or teamwork. The employees must ensure that teammates know of their proposed schedules and have sufficient information on the job at hand to continue in their absence. What emerges from this increased communication is a heightened sense of cooperation and team spirit, in which one person can rely on another to act as his or her "deputy." Increased willingness to cover for one another means more overall flexibility. Employees are ready and able to perform the jobs of other employees when necessary.

Another consequence of improved communications is better management skills. Flexitime may mean that managers are absent during part of the day when employees are working; managers must therefore plan daily work assignments and projects and communicate them to their employees so that they can perform effectively in the manager's absence.

However, if communications problems existed before the implementation of flexitime, FWH can aggravate them. If workers are unwilling or unable to communicate their schedules to other workers, the results can be a lack of work, idleness, standstills, and pervasive friction between workers. This is particularly true in environments requiring teamwork. Unless resolved, these communications problems may jeopardize the implementation of flexitime and may disrupt the organization's functioning.

Since all personnel are available only during core time, internal and external communications may deteriorate. Most organizations have not found this to be a problem internally because employees make an effort to schedule meetings during core time and to work independently during the flexbands. In dealing with external communications, most service organizations establish some type of minimum schedule to ensure that there are full services available to customers all day. In some cases, this means extending service hours.

In highly interdependent jobs, such as assembly lines or certain clerical input, flexitime can create problems at points of interface if not implemented properly. Again, workers must establish adequate systems design and communications so that teams can plan and coordinate their schedules. This may require careful supervision at first to ensure that workers are cooperating sufficiently.

Recruiting/Reduced Turnover

Flexitime can have a positive impact on organizational climate by improving recruitment and reducing turnover. Because flexitime is appealing and because relatively few organizations offer this benefit, organizations under flexitime who actively recruit employees have found the responses to their programs have significantly increased.

The stringent Equal Employment Opportunity requirements imposed by the government have made the recruiting of minorities and women a particular problem for certain firms. Flexitime has been a significant advantage for those firms because it can attract staff in a tight minority-labor market. An applicant who selected the organization because of the opportunity for flexible working hours will probably have a higher level of commitment to the firm, thus improving the organizational climate.

Since flexible working hours may be an important criterion for choosing the firm, employees will not be as hasty to leave the firm as they might be otherwise. Many firms have experienced a reduction in labor turnover. Once accustomed to flexitime, the employee is unlikely to be attracted to a firm lacking this possibility. Furthermore, flexitime may accommodate changes in situations that might have led to turnover in the past. If an employee's carpool disbands, for instance, the employee might not have other alternatives for transportation to work under the nonflexible system. In contrast, flexitime might allow the employee to join other carpools leaving at a different time.

Availability of Flexitime to all Employees

It may be difficult to provide flexitime for certain types of employees within an organization. Examples are security personnel, maintenance personnel, switchboard operators, receptionists, and cafeteria employees. Implementing flexitime for other employees may aggravate the problem of these workers' perceived inferior status and low job satisfaction, since they are unable to participate in the system.

We recommend that the firm try to implement flexible scheduling for these employees, even if on a more limited basis. An alternative some firms have considered is a wage differential for employees unable to participate in FWH. Of course, this may pose problems for workers who could participate in flexitime but would prefer to earn additional money. Furthermore, unionized institutions may require extensive negotiations.

Misuse of Flexitime

Many firms are concerned that employees might attempt to cheat the system. We must emphasize that by choosing to implement flexitime, the organization is making the commitment to trust its employees. FWH demands a sense of mutual responsibility and trust between the employee and the organization. This mutual trust and responsibility can be jeopardized if employees attempt to cheat on their hours. The firm would suffer significant financial loss if cheating were to occur on a broad scale.

We have not heard of any cases of extensive cheating. Most firms have been pleased to state that employees themselves have reported the few instances of cheating. Cheating the system jeopardizes the privilege for all, and employees are willing to risk the sanctions necessary to avoid losing the system.

Implications for First-Line Supervisors

First-line supervisors are critical as a group; their support is absolutely necessary for successfully implementing a flexible schedule. Because flexitime has major consequences for a supervisor's job, we will discuss it here in detail.

The data describing front-line supervisors' perceptions of flexitime reflects the changes required of them. For example, when we compared reports of employees and supervisors within the same organization, our data revealed that employees sometimes perceived greater improvements in productivity than supervisors did (although the supervisors were consistently positive as well). In fact, the one negative report from the private sector described a manager's concern that the limited supervision characteristic of flexitime might increase inefficiency. In general, nonmanager employees perceive flexitime as influencing performance more positively than their supervisors do, although both groups report that flexitime has positive effects on productivity. It may be that supervisor perceptions are indeed more accurate than those of employees, who tend to exaggerate the benefits of flexitime. On the other hand, supervisors may be less positive in their reports because they perceive additional burdens placed on them to continue supervising employees whose schedule may not coincide with their own.

First-line supervisors . . . absorb the scheduling problems associated with these systems, which is clearly added work and compounds the problems of work flow. . . . And additionally, these exempt employees probably feel as though they have to be on the job when the first worker appears and until the last leaves. If these first-line supervisors are feeling put upon by this groovy new concept, then all subordinates will probably pay the price.[25]

Several studies have investigated the nature of the change required of first-line supervisors. In their study of how flexitime changed a supervisor's job, Dowell and Wexley found that the supervisor's job will be more complex.[26] Flexitime will certainly influence relationships with subordinates.

A supervisor may perceive a decrease in authority, since he or she will not have control over (nor in some cases even have to verify) employee starting and quitting times. Some supervisors have objected to this aspect of flexible scheduling because they feel threatened by a loss of power. Other supervisors have welcomed flexitime because in many cases it eliminates the necessity for time recording, which is a source of friction with employees and a time-consuming, nonproductive task. How supervisors react depends upon how much importance they attach to their monitoring function and how well they have been prepared to accept the new system.

With respect to work planning and scheduling, supervisors will no longer have the stability of a fixed schedule to work from. Work must be organized and scheduled to the point that the supervisor's presence is not required at all times. The supervisor must increase his or her awareness and responsiveness to all levels of interaction with subordinates, since there may be less total time for interaction.

Some current research has considered the general impact of FWH on the first supervisors working under flexitime.[27] These first-line supervisors came from different U.S. organizations using a wide variety of flexitime systems. According to Graf's results, the supervisors noted an increase in the amount of long- and short-term planning required on the job and a decrease in their own concern with direct control of employees. These supervisors also reported that there was a significant increase in the amount of both written and oral communication between themselves and employees, in spite of decreased opportunities to interact. We may surmise that this perceived increase in communication implies a more participatory style of supervisor.

Graf also found that supervisors had to generate more formal rules and regulations to ensure smooth work flow in their absence. Furthermore, the results indicated that supervisors believe they are more actively involved in the employee-appraisal process. What explains these results? Perhaps supervisors perceive a decrease in their direct control over the work unit because flexitime limits their ability to monitor all employees all the time. The increase in rules and appraisal activity may represent a compensation through indirect control. The supervisors must provide contingencies for the times they are unavailable, and some form of guidance is needed. Additional rules and appraisals may help to fill this void.

Another study measured the attitudes of first-line supervisors at Smith/Kline Corporation.[28] The supervisors reported first as employees, then as supervisors, regarding impact on their jobs six months after implementation. The researchers found that when the supervisors reported as employees, work attitudes improved after the implementation of flexitime. When they reported as supervisors, however, their attitudes did not show improvement at all after the implementation of flexitime. We observed the same effect in our public sector data. This indicates the role conflict supervisors experience. As employees, supervisors enjoy the system's benefits, yet as supervisors they may encounter problems in the work unit that result from flexitime. Consequently, their overall attitudes are less positive than those of the rank-and-file workers, who are accountable only for their immediate, discrete tasks.

Golembiewski, Fox, and Proehl investigated the impact of flexitime on supervisors after three years and found more positive results.[29] Of the 48 supervisors who participated in the study, more than 70 percent reported that productivity had increased; 20 percent reported no change. Furthermore, about 80 percent of first-line supervisors believed that after the three years, flexitime still had a positive effect on morale. These researchers concluded:

First-line supervisors continue to see a very favorable ratio of benefits to costs in flexitime over the long run. Flexitime applications do require changes in supervisory attitudes and behaviors, but these changes were within the competencies of most supervisors, and the advantages of flexitime probably motivated and reinforced the changes.[30]

From the results described in our review and from other researchers' findings, there is substantial evidence that flexitime requires major adjustments from first-line supervisors. The degree of change required in supervisory style and in ability to cope with change will clearly influence this group's attitudes and perceptions. How well the organization recognizes these needs and facilitates such change will have a bearing not only on the supervisors' attitudes, but on the success of the system itself. We should emphasize that if an organization's first-line supervisors do not support implementation of flexitime or if they feel threatened by it, the chances for success of the system drop significantly. In Chapter 10, Implementation, we will discuss steps the organization can take to recognize first-line supervisors' needs and to gain their support.

The trend of improved attitudes visible in Golembiewski's two studies indicates that flexitime should benefit first-line supervisors in their role as employees; and it should benefit them as managers, too, since they will see its positive effects on subordinates' attitudes and performance. Cases of successful implementation, where supervisors have adopted a management style responsive to the employer's needs and receptive to participation, have been associated with employee willingness to schedule time to meet organizational needs.

Of the few reported failures of flexitime experiments, most have resulted from situations in which uncooperative, authoritarian supervisors have been unwilling to try altering their supervisory style to accommodate the new system. Conversely, a participatory, humanistic supervisory style can favorably affect work climate. This approach heightens employee commitment to the task; this in turn refocuses attention away from the clock and toward the task at hand.

Implications for the Employee

When evaluating how flexitime affects the worker, one must remember that the quality of work life affects the individual's total life situation. Factors influencing the worker's quality of work life include task, physical work environment, social environment within the work situation, administrative system of the company, and relationship between work and personal life.[31] A work environment increasingly dominated by technology has prompted many people to accept worker alienation and disorientation as the cost of more jobs and higher wages. Socioeconomic norms have been evolving to resist these developments, however. Significant numbers of workers are protesting them—either actively, through their unions or other channels, or passively, through their work product and productivity levels. These workers are unwilling to work in a dehumanized setting in which they are considered replaceable parts.

This problem is not confined to the blue-collar worker. In order to promote productivity and efficiency, principles derived from scientific management, systems analysis, operations research, and other techniques traditionally applied to the industrial setting have also been used to evaluate white-collar jobs. The result is that the atmosphere in many white-collar jobs resembles that of the assembly line, with associated job insecurity and concern over job availability.

Flexitime is not a panacea for these concerns but can have a significant impact by improving the quality of life for both the blue- and white-collar worker. Flexitime affects the quality of work life through improved personal control over the work environment and affects the quality of life outside work through better adjustment of one's work life to personal lifestyle. Flexitime provides employees with greater freedom by allowing them to determine their working schedule within certain limits, according to their own personal needs. Not only are employees granted the right to decide, but they are also given the privacy of not having to explain or account for their decisions, so long as they remain within the bounds already agreed upon. This twofold freedom can help to offset the negative aspects of technological change described earlier. Specifically, flexitime can help workers and the organization to deal with feelings of alienation from jobs. Involvement in the decisions and the teamwork necessary to coordinate flexible hours can encourage workers to feel themselves to be active participants in the organization, not just anonymous, replaceable parts. The routinized aspects of certain jobs can also be reduced, as flexitime gives workers some control over their time on the job and their schedules for completing tasks.

We will discuss the implications of flexitime for the employee in three areas: (1) the work environment or climate, (2) work performance, and (3) the nonwork domain.

Work Climate

Flexitime affects the work climate related to the employee's bio-clock, tardiness, unpaid overtime for exempt employees, economic benefits realized by the firm, loss of personal absence privileges, time recording, and the need for structure.

Bioclock. People now generally recognize that individuals vary in their psychological and physiological needs. Not only do needs vary among individuals, but the needs vary within the individual during the day or over different stages of life. Most organizations, however, have either failed to recognize this aspect of the individual or have chosen to ignore it. The result is that the organization places a higher priority on the "appropriate" membership behaviors of attendance and punctuality than on working efficiently and productively. Flexitime reverses these priorities by giving performance more weight than membership behavior and allowing employees to choose the attendance patterns most appropriate for them. A system of flexible working hours thus allows some degree of adjustment in work schedule to accommodate variations in individual bioclocks or paces of life.

For instance, some employees who prefer to sleep late in the mornings may spend the time between 9:00 A.M. and 10:00 A.M. at work in a semisomnolent state. On the other hand, some employees wake at the crack of dawn but begin to fade by 4:00 P.M. Under flexitime both types can arrange their workday better to suit their own biological clock. They are more likely to work effectively on the job if they have some control in choosing these hours. Flexitime also means that an employee who was out particularly late at night or is tired can come to work later and proceed to work effectively and efficiently from the moment of arrival. Under a nonflexible system (or a less flexible one), the same employee would either arrive on time and work at less than top efficiency or would be tardy or absent.

Because employees can choose the working hours that coincide with their efficiency cycle, they will be more alert and take greater interest in their work. When the employees arrive at work, they are ready to begin. As a result, work atmosphere improves because workers feel healthier, more energetic, and better able to contribute more to their jobs.

Tardiness.   Tardiness has been a continuous and irksome problem for many organizations. For workers the possibility of such disciplinary actions as a note in personal records, a warning from management, and docked pay or reduced time off intensify the pressure to be on time. Employees often feel embarrassment or even shame over such actions. The responsibility most employees feel toward fulfilling their jobs and the threat of disciplinary action can provoke guilt and anxiety in a tardy employee. The demoralizing experience of having to account for one's whereabouts to the supervisor reinforces this guilt.

The cycle of tardiness, possible disciplinary action, and guilt wastes time and energy that everyone involved could devote to productive activity. Tardiness or membership behavior is not related to on-the-job productivity but to attendance at work. Productivity is affected only indirectly, in that tardy employees spend less time on the job. Both the organization and the individual misplace their goals by focusing on membership behavior rather than on task completion. Too often, organizations and individuals place greater emphasis on attendance and other associated behavior.

Flexitime eliminates the problems of tardiness and punctuality. Because the workday for an employee starts when he or she arrives, the missed trains or the unexpected traffic jams no longer mean tardiness. Flexitime removes the need to reach work on time and, accordingly, eliminates the fear of being late for an appointment or engagement outside work.

However, one form of tardiness that often concerns supervisors is an employee's late arrival for work during the core time. The organization must decide the seriousness of this offence and clearly define disciplinary action to employees. One suggestion is to require employees to make up this time twice over. For example, an employee who arrived 15 minutes after core time began would have to work an extra half hour to make up this time. Note that the shorter the core time period, the less likely this problem will be. We should note, however, that none of the organizations in the public or private sector reported this as a serious problem, since most employees choose to arrive during the early half of the morning flexband.

For the organization, reducing tardiness has significant benefits. The supervisor need not monitor the arrival times of employees or deal with offenders. Within the work group, relations between punctual and tardy employees can improve. Finally, both the organization and the worker can refocus their efforts on task completion, instead of wasting emotional economic resources reinforcing appropriate membership behavior.

Unpaid Overtime for Exempt Employees. Many management and upper-level employees work long hours without overtime. In the past this has been expected of management; supposedly the status of membership in management is compensation. Furthermore, company policy has usually dictated that staying late in the evening was no excuse for being late to work the next morning.

With the implementation of flexitime, the additional hours management employees work are at least recorded and reported to the personnel department. These employees are thus credited with the additional time worked. Since exempt employees use the same time-recording system as do nonexempt employees, extra time on the job allows commensurate time off later (up to certain limits and as long as banking is allowed); the time is no longer simply donated to the firm. This does *not* necessarily mean that time off accrues at overtime rates, however.

Exclusion from Economic Benefits Realized by the Firm. A source of controversy between labor and management has been the redistribution of any financial benefits resulting from flexitime. With the implementation of flexitime, many firms have realized savings through productivity increases and better use of capital assets. Workers (and especially labor unions) have questioned the rationale for permitting management to retain all residual benefits from introducing the system. According to this view, if higher productivity results from a more intensive use of labor, then workers should receive at least part of the resulting gain in the form of higher earnings, bonuses, profit sharing, or improved benefits (such as increased paid vacation or improved medical insurance).

Personal Absence Privileges. Employees in many firms routinely receive time off with pay for personal needs, such as doctor's appointments, which cannot be scheduled during nonbusiness hours. This paid time off can accumulate substantially during the year, depending upon the leniency of the firm. It thus represents a perquisite, and not just an economic commodity, for the employee.

One of the firm's chief advantages when implementing flexitime is the reduction of paid personal time off. Concomitantly, we can also view it as a disadvantage to employees. Under flexitime, employees can use the flexbands for personal time off, but must ensure that they make up these hours during flexbands. The company no longer absorbs employee time away from the job as unproductive or lost time.

In contrast, many employers permit employees to take personal time off but dock their pay for the hours not worked. These employees may well see flexitime as an advantage because it gives them the opportunity to take occasional time off without having to sacrifice their income level.

Time Recording. Some employees consider the reintroduction of the time-recording device (e.g., the punch clock) to be a disadvantage of flexitime. Time recording devices have often been considered a means of differentiating management from nonmanagement status. In addition, people have viewed time recording as a technique for controlling tardiness and absence for punitive purposes. Workers were docked pay, reprimanded, or put on probation if they punched in late.

However, recording time is a necessary part of individual freedom to distribute time. Furthermore, the system is indiscriminate, since all management and nonmanagement employees must use the device. There is no status differentiation involved. Once people understand this system, they usually drop any objections to mechanical time recording, and they cease to regard the necessary devices as disadvantageous.

Need for Structure. Many individuals depend upon a full and consistent work schedule with clearly defined hours to structure their lives. This structure is important to their psychological well-being. Long periods of unprogrammed time, which certain flexitime arrangements can produce, and the recurrent requirement to choose alternatives may prove unsettling to such employees.

People whose jobs are their chief interest and purposeful activity or those who have unhappy family lives may find the opportunity to schedule their own time and leisure or personal time undesirable. When given more time off the job, their frustrations, conflict, and boredom increase. This may take the form of aggressive or antisocial behavior toward the organization.

Planning and Teamwork

Implementing flexitime can have a direct impact on work performance in terms of planning and teamwork, particularly in service organizations and organizations in which the tasks performed are continuous processes.

In the case of service organization, employees must be available to clients throughout a defined period of the day—usually longer than the core time. This requires that employees coordinate their schedules to ensure complete coverage. Either the organization or the workers themselves can undertake such planning. If the organization imposes planning, then the employees have less flexibility. The organization should limit its control to the minimum.

For example, employees might rotate responsibility for coverage during early morning hours on a daily or weekly basis. Employees assigned to this coverage would lose their flexibility for this period, and other employees in the unit would be free to utilize the flexitime privilege as they desire. It is preferable, however, to give employees the opportunity to plan required scheduling themselves. This additional responsibility and the opportunity for decision making reinforces the concept behind flexitime—namely, the emphasis on the individual within the organization. Furthermore, employee decision making requires the work group to develop the cooperation, teamwork, and group problem-solving skills necessary to deal with this new responsibility. The work group will be motivated to develop these skills and maintain these newly acquired freedoms to avoid the imposition of management control. In many cases employees can easily solve scheduling problems if one worker plans to arrive early or leave late each day under flexitime. When maintaining coverage means more of an inconvenience for employees, the supervisor should observe group interaction and be alert to the possibility of one employee dominating others or of one employee being exploited.

If the work group successfully handles planning without intervention from management, then the skills in decision making and problem solving the group acquires will probably affect other aspects of the job. Exercising new rights can produce a significant improvement in the quality of the employee's work life. Moreover, the organization benefits as efficiency and productivity improves. Studies at one firm showed that morale had improved because of the team spirit that developed; employees felt that they belonged to an identifiable group.[32]

Because flexitime is more difficult to implement in such continuous-process operations as assembly lines, planning and teamwork become even more critical. In fact, these aspects become the prerequisites for successful implementation. If the system is successful, however, employees can receive benefits similar to those described for a service organization.

Efficiency and Task Completion

Research has shown that many individuals will make strong efforts to complete tasks they have begun and that employees find the act of completion itself a rewarding experience. Through flexitime the organization can play a major role in providing this reward by creating conditions in which the individual experiences the satisfaction of completing a task. Having experienced this reward, the employees should be motivated to repeat the experience, knowing that they will receive credit not only for hours worked, but also for completing the project.

Flexitime helps to improve the quality of working life by making task completion easier, if not actually encouraging it. Under flexitime employees receive credit for extra hours worked by *their own choice* during the day. (Overtime premiums would not apply if the employee decided to work more than the usual number of hours.)

Workers would not have to stop in the middle of a job at quitting time to put equipment away and clean up the work site, only to waste precious time the next morning setting up the task and getting underway again. This advantage applies to both blue- and white-collar workers. A manager can finish a report; a secretary can finish a typing assignment; an assembly line can finish a batch of goods.

For the employee one potentially negative aspect of this improved efficiency and orientation toward task completion is a reduction in overtime earnings. Though benefitting the firm, such a reduction can decrease the employee's income. This reduction can become a serious problem for the worker if the overtime was regularly scheduled and relied upon as a source of income.

Another concern to employees and many unions is that management may pressure workers to reduce overtime by scheduling their time according to the needs of the firm. This pressure may be overt, by limiting the worker's choice of hours over and above those embodied in the formal flexitime agreement, or may be more subtle. The employer might indicate which schedule the employee should "volunteer" to work and either directly or indirectly threaten sanctions should the employee choose otherwise. For example, employees could be made to feel that being available at straight-time pay would determine pay raises and promotions. The decision still remains with the employee, but the implications of the decision are now far more significant. Whether or not employees perceive the situation as coercion, they will resent the system, and its probability of success will diminish.

Even under a flexible working hours system, there can be legitimate needs for overtime during periods of heavy workloads, during seasonal trends, and for backlogs of work. The firm must carefully define overtime rules to avoid disadvantageous results for the employee.

Increased Job Knowledge

As a corollary of the increased planning and teamwork required when implementing flexitime, many workers have gained significant knowledge of their own tasks as well as of others' tasks. In order to maximize flexibility, many employees agree to cover for one another both horizontally and vertically within the organization. They may be required to accept additional responsibility when peers or supervisors are absent. To do so employees must be willing and able to exchange job functions and roles. As a result the employees develop skills and abilities otherwise denied them. These circumstances not only improve advancement opportunity, but also reduce the boredom and staleness associated with repetitive tasks.

Such activities encourage the members of a work group to utilize their group decision-making skills. They also require cooperation and reinforce teamwork. Often job knowledge requirements have opened previously nonexistent channels of communications among workers. Some organizations have recognized this phenomenon and have encouraged it through formal training programs. However, we recommend that management monitor this type of activity carefully to ensure that unqualified personnel do not accept positions of responsibility.

According to one company, "The program has forced us to develop people who have knowledge of more than one job. Therefore, job knowledge has increased dramatically."[33] Increased job knowledge for employees can result in higher skill-level ratings which, in a union environment, makes them eligible to bid on more highly rated jobs. In both union and nonunion environments, the employee can demand better wages based on increased job knowledge and the resulting increased value to the company.

The Nonwork Domain

Implications for change in the nonwork domain of the employee include changes in family, social, and recreational activities; educational pursuits; and changes in mode and duration of commuting patterns.

Family/Social/Recreation. Flexitime can bring about significant change in an individual's family and social life by effectively increasing the amount of leisure time available through a more convenient or appropriate schedule. Increased control over the availability of leisure time can have a significant impact on the structure of family life. Many of the traditional roles within family life—the husband as breadwinner, the wife as homemaker and babysitter—have been reinforced by rigid schedules of working hours. At one time the "typical" husband left early in the morning, was gone all day, and arrived home so late that he had little opportunity to interact with his children. The wife assumed the responsibility of delivering the children to school, picking them up, performing household chores, and cooking the evening meal. Flexitime provides the opportunity for both parents to participate in these activities. For example, the husband might leave later in the morning to have breakfast with his children and drive them to school; he might schedule a longer midday break to go home for lunch; or he might leave work early in the day to spend more meaningful time with his family. For the wife, benefits include a husband who is more active in family life and able to share some of the responsibilities previously delegated to her.

If both husband and wife are employed, they can adjust their starting and finishing times to one another or to the children's school schedules. They can coordinate their nonwork time to maximize efficiency in performing required household chores. In situations where parents must take time off from work for doctor's appointments, parent/teacher meetings, and school functions, flexitime can help by giving the parent an opportunity to participate in these activities without losing time at work.

As the two-parent, wife-at-home family is becoming atypical, a flexible schedule becomes more important. For the single parent who balances work and family requirements under great stress, flexitime is an answer to the double bind.

Because employees have a choice concerning their leisure time, a host of new possibilities arise. For example, employees can use recreational areas during nonpeak or daylight hours, and previously impossible social activities and hobbies become feasible.

When we described the variations possible in a flexitime system, we mentioned the concepts of core time and floating weekend. Core time off means that the employee may take half or full days off from work. The implications for leisure time are numerous. Most important, employees may create large blocks of time for hobbies, social clubs, community activities, and sports. Employees may combine this time with the weekend for early getaways or late returns, thus extending weekends into minivacations. The floating weekend may allow grouping two weekends together for a longer vacation and utilizing recreational facilities or resorts during off-peak periods. In addition to increasing enjoyment of less crowded facilities, employees may realize cost savings through reduced midweek rates at resorts.

Education.   Flexible scheduling may also result in educational opportunities, since flexible scheduling allows access to courses previously unavailable to employees. Depending on core hours, employees may be able to attend classes during their lunch hour, early in the morning, or in the late afternoon. If the organization allows core time off, employees can pursue educational activities at any time during the day. Organizations may wish to encourage continued education in fields that would help employees perform their jobs more effectively, by paying for all or a portion of the tuition. As a result both employees and the organization will be enriched as employees gain additional knowledge and skills.

Transportation.   When organizations define the workday for their employees, they do not include travel time to and from the workplace. This time is considered part of employee free time. Employees may choose to live a great distance from work, traveling a long way each day in order to have the opportunity to benefit from suburban life. (A recent newspaper article reported that 1.3 million workers travel 50 miles or more to work each day.) Or they may prefer to live near their place of work. The other major aspect of time spent traveling is the method of transportation. Public transportation can be faster or slower depending on its convenience to home and work, depending also on the level of traffic congestion along the route.

Flexitime simplifies transportation for the worker in several ways. Employees traveling on public transportation may be able to schedule their traveling at off-peak ticket prices. Furthermore, employees may be able to schedule better connections, thereby reducing waiting times for trains or buses. Those traveling by car at off-peak hours avoid traffic delays and reduce associated pressure and tension. Traveling is safer during less congested periods of the day and can take significantly less time. It may become possible for the worker to form carpools with neighbors who previously worked on different schedules. Cost savings can be substantial if a family can now function with one car instead of two. Finally, traveling (especially driving) can be arranged to avoid extreme and dangerous weather conditions.

All of this can mean a significant improvement in the quality of free time for the worker. By minimizing the unproductive time associated with commuting, employees have more free time to spend as they wish outside the work environment. They may be better able to schedule their work hours around their families' needs. The overall result is an improvement in the quality and quantity of time *spent* outside of work. It is interesting that most employees choose a new, comfortable arrival and departure time and, with few exceptions, follow a consistent and stable schedule.[34]

Notes

1. Nollen and Martin, 1978
2. Ibid.; Long and Post, 1981.
3. Nollen and Martin, 1978.
4. Ronen, 1981*b*.
5. Ronen, 1981*b;* Ronen and Primps, 1980.
6. Ronen, 1981*b*.
7. Nollen and Martin, 1978.
8. Nollen, 1979.
9. Ronen, 1981*b*.
10. Nollen, 1979.
11. Nollen and Martin, 1978.
12. Nollen and Martin, 1978.
13. Nollen and Martin, 1978.
14. Nollen, 1979.
15. Narayanan and Nath, 1982; Kim and Campagna, 1981.
16. Nollen and Martin, 1978; Nollen, 1979.
17. Ronen, 1981*a;* 1981*b*.
18. Nollen and Martin, 1978; Nollen, 1979.
19. Nollen and Martin, 1978.

20. Hicks and Klimoski, 1981; Glickman and Brown, 1974; Orpen, 1981; Shamir, 1980.

21. Nollen and Martin, 1978.

22. Jaeger and Groushko, 1976.

23. Nollen, 1979; Cowley and Fiss, 1977; Fields, 1974; Golembiewski, Hilles, and Kagno, 1974; Gomez-Mejia, Hopp, and Sommerstad, 1978; Nollen and Martin, 1978; Port Authority of New York, 1975; Ronen, 1981*b;* Schein, Maurer, and Novak, 1977; Swart, 1978.

24. Golembiewski and Proehl, 1978.

25. Zaluski, 1977.

26. Dowell and Wexley, 1973.

27. Graf, 1978.

28. Golembiewski, Hilles, and Kagno, 1974.

29. Golembiewski, Fox, and Proehl, 1980.

30. Ibid.

31. Davis and Cherns, 1975.

32. Conference Board in Canada, 1973.

33. Ibid.

34. Ronen, 1981*b.*

CHAPTER FIVE

Part-Time Employment

Definitions, Variations, and Examples

Like flexitime, part-time work in its many forms offers another important group of options for employees and employers in dealing with change and in developing more meaningful work. In this chapter we will define various part-time programs and evaluate advantages, disadvantages, and current trends in the part-time work force.

Part-time employment differs somewhat from flexitime and the compressed work week in that it has been well established and accepted by many firms for years, especially in certain industries. Although many employees do not consider it as an innovation in alternative work scheduling, it is nonetheless relevant for us to include part-time work here for several reasons.

First, demand for part-time employment has grown substantially at all levels of employment as more mothers, elderly citizens, and students seek to enter the work force. Second, in response to this increased demand, there have been a few innovations in part-time employment, such as *job sharing* (which will be discussed in Chapter 6). Third (perhaps associated with its established acceptance), the availability of part-time work has been unnecessarily confined to serving specific employee groups at lower job levels within the organization and is usually considered a temporary solution only. Finally, because many managers have held negative stereotypes of the part-time work force, it is important to discuss the nature of this problem and the accuracy or inaccuracy of such stereotypes.

On the one hand, the stereotyped image of the part-time employee had its real (although segmented) sources. For example, 3 million of the 15 million people who worked part-time in 1974 wanted full-time work but were working part-time involuntarily for economic reasons. This is in part a consequence of unemployment, which reflects losses for individuals as well as for the economy (i.e., a less productive society with less utilization of human resources). Involuntary part-time work was disproportionately common among the unskilled, the less educated, and the young. There were racial disproportions also; the proportion of blacks affected was much higher than whites.[1]

On the other hand, the part-time work force is just beginning to gain acceptance as more than a marginal supplement to the full-time work force. Perhaps because part-time employees have been considered marginal or temporary workers, few systematic studies have been conducted to examine this group's effectiveness, attitudes, or quality of work life. Only recently have researchers undertaken to study this group in a serious way. The data available thus far will be presented in this chapter, following a discussion of trends in the part-time labor force and definitions of possible variations and categories of part-time employment. Because we consider job sharing an important innovation in part-time employment, we discuss its implications in a separate chapter.

Trends in the Part-Time Labor Force

Significant changes have been taking place in the part-time work force during recent years. Since 1954 the number of part-time workers has been increasing by approximately 4 percent per year, which is a higher growth rate than for full-time employees. In May 1981, 22.3 percent of the 88 million nonagricultural employees in the United States were working part-time. At that time 12 million people (61 percent of all part-time employees) were working part-time by choice (voluntary part-timers). A more accurate trend can be seen in Table 5–1.

The following examples provide further insight into the extent of the part-time employment in various fields in 1980:

At S. S. Kresge Company, 34,000 of the 133,000 employees work 24 hours a week or less.

At Howard Johnson Company, half of the 25,000 employees are part-timers.

At the headquarters of Prudential Life Insurance Company in New York City, 1,000 employees are part-timers.

Table 5-1

Percent Distribution of Wage and Salary Workers in Nonagricultural Industries, by Full- and Part-Time Status and Sex, May 1954 to May 1983

Year and Sex	Total		Full-Time*	Part-Time†	Usually Full Time		Usually Part-Time		Employed but Not at Work
	Number in Thousands	Percent		Total	Involuntary of Economic Reasons	Voluntary or Noneconomic Reasons	Involuntary or Economic Reasons	Voluntary of Noneconomic Reasons	
Both Sexes:									
1954	48,063	100.0	81.0	15.4	3.0	2.6	1.7	8.0	3.7
1955	49,374	100.0	82.4	14.3	1.7	2.8	1.6	8.2	3.4
1956	51,475	100.0	80.4	16.3	2.1	3.2	1.5	9.4	3.3
1957	51,727	100.0	80.8	16.0	2.2	2.8	1.7	9.4	3.1
1958	51,085	100.0	79.0	18.0	3.5	2.6	2.4	9.5	3.0
1959	52,727	100.0	80.9	16.1	1.6	2.6	2.0	9.9	3.1
1960	54,365	100.0	79.6	17.3	2.0	2.9	2.0	10.4	3.1
1961	54,115	100.0	78.8	18.2	2.2	2.9	2.6	10.5	3.0
1962	55,569	100.0	79.7	17.3	1.8	2.3	1.9	11.4	2.9
1963	57,087	100.0	79.5	17.4	1.6	2.5	1.8	11.5	3.1
1964	59,067	100.0	78.3	18.3	1.4	2.7	1.8	12.4	3.4
1965	59,993	100.0	79.2	17.4	1.4	2.6	1.3	12.0	3.4
1966	62,530	100.0	78.7	18.0	1.2	3.2	1.0	12.7	3.3
1966††	61,709	100.0	79.7	17.0	1.2	3.2	1.0	11.5	3.4
1967	64,020	100.0	77.7	19.0	1.3	4.3	.8	12.6	3.4
1968	66,353	100.0	77.0	19.4	1.1	4.4	.9	13.0	3.6
1969	67,536	100.0	76.7	19.6	1.1	4.4	.9	13.3	3.7
1970	68,904	100.0	75.1	20.8	1.5	4.5	1.1	13.8	4.0
1971	69,150	100.0	74.9	21.1	1.5	4.8	1.4	13.5	4.0
1972	71,631	100.0	74.9	21.2	1.2	4.6	1.4	14.0	3.9
1973	74,143	100.0	74.9	21.2	1.2	4.9	1.3	13.9	3.9
1974	75,839	100.0	74.7	21.2	1.4	4.5	1.5	13.8	4.1
1975	74,271	100.0	73.5	22.2	2.0	4.3	2.1	13.8	4.3

Year									
1976	77,447	100.0	73.7	21.9	1.5	4.6	2.0	13.8	4.4
1977	79,759	100.0	73.8	22.1	1.3	4.8	2.1	13.9	4.1
1978	83,412	100.0	73.7	22.5	1.2	4.9	2.1	14.3	3.9
1979	85,509	100.0	74.0	22.2	1.2	5.2	2.0	13.8	3.9
1980	85,891	100.0	72.6	23.0	2.0	5.0	2.2	13.8	4.4
1981	88,005	100.0	73.2	22.3	1.5	4.7	2.5	13.7	4.4
1982	94,100	100.0	75.1	21.1	2.0	4.2	2.9	12.1	3.8
1983	93,949	100.0	74.4	21.1	1.5	4.3	3.6	11.7	3.5
Men:									
1965	37,983	100.0	85.1	11.7	1.4	2.4	.9	7.0	3.2
1966	39,211	100.0	84.3	12.5	1.1	3.3	.6	7.5	3.2
1966††	35,758	100.0	85.3	11.5	1.1	3.3	.6	6.4	3.2
1967	39,971	100.0	83.6	12.9	1.2	4.1	.5	7.1	3.3
1968	40,912	100.0	83.7	12.9	.9	4.2	.6	7.2	3.4
1969	41,340	100.0	83.3	13.0	.9	4.1	.6	7.4	3.7
1970	41,885	100.0	82.5	13.6	1.3	4.2	.7	7.4	3.9
1971	42,077	100.0	82.2	14.2	1.4	4.5	.8	7.4	3.6
1972	43,332	100.0	82.3	14.2	1.2	4.5	.8	7.6	3.6
1973	44,438	100.0	82.2	14.1	1.1	4.6	.7	7.6	3.7
1974	45,128	100.0	82.2	13.7	1.3	4.3	.8	7.3	4.1
1975	43,678	100.0	81.1	14.7	2.0	4.1	1.3	7.4	4.2
1976	45,080	100.0	81.2	14.6	1.6	4.3	1.3	7.3	4.3
1977	46,194	100.0	81.5	14.5	1.2	4.4	1.3	7.6	4.0
1978	47,888	100.0	81.5	14.9	1.2	4.7	1.3	7.7	3.7
1979	48,683	100.0	81.7	14.6	1.3	4.8	1.1	7.4	3.7
1980	48,130	100.0	80.2	15.5	1.9	4.6	1.4	7.6	4.3
1981	48,949	100.0	81.2	14.6	1.5	4.4	1.5	7.3	4.2
1982	52,149	100.0	81.9	14.6	2.1	3.8	2.1	6.6	3.5
1983	51,606	100.0	82.3	14.5	1.5	4.1	2.5	6.4	3.2
Women:									
1965	22,011	100.0	69.2	27.2	1.4	3.0	2.1	20.7	3.8
1966	23,319	100.0	69.1	27.3	1.3	2.9	1.7	21.4	3.5

Table 5–1 (concluded)

1966††	22,953	100.0	70.3	26.2	1.3	3.0	1.7	20.2	3.6
1967	24,051	100.0	67.5	29.0	1.3	4.6	1.3	21.8	3.5
1968	25,440	100.0	66.3	29.9	1.4	4.7	1.5	22.3	3.8
1969	26,195	100.0	66.2	30.0	1.3	4.7	1.4	22.5	3.8
1970	27,018	100.0	63.8	32.0	1.7	4.9	1.8	23.7	4.2
1971	27,075	100.0	63.5	31.9	1.6	5.1	2.3	22.9	4.6
1972	28,299	100.0	63.7	32.0	1.3	4.7	2.3	23.7	4.3
1973	29,707	100.0	64.0	31.9	1.2	5.2	2.1	23.4	4.2
1974	30,711	100.0	63.7	32.1	1.5	4.8	2.5	23.3	4.2
1975	30,693	100.0	62.6	32.9	2.0	4.7	3.3	23.0	4.5
1976	32,368	100.0	63.3	32.1	1.5	5.0	2.9	22.7	4.6
1977	33,565	100.0	63.3	32.6	1.5	5.2	3.1	22.7	4.2
1978	35,525	100.0	63.2	32.7	1.3	5.2	3.1	23.1	4.1
1979	36,826	100.0	63.8	32.1	1.2	5.7	3.1	22.1	4.0
1980	37,760	100.0	63.1	32.5	2.1	5.4	3.3	21.7	4.5
1981	39,056	100.0	63.3	32.0	1.5	5.1	3.7	21.8	4.7
1982	41,951	100.0	66.6	29.3	1.8	4.5	4.0	18.8	4.1
1983	42,343	100.0	67.0	29.1	1.4	4.6	4.9	18.2	3.9

* 35 hours or more.
† 1 to 34 hours.
†† Revised data for 1966. Data prior to this are not strictly comparable with those for later years because of differences in methodology and population. Data for the earlier period refer to persons 14 years of over; data for the subsequent period refer to persons 16 years or over.
Note: Because of rounding, detail may not equal totals.

Departments stores have also used part-time schedules intensively:

At J. L. Hudson, in the Detroit area, 65 percent of employees are part-timers.

At Gimbel Brothers, Inc., in New York City, 60 percent are part-time employees.[2]

•Organizations employing permanent part-time employees include Massachusetts Mutual Life Insurance Company; Campbell Soup, Inc.; Trans World Airlines, Inc.; Maytag Company; and Lockheed Missiles and Space Company, Inc. These are just a few of the firms that use permanent part-timers.

The high percentage of part-time employment in the United States is matched only by Sweden (21 percent); in other countries the percentage is much lower (France, 11 percent; Germany, 8 percent; U.K., 4 percent; Switzerland 5 percent).

Increased participation by women in the work force has been associated with some of this growth. The proportion of women who were voluntary part-time employees rose from 16 percent to 22 percent during the past two decades, and 32 percent of all women employees now work part-time. Other groups want part-time work as well. Fifteen percent of male employees work part-time. Half of these male part-time employees work part-time regularly and voluntarily.

Since 1968 persons under 25 years of age, many of whom are students, have represented 55 percent of the growth in regular, voluntary part-time work. This growth has primarily been attributed to the World War II baby boom. However, increased youth participation in part-time employment has also been encouraged by federal and state programs for high school and college students, as well as by student loan programs and the Veteran's Readjustment Act of 1966. Men and women under 25 represent 17 percent of the full-time labor force and 47 percent of the part-time labor force.[3]

In addition to increased demand for part-time employment by women and youths, part-time growth has resulted from participation in the work force by people over 65 years of age. Our social security system encourages part-time employment, since pension recipients can receive limited earnings before losing benefits. Among workers 65 and older, the likelihood of working part-time rose from 38 percent in 1968 to 49 percent in 1977.[4]

In 1973 close to 200,000 civil service employees worked part-time, and in 1981, 35 state governments indicated that they employed workers on a permanent part-time basis—29 percent of those holding permanent positions are part-timers. Of the 6 out of 10 postal service employees occupying permanent part-time positions, 48 percent were men.[5] Since these jobs were concentrated at lower pay levels, several government programs were instituted to encourage part-time employment in professional and managerial positions. In 1978 Congress passed legislation to expand part-time career opportunities within the government, through the Federal Employees Part-Time Career Employment Act of 1978 (PL 95–437). The legislative branch has not been alone in its encouragement of part-time employment. In 1977 President Carter issued to the heads of executive departments and agencies a memorandum encouraging them to "establish innovative programs to expand opportunities for men and women seeking part-time employment" and requesting that they conduct "pilot and research studies to determine where part-time employees can make the maximum contribution."

The highest concentration of part-time positions is in service industries. According to Deutermann and Brown, 90 percent of all voluntary part-time employees are members of this group.[6] In retail and wholesale firms, 25 percent are part-timers; compare this with 6 percent in railroad, mining, and manufacturing and 18 percent in clerical positions. The percentage of employees who work part-time has been broken down by occupation and by industry in Table 5–2.

Reviewing the composition of the part-time labor force, it seems that most part-time positions are available in service and sales industries and that participation is concentrated among women, youth under 25 (male and female), and people 65 years and older. We can readily attribute this pattern to the various advantages of part-time work, which we will discuss in detail.

Definitions, Variations, and Examples

Part-time employment has been defined in many ways, although most definitions incorporate the notions that the employee reports to work for fewer hours per day and/or fewer days per week than the contracted attendance hours required of full-time employees. For the purposes of our discussions here, we have chosen to define part-time work as follows: Part-time employment means work on a regular and voluntary basis for a daily, weekly or monthly period of substantially shorter duration than a 40-hour week or a normal 8-hour day (normal or statutory hours of work). This employment is stable and differentiated from temporary, casual, or intermittent labor. It can include part-day, part-week, part-month, or part-year work.

Table 5–2

	Percent of All Workers Who Are Regular and Voluntary Part-Time Workers
By occupation:	
Professional/technical	10.9
Managerial	3.3
Sales	23.8
Clerical	17.2
Skilled blue-collar	2.9
Operatives excluding transport equipment operatives	5.5
Laborer	18.9
By industry:	
Manufacturing	3.4
Wholesale/retail trade	25.4
Finance, insurance, real estate	9.1
Service	19.9
Public administration	5.2

Percentages of employees who work part-time, by occupation and by industry.

Source: Adapted from W. V. Deutermann, Jr., and S. C. Brown, "Voluntary Part-Time Workers: A Growing Part of the Labor Force," *Monthly Labor Review,* June 1978.

The Federal Employees Part-Time Career Employment Act of 1978 (PL 95–437) promotes the expansion of part-time employment opportunities in the federal service. It narrows the part-time definition from scheduled work of "less than 40 hours per week" to "scheduled work between 16 and 32 hours per week." It also sets guidelines to convert full-time jobs to part-time positions. There are different ways of evaluating benefits for part-time employees. For retirement, employers consider the calendar week; for such other aspects as promotions, employers consider prorated periods based on percentage of hours worked per week divided by 40. Note that at present the most common part-time schedule is the part-day/full-week, and only a quarter of part-time employees work the full-day/part-week schedule.

Reasons for Working Part-Time

In addition to differentiating between part-time workers with respect to the actual schedule worked, we should also distinguish employment in terms of the employee's reasons for working less than full-time. Outcomes associated with these different segments of the part-time work force may be very different. For example, one might predict that involuntary part-time workers may be less committed to the organization, since they would prefer to be working full-time. If a full-time job becomes available in another organization, it is likely that they will quit their part-time jobs for the full-time opportunity without much hesitation. Most of our discussion will center on permanent voluntary part-time employees, their impact on the organization, and the effects of the schedule on them as individuals.

Stereotypes of the Part-Time Work Force

One of the problems associated with part-time employment has been the negative stereotypes many managers and employers hold. One group of researchers summarized the problem as follows:

> Among many employers there is a stereotype of part-time employment. It is often viewed as marginal and unnecessary except as an expedient to cope with special work needs, appropriate only for certain work technologies, and suitable mainly for entry-level and less desirable jobs. Managerial jobs are thought to be unsuited to less than full-time work, and professional jobs only if there are no administrative responsibilities. . . . Part-time job holders are correspondingly often viewed as temporary, secondary wage earners and not serious about careers or committed to the labor force.[7]

Such stereotyping has further limited the availability of part-time employment except at low levels within the organization. Such jobs are typically routine and require little skill. The low percentage of part-timers who hold managerial positions supports this contention (see Table 5–1). Managers are often unwilling to invest training in part-time employees because they believe this work force to be marginal in nature and believe that turnover within this group is high. These negative stereotypes have also limited the promotional opportunities and career paths available for part-time employees. Finally, since these workers are assumed to be secondary wage earners, employers often do not feel compelled to provide wages and benefits commensurate with those that full-time employees receive.[8]

With the use of research results, we hope to dispel and invalidate some of these negative stereotypes. We must reevaluate our notions of the part-time work force, since many of these negative attitudes may be self-fulfilling for the part-time employee. Lower salaries and lack of fringe benefits give part-time employees little incentive to form strong commitments to the organization or to their jobs. Such negative attitudes may be reinforced by an awareness of the employer's negative perceptions. As demand for part-time employment increases at all levels within the work force, such negative stereotyping must diminish so that part-time employees can maximize their opportunity for effectiveness and their possible contribution to the organization.

Field Results

Of the alternative work schedules we have discussed, it is surprising that part-time work, as the most widely recognized and established schedule, is also the one that has been least systematically studied. Despite the acceptance and popularity of part-time scheduling, the lack of available data in this area indicates a certain bias held by industry to be present also in academia; that is, that part-time workers are marginal in ability, attitude, and commitment to the organization. We hope to be able to dispel some of these notions through a presentation and discussion of the available data.

The results presented here are from a few surveys and studies that investigated part-time employment in the public and the private sector. Among them, 10 concentrated on attitudinal outcomes where behavioral and performance data was very scarce; they depend largely on surveys of managers from organizations using part-time employees. We will discuss these results in the next section. They allow us to draw some tenuous conclusions about the schedule's effects on the organization and on the individual. We do not, however, have enough information to allow us to synthesize the data in summary form and to draw conclusions about overall trends, as we did for flexitime and the compressed work week.

Consistent with the format used thus far, we will present results associated with aspects of organizational effectiveness, including productivity and membership; we will then describe data associated with part-time employee attitudes and impact on the nonwork domain.

Organizational Effectiveness

Productivity

Especially those managers who do not themselves employ part-time employees believe that part-timers are less productive than are full-time employees. However, the available data have not supported this conclusion. As indicated in Table 5–3, 62 percent of managers employing part-time workers associated these employees with increases in productivity, and only 5 percent reported lower productivity.

Table 5-3

Reports from Firms Using Part-Time Employment (percent)

Criteria	American Management Association Survey*	U.S. Department of Labor Survey†
Participants of the Survey	Senior manager from 481 organizations using part-time employment were surveyed through mail questionnaires: 90%—private sector. 10%—public sector. Number of employees in organizations: 5%—less than 100. 25%—100 to 499. 17%—500 to 1000. 53%—more than 1000.	Thirty-nine firms from the private sector using part-time employment were surveyed. In most cases two persons from each firm responded—an employment expert (usually the vice president of personnel or the personnel director) and a work-unit supervisor. Of the supervisors, 39 were personally interviewed, and 30 responded to mail questionnaires (77 percent response rate). Thirty-nine employment experts responded to personal interviews and 24 responded to mail questionnaires (62 percent response rate).

	Managers*			Supervisors†			Employment Experts†		
	Improvement or Increase	No Change	Decrease	Better than Full-Time	Equal	Worse	Better than Full-time	Equal	Worse
Effects on Effectiveness									
Productivity	62%	33%	5%	26%	62%	13%	43%	38%	19%
Turnover	40	41	19	21	44	36	32	32	35
Absenteeism	47	47	6	44	33	23	53	40	7
Tardiness	39	56	5						
Fatigue	59	40	1						
Effects on Costs									
Unit labor costs of production	52%	42%	6%	21%	66%	13%	24%	71%	5%
Wage costs	58	39	3	68	29	3	76	22	3
Overtime	69	29	2						

Fringe benefit costs	57	25	19	67	25	8	50	26	24
Personnel administration costs (recordkeeping)	16	45	39	0	69	31	0	68	32
Recruiting	46	37	17	17	54	29	35	41	24
Training	12	55	33	21	54	26	21	61	18
Equipment and facilities costs	15	71	14	18	61	21	14	76	11
Effects on Workers, Customers and the Public									
Promotability				11%	63%	26%	8%	43%	49%
Loyalty				3	49	49	5	53	42
Relationship with employees	31%	56%	13%						
Relationship with customers	12	78	10	5	87	8	6	92	3
Public relations	24	72	4						
Effects on Management Aspects									
General Supervision (scheduling, coordination, communication)	56%	22%	22%						
Coverage of work situations				0%	51%	49%	8%	57%	35%
Employee scheduling	35	30	35						
Work scheduling	41	29	30						
Difficulty of management job	14	48	38						
Effects on Communication									
Internal communication	6%	59%	35%						
External communication	6	76	18						

* S. D. Nollen and V. H. Martin, *Alternative Work Schedules, Part 2: Permanent Part-Time Employment* (New York: American Management Association, 1978).

† S. D. Nollen, B. B. Eddy, and V. H. Martin, *Permanent Part-Time Employment: The Manager's Perspective* (New York: Praeger Publishers, 1978).

A two-year study of the Massachusetts Department of Public Welfare in Boston concluded that employees working half days were carrying 89 percent of a normal, full-time case load.[9] Turnover among these part-time employees was 14 percent, compared with 40 percent for full-time employees in the same types of positions.

In 1974 the Control Data Corporation opened a bindery in St. Paul, Minnesota, staffed entirely with part-time employees. This staffing decision was made because the bindery was located in an area of low unemployment and having a high proportion on one-parent households. Productivity has continued to rise since its opening. Furthermore, rates of sick leave, tardiness, and absenteeism are lower than for comparable groups working full-time at other Control Data Corporation facilities.

In a study of job performance at Macy's Department Store in New York City, which employs permanent part-time workers (25–38 hours per week) to augment its sales force, the part-time group was highly stable, having low turnover and long service records.[10] One reason for this stability might well be the difficulty of finding alternative part-time positions. A similar explanation was given in another study, where favorable job performance outcomes were associated with the excess supply of those looking for part-time employment, especially women and students.

One study also reported that outcomes were more positive for clerical jobs than for production jobs.[11] It may be that part-time employees in clerical jobs are more typically voluntary and that part-time employment is scarce. The results lead one to assume that there are demographic differences between these groups as well, in terms of educational level and socioeconomic status, but we have no data to support this view. One could hypothesize that involuntary part-timers have less commitment to the organization because they want or seek other forms of employment. It could also be that the routineness, physical demands, and less pleasant environment of production work may be associated with lower levels of productivity for production workers than for clerical workers. This generalization must be made carefully, since no data is available on differences of productivity in full-time workers in the same types of jobs.

Further comparison across these types of jobs is tenuous, since the criteria for measuring productivity are quite different. For example, how does one compare orders processed in a clerical job with units completed and assembled in a production environment? Another reason part-time workers may be more productive than full-time workers is that the shorter workday reduces fatigue. As indicated in Table 5–3, 59 percent of managers surveyed believed that part-time employment reduced fatigue.

For the most part, part-time employment schedules have not lent themselves to the kinds of job and organizational changes that would be associated with higher productivity. Unlike flexitime and the compressed work week, part-time employees are usually confined to lower-level jobs that are typically more routine and highly controlled—whether in a production or clerical environment. The part-time employees themselves are often viewed by managers as marginal members of the organization who have little incentive to stay employed if another opportunity arises. Finally, in most cases there is little task interdependence between part-time and full-time workers, requiring little additional effort in terms of job coverage, communications (except for supervisors), and interpersonal relations. Thus, as long as part-time work continues to be characterized along these lines, one would expect few of the intrinsic rewards associated with part-time employment. The one major exception to this would be in the area of job sharing (which we will discuss in Chapter 6).

Scheduling

Of the organizational changes associated with part-time employment, perhaps the more important are scheduling problems, meeting peak workloads, and extending hours of operation.[12] A part-time work force extends the organization's flexibility to meet fluctuations in work demands without hiring temporary employees, who may be unfamiliar with the job, or to extending hours of overtime, which are costly to the organization and exhausting for full-time employees. Fifty-eight managers in 21 government agencies reported that the main advantage of part-time employment was greater flexibility in meeting work requirements.[13]

Despite these advantages associated with the part-time schedule, managers have reported that scheduling accounts for 26 percent of the problems of a part-time work force. One third of the managers who have part-time employees reported that their jobs were harder as a result; one third reported no change; and one third reported improvement in scheduling (Table 5–3). Specifically, supervisors encountered difficulty scheduling work to accommodate the part-time employee's availability. Problems also arose with a lack of continuity between full- and part-time workers. The same study found that some communications problems were created with part-timers. Evidently, some supervisors found it difficult to communicate job assignments and instructions, since part-timers were available for fewer hours during the day—sometimes during times the supervisor was unavailable. If there was little or no overlap between part- and full-time employees, one would expect the organization to provide a part-time supervisor to alleviate this type of problem.

Costs (Overtime and Fringe Benefits)

With respect to the hiring and maintenance of the work force itself, reports from studies are mixed regarding costs. In one survey one in three users of part-time employees reported increased personnel administration and training costs.[14] This is no surprise, considering that the use of part-time scheduling usually means expanding the number of employees in a firm. Furthermore, because of the reduced schedule, more part-time employees must be trained to equal one full-time employee. One study also reported higher personnel costs associated with high turnover among part-time employees in the public sector, although the same study reported a saving associated with lower personnel cost resulting from savings in overtime, availability of quality part-time personnel, and flexibility in meeting work requirements.[15]

With respect to overtime, one can make a strong argument that such costs should be substantially reduced. This is a primary reason for utilizing part-time scheduling for many organizations (the mini-shift). The managerial survey found that 69 percent of employers reported overtime savings (see Table 5–3).

An area of costs associated with part-time employees that has become quite controversial is fringe benefits. Studies indicate that most organizations employing part-timers do not provide the same level of fringe benefits as for full-time employees.[16] These studies found that employers typically granted vacations on a prorated basis but that other types of benefits, such as sick leave, life or health insurance, and pension plans, were substantially reduced. Table 5–4 compares benefits offered to part-time employees and to full-time employees.

Employers do not pay full fringe benefits to part-time employees, and this reprsents a substantial cost savings and an incentive to utilize part-time schedules. This policy has become increasingly controversial because those who must work part-time schedules but are fully committed to their jobs and their organization are penalized. Although providing full benefits might make costs prohibitive for many employers, there must be a way of prorating these benefits (beyond vacation time) in order to minimize this type of discrimination. Associated with such a change in policy is the acceptance of

Table 5–4

Fringe Benefit	Percent of Organizations Offering Benefits to Full-Timers	Percent of Organizations Offering Benefits to Part-Timers	Percent of Organizations Offering Prorated Benefits	Percent of Organizations Offering benefits Same as Full-Time
Vacation	95	80	75	5
Sick leave	95	55	49	6
Life insurance	96	51	27	24
Health insurance	97	52	19	33
Pension	93	59	42	17
Profit sharing	61	28	20	8

Source: Adapted from Stanley D. Nollen and Virginia H. Martin, *Alternative Work Schedules, Part 2: Permanent Part-Time Employment* (New York: AMACOM, 1978).

part-time workers as more than marginal employees of the organization.

Cost considerations associated with problems of fluctuating workloads, the efficient use of equipment and machinery, and the desire to reduce the demand for overtime prompt a company to consider part-time employment. Part-time schedules are just now being recognized for their value to employees. Perhaps with the exception of the public sector, employers still tend to be economically motivated when they consider implementing part-time schedules. As a result one would anticipate a reduction in economic costs associated with the schedule as the major criteria for willingness to implement it. In fact, it was found that the costs and benefits associated with the schedule were favorable.[17]

Membership

As with productivity there is little systematic data available on membership behavior associated with part-time schedules, but there are many assumptions and expectations consistent with the old, negative stereotypes of part-time employees. Specifically, employers without experience with part-time employees expected absenteeism to be high for this group. Contrary to this expectation, however, 47 percent of part-time employers reported that absenteeism declined, as indicated in Table 5–3.

There were no data regarding changes in tardiness. One would not predict any particular changes associated with tardiness, since there is usually no flexibility associated with part-time schedules.

It does appear that part-time scheduling facilitates recruiting, as reported by 25 percent of part-time employers in the survey. The reason is part-time jobs make new segments of the labor force available. To the extent that part-time schedules are desirable or necessary for many who wish to work, demand will increase for them. Another study added that the part-time schedule made available quality personnel who might otherwise be unavailable.[18] Although recruiting is apparently easier, employers still associated part-time employment with higher turnover than for full-time employees. According to employers surveyed in the study, part-time employees have other interests outside the job.[19] One might predict differences in rate of turnover based on the part-time employee's level in the organization. For example, voluntary employees at the professional or managerial level within the organization may have lower levels of turnover than involuntary part-time production workers. Perhaps consistent with this is the Gannon and Nothern finding that turnover was unrelated to job satisfaction for part-time employees, whereas several studies have established such a relationship for full-time workers.[20] This area requires further research which should distinguish clearly between the different kinds of part-time employees.

Attitudes

Of the 10 studies that have appeared in the literature, virtually all examine employees' job-related attitudes toward part-time or other types of part-time schedules. Seven of the 10 studies investigated various facets of job satisfaction. The instrument most commonly used was the Job Descriptive Index, although a few studies used internally developed or other similar instruments examining many of the same facets.[21] Four studies also attempted to measure overall job satisfaction (most often using the GM Faces Scale). Three of these examined job facets and overall satisfaction independently, and one study attempted to discern differences in patterns of job satisfaction through the differential contribution of job-facets-satisfaction to overall job satisfaction.[22]

Another study concerned nonjob-related attitudes—specifically, happiness and role conflict—as dependent variables, in addition to satisfaction with career,[23] job tenure,[24] commitment,[25] and measure of work motivation.[26]

In describing this list of dependent variables, we can see that none of these studies has included behavioral outcomes, with the exception of job tenure. (The two studies that used tenure as a dependent variables measured it differently: Gannon and Nothern compared employees who left the organization before completing two years of work to those who remained; Katerberg, Hom, and Hulin used intention and actual reinlistment in the National Guard as their criteria.[27] Beyond these, however, there are no objective measures of behavioral outcomes, either with respect to membership or pro ductivity).

Yet, despite the paucity of hard data, an examination of this literature is useful for two reasons. First, to the extent that we can associate job attitudes with behavioral outcomes (in particular, membership behavior), we can make certain predictions about the expected behaviors of part-time employees. Second, similarities in attitudes between part-time and full-time employees may allow us to predict behavioral similarities. Such generalizations require that we control for certain variables and allow for moderating effects of others.

Description of Studies

Having established that the studies in this field are predominantly attitudinal in nature, it is important to qualify this review further by describing the variety of instruments used, the various moderators and groups of covariates, and differences in samples. Another major source of variation in the studies is the type of part-time schedule under study; it is reasonable to assume that outcomes may be different for different schedules. In this section, we will examine in more detail each aspect of the studies.

With respect to instruments, the Job Descriptive Index was most commonly used to measure facets of job satisfaction; four studies used this instrument.[28] Miller and Terborg used an instrument that was similar to the JDI, and that had been developed internally. The job facets by this instrument were pay, advancement, work, subordinates, and benefits.[29] Hom investigated seven facets of job satisfaction, including supervisor, company identification, co-worker, physical work conditions, pay, job security, and work itself. Jackson, Keaveny, and Allen had the employees in their sample rank the following five aspects: importance of work, chance for advancement, high income, short working hours, and job security.[30] The studies including measure of overall job satisfaction all used the GM Faces Scale developed by Kunin.[31] These studies included Logan, O'Reilly, and Roberts; Katerberg; and Miller and Terborg.[32] Similarities in the instruments in these studies should allow some degree of comparison, however. It is more difficult to compare these, as a group, to studies that used other dependent variables, such as job tenure[33] and role conflict.[34]

One study used attitudes (supervision, other managers, work, social climate, performance evaluation, and pay) as an independent variable where job tenure was the dependent variable.[35] Another study used various facets as moderating variables (pay satisfaction, co-worker, supervisor, and job involvement).[36]

With respect to covariates, one study used occupation[37] and another controlled for demographic variables (marital status, number of children, and family income[38]). Because one would predict that occupational level and demographic data would be major sources of variance in predicting attitudes of part-time employees, we should compare the samples taken in the studies reviewed here. Perhaps we can explain some of the differences in findings as a function of certain demographic variables or occupational level. To compare studies where these variables were not controlled, we describe the samples for each study in Table 5–5.

In four studies the subjects worked in a variety of jobs.[39] In three studies the samples were taken from retail sales organizations; this should not surprise us, considering the concentration of part-time employees in this industry.[40] Interestingly, two studies investigated part-time employees in the nursing profession, although the Logan study included various occupational levels, as mentioned previously.[41] It seems plausible to predict that job attitudes will, as outcomes, be related to occupation and job level. Thus comparing attitudes across studies where this variable was not controlled may confuse otherwise consistent results. Katerberg found that the job type was determined by the job status (part-time versus full-time).[42]

With respect to demographic variables, we may also predict that outcomes will vary by sex, marital status, number of children, incomes and occupation of spouse, and so forth. More specifically, people who are restricted by circumstances in their nonwork domain from working full-time and who are working part-time out of necessity may have different attitudes toward their jobs than individuals who, for example, have a lesser economic need to work and have chosen a part-time job for intrinsic rewards and/or social interaction, or for other sources of stimulation. Most of the studies (7 out of 10) examined here compare part-time to full-time employees with respect to these outcomes. As with job level, it may be inappropriate to group all part-time employees together for comparison with full-time workers. If demographic variables are grouped together to describe the socioeconomic status and life cycle of the part-time employee, we may find differential outcomes associated with these groups. Of the two studies investigating differences based on demo-

Table 5-5

Description of Samples and PT Schedules of the Studies

	Sample	Schedule
Brief, Van Sell, and Aldag (1979)	N = 109 PT* EEs.† N = 109 FT EEs. All were female nurses.	PT EEs worked less than 34 hours/week PT schedule not designated.
Gannon and Nothern (1971)	N = 36 short-term PT EEs. N = 96 long-term PT EEs. All were checkers in a supermarket.	Schedule not described, although PT at night and Saturday differentiated from other PT.
Goldberg (1981)	N = 93PT N = 68FT EEs of central office of U.S. Office of Personnel management— various job levels— clerk typist, personnel staffing assistant, development specialist, library technician, personnel research. PT EEs matched to FT EEs.	PT schedules not indicated.
Hall and Gordon (1973)	Women on mailing lists of alumnae clubs. 2 samples: N = 109 N = 261 Differentiation between: full-time homemaker full-time volunteer PT volunteer FT employee PT employee	Different PT schedules, but not differentiated.
Hom (1979)	N = 10,000 PT EEs in retail sales from 84 stores.	Sixteen groups created by classifying according to number or hours worked per week—and steady versus seasonal employment. PT schedule not designated.

Table 5–5 (concluded)

	Sample	Schedule
Jackson, Keaveny and Allen (1977)	NORC/ROPER data: N = 1253 FT. N = 237 PT. Four occupational levels.	No indication of schedule.
Katerberg (1980)	N = 160 PT; and N = 66 FT Air National Guardsmen. Five job types— aircraft mechanic, jet engine mechanic, aerospace ground equipment, military police, and supply.	PT EEs work 2 days/ month (weekend) FT EEs cover remaining 28 days/month. Schedule not described, although PT at night and Saturday differentiated from other PT.
Katerberg, Hom, and Hulin (1974)	National Guardsmen. N = 534.	Part week and part month, but not differentiated.
Logan, O'Reilly, and Roberts (1973)	PT, N = 47. FT, N = 104. EEs were all female, white RNs, vocational nurses, aides, or clerical personnel.	PT EEs working 23 hrs/ week on average. FT EEs working 39 hrs/ week on average.
Miller and Terborg (1979)	N = 660 FT EEs N = 404 PT EEs. EEs in same job classification across 55 stores in a midwest retail organization.	Type of PT schedule not designated.

* PT: part-time.
† EEs: employees.

graphic variables, the Hom study found differences in outcomes associated with these variables, whereas Brief et al. did not.[43] It is clear that demographic variables, as descriptors of life cycle and socioeconomic status, may help us to understand why attitudes differ for various groups of part-time employees.

In addition to occupational level, life cycle, and socioeconomic status, another important variable to consider is type of part-time schedule. Table 5–1, column 2, describes the type of schedule used in each study. As can be seen, exactly half (5 out of 10) of the studies did not specify the type of schedule. Of the studies that did provide this information, four described only the number of hours worked per week (or days per month, in one case).[44] Hom used discriminant analysis to break out 16 groups of employees along two dimensions of part-time work: (1) hours worked per week and (2) steady versus seasonal employment.[45]

The lack of information on actual schedules is rather surprising, considering the most of these studies have set out to examine outcomes specifically associated with part-time schedules. In addition to hours worked per week and steady versus seasonal employment, there are other dimensions that should be indicated. The first and most obvious is number of days worked per week and the specification of which days. Part-time employees have often been called peripheral workers because of their reduced schedule and intermittent work experience.[46] If one could envision "peripherality" as a continuum, one might hypothesize that the less peripheral the employees perceive themselves to be with respect to the organization, the more their attitudes will resemble those of full-time employees with the same demographic profile and the same job. When we consider the notion of peripherality, it seems clear that hours worked per week does not provide enough information to position the employee on our hypothetical continuum.

Days worked per week and the specification of which days may further help to define employee sense of peripherality. For example, an employee who works 15 hours may be considered quite peripheral to the organization. If these 15 hours were allocated at three hours per day, five days per week, the employee might indeed feel little organizational commitment, involvement, or attachment to peers. On the other hand, if the 15 hours were scheduled for two days per week, 7½ hours per day, the employee might feel less peripheral. In particular, the full day of work allows for full participation in all membership activities (such as coffee breaks and lunch) and may provide greater opportunity for interaction with supervisors and managers. In this instance, both schedules require 15 hours per week, yet the outcomes associated with them might be quite different. Finally, if the employee were to work two full days per week, but if these days happened to be Saturday and Sunday (which other employees had off), the employee's sense of peripherality might be the highest of the three examples. One could predict commitment to the organization to be low and turnover and absenteeism to be high. Hom found that part-time employees whose work status was highly peripheral (based on hours worked per week and seasonal versus steady employment only) had poorer job attitudes, although controlling for demographic variables mitigated this affect.[47]

However, a moderating variable in each of these examples is the employees' choice of peers. If the employees choose full-time workers as a frame of reference, their job attitudes might be poorer than if they had chosen other part-time employees as co-workers. Logan, O'Reilly, and Roberts use the frame of reference notion in a somewhat broader context to help explain differences in patterns of job satisfaction between part- and full-time employees:

> Because of job availability to them and the degree to which "partial inclusion in" the work force differentially operates for these two populations, part-time workers view their job in relation to what they expect to find in other part-time jobs, and full-time employees do likewise for full-time jobs.[48]

Logan et al. found differences in outcomes between part- and full-time employees, and they offer the frame of reference notion as one explanation of their findings. Their data compare employees working an average of 23 hours per week with employees working an average of 39 hours per week, although they do not specify hours worked per day. Whatever the schedule in this case, the peripherality of the part-time employees was enough to differentiate attitudes of the two groups. Occupational levels were roughly equivalent for the two groups, and demographic profiles were similar.

Thus far the dimensions of part-time work described are number of hours worked per week, seasonal versus steady employment, and schedule of hours in terms of hours per day and days per week; but one additional dimension is important to consider. Many employees hold part-time jobs because full-time jobs in the same occupation are unavailable. In this case one might predict that the frame of reference the individual employee chooses would be full-time employees occupying the desired job, regardless of level of peripherality of the part-time employee. This may have additional implications for attitudes we haven't described. For example, Goldberg notes that for employees who worked long-hour part-time schedules (LPT), the relationship between participative decision making was reduced in comparison with short-hour part-timers (SPT).[49] Goldberg concludes that this finding is an artifact, associated with the fact that the LPT groups were all involuntary part-time employees desiring full-time work.

We should consider the frame of reference for part-time employees in any study investigating this group, but we should also note that the frame of reference may be influenced by type of schedule, degree of peripherality, reason for working part-time (including voluntary versus involuntary), and life-cycle and socioeconomic status. The studies reviewed here consider few if any of these factors individually; certainly none of the research to date has attempted to include all of them in comparing outcomes of employees on different schedules.

Having discussed the limitations of these studies, we will now attempt to compile results comparing job attitudes between groups of employees. These results are grouped together and discussed for each facet of job satisfaction because the methodologies are so similar for the majority of studies. Results are also compiled for findings on overall job satisfaction.

Intrinsic Aspects—Work Itself

Six studies reported on attitudes toward intrinsic aspects of work. Three studies found that full-time employees were more satisfied with work itself than were part-time employees.[50] In the Goldberg study, subjects were civil servants occupying one of several job levels. In the Miller and Terborg study, the sample was taken from retail sales personnel—presumably these employees are sales clerks. Katerberg's study includes five occupational levels, but when controlling for job type, a significant main effect showed up between internal work motivation and job status: Full-time employees reported being more highly motivated than did the part-time group. In his classification of 16 groups of part-timers (based on hours worked per week and steady versus seasonal work), Hom found that employees working intermediate numbers of hours were more satisfied with work itself than were those working long or short hours.[51] Brief, Van Sell, and Aldag reported no differences between the two groups in a sample of female nurses.[52] In their study, Logan et al. investigated the components of work-facet satisfaction. They found that, although both groups value work itself, the part-timers define work satisfaction in terms of co-workers, whereas full-timers perceive work satisfaction in terms of the other four Job Description Index (JDI) facets.[53]

Jackson et al. investigated differences over four occupational levels and found that at lower levels part-time employees were more satisfied than were full-time employees, but there were no differences in higher job levels.[54] We should mention, however, that in this study, employees were asked to *rank* five facets according to importance. In this context, importance of work may take on a different meaning than satisfaction with work itself. For the part-time employees at lower occupational levels, one might hypothesize a need to work for financial reasons, which may outweigh the importance of intrinsic rewards. An investigation of demographic variables might bear this out. At higher occupational levels, importance of work may include more of a desire for intrinsic rewards, which would explain part of the rank assigned to this variable. Another problem with comparing this study with others is the methodology itself. Ranking represents a forced choice wherein one facet is chosen at the expense of others, unlike the JDI, in which each facet is evaluated independently of the others.

From these results, there does appear to be some support for the notion that full-time employees are more satisfied than part-time employees with the intrinsic rewards offered by these jobs. Two cases investigating higher occupational level jobs found no differences, however.[55] We discuss these results here in terms of occupational level as a moderating variable, the presumption being that those in higher occupations have more opportunities for intrinsic rewards.

Peripherality of the Employee

Another important variable to consider is peripherality of the employee as perceived by the supervisor. If the supervisor perceived the part-time employee as a marginal member of the work unit and therefore delegated to her or him the less desirable tasks, we might predict lower work satisfaction. On the other hand, supervisors may be forced to delegate responsibility to part-time employees for certain tasks if the supervisor is unavailable during the part-timers' work hours. In this case the additional autonomy and responsibility may be associated with an equal or higher level of intrinsic satisfaction than for full-time employees in the same work group.[56] Currently available information does not allow us to determine whether or not this argument applies in the Jackson study.

According to Logan et al., the importance of co-workers in defining the intrinsic facet perhaps suggests that these employees have established a support system to function more effectively in other jobs—although we can only guess whether this is caused by the supervisor. Thus, with respect to the intrinsic facet, we should note the degree of peripherality as perceived by both employee and supervisor as well as the occupational level before we can fully understand differences between these two groups on this facet.

Katerberg, Hom, and Hulin used several facets as moderators and used work satisfaction as a dependent variable.[57] These researchers found that job scope was related to work satisfaction but that the moderating effects of these attitudes were inconsistent. They conclude that intrinsic rewards may be as viable a means of increasing work motivation for part-timers as for full-time employees, rather than relying exclusively on extrinsic rewards, as is often done for part-timers.

Pay

Five studies reported differences based on income for the two-job-status groups, with mixed results. Three studies reported no differences.[58] Jackson et al. reported that high income was more important to full-time semiskilled and unskilled employees than to part-time employees. This finding is not surprising if one assumes that the full-time groups have greater economic demands placed on them. Logan et al. found that part-time employees were slightly more satisfied than were full-time employees. These results are also not surprising, given their sample of white female nurses, aides, and clerical personnel.[59] Again, one can hypothesize that the demographics of sex and family income mitigate satisfaction with pay–job-status relationship. Assuming that pay scales are equivalent for the two groups, there should be little justification overall for differences in attitudes towards pay. The differences found appear to be related to occupational level and sex. More research is necessary in this area before drawing conclusions.

Promotion

One of the part-time employees' most frequent complaints is that there is no career path available to them. As peripheral employees they are considered out of the organizational mainstream. The organization often justifies the lack of promotion opportunities by arguing that the part-time work force is less committed to organizational goals and objectives. Given this background one would expect part-time employees to be less satisfied with promotional opportunities than are full-time employees. In two studies this was true.[60] More specifically, Logan et al. found that promotion did not contribute to overall satisfaction for part-time employees, whereas it did for full-timers. The finding is consistent with the notion that part-timers in this study simply did not perceive promotion opportunities available for them. Two studies found no differences.[61] It could be argued that in the latter cases the subjects were in professions (nursing and retail sales, respectively) in which part-time employment is widely used and accepted. It may be that these occupations have by now incorporated career paths for the part-time group. The one study that reported part-time employees more satisfied than full-time employees was Katerberg.[62] Katerberg's sample was taken from National Guardsmen, and part-time employment was defined as two days of work per month. The context of the military and unusual nature of the schedule makes it difficult to generalize these results into other studies. It may also be that the National Guard has clearly defined promotional opportunities for part-timers. Thus it is easy to explain the inconsistency of this result compared to the other studies but more difficult to explain why part-timers are more satisfied than full-time employees.

Supervisor

With respect to supervisor-employee relations, one might predict part-time employees to have negative attitudes toward their first supervisors for a variety of reasons. For example, if the supervisor perceives the employee as peripheral to the organization, this may influence the type of work assigned to the part-timer. Part-time employees with the same job title as full-timers may be assigned less interesting work with reduced opportunities for intrinsic satisfaction. On the other hand, if the part-timers' schedule does not overlap sufficiently with the supervisor's to allow adequate help and supervision, the employees' frustration and needs may also lead to more negative attitudes.

Despite the general recurrence of such views, the studies reviewed here did not reflect them. The five studies offering results on attitudes toward supervisors found no significant differences.[63] In Logan et al. part-timers showed slightly more, but not significantly more, satisfaction with this facet.

If we examine the samples used in these studies, the results should not be surprising. In Miller and Terborg the sample was taken from retail sales. Brief et al. and Logan et al. studied nurses, and Katerberg sampled the attitudes of National Guardsmen toward their officer in charge and noncom officer in charge. As mentioned earlier, part-time employment has long been accepted in sales, and the preprofessional level associated with nursing might encourage negative stereotypes in this field. Although not specified in either study, it is also possible that the first-line supervisors were themselves part-time employees. This may be the case for the National Guard sample (and is possible in the other two studies as well). If so, there would be little or no reason to hypothesize differences in attitudes on this facet based on job status. One would predict, if anything, a positive relationship between job status and promotion because of the highly visible promotion opportunities available.

Co-Workers

Five studies investigated attitudes toward co-workers. Brief et al. and Katerberg, Jackson et al., and Miller and Terborg found no differences between part- and full-time workers on this job-satisfaction facet.[64] Logan et al., in a sample of female nurses, aides, and vocational personnel, found part-time employees to be slightly more, but not significantly more, satisfied with co-workers than were full-timers. More interesting was the fact that part-time employees interpreted the work facet in terms of co-workers only, whereas full-time employees perceived the work facet in terms of all four remaining facets. Hom found that short-hour and long-hour part-timers were less satisfied than were medium-hour employees.[65] However, when he controlled for the effects of demographic characteristics, these differences were eliminated. Given Hom's findings and the demographic profile of the Logan et al. sample, there is some basis for concluding that demographic variables are more useful in explaining differences in job attitudes than job status. It is clear that more studies are needed before we can reach any conclusion.

Other Facets

Several of the studies included such other facets as satisfaction with schedule, work motivation, job security, and benefits. We do not discuss them because only one study reported a result for each of these facets. A significant result, however, appeared in Gannon and Nothern's study, which related several facets of attitudes (supervision, other managers, social climate, job, evaluation of performance, and pay) to job tenure for part-time employees.[66] This study found that job-related attitudes failed to predict tenure for this group.

Overall Job Satisfaction

Six studies reported comparisons between part-time and full-time employees based on overall job satisfaction and had mixed results. There appears to be little or no support for the notion that part-timers differ from full-time employees in their job satisfaction. Katerberg reported no differences when he controlled for job types.[67] Logan et al. found little difference in level of overall job satisfaction but also found that the facets contributing to OAJS differed for part- and full-time workers.[68] Specifically, the part-timers responded more to contextual factors than did the other group. In two studies overall job satisfaction was lower for part-timers than for full-timers.[69]

These results are what one would predict for part-time employees, given the context of negative stereotypes of low job level, high turnover, and in general low organizational commitment. Miller and Terborg explain their findings by theorizing that the part-time and the full-time group have a common frame of reference. If this is the case, we could expect that differential treatment based on negative stereotypes would create negative attitudes. The Hall and Gordon study is interesting because it incorporates influences from the non-work domain to explain the differences in attitudes. In particular, it considered pressures from home and family and from role conflict to cause lower satisfaction. Regardless, however, more women expressed a preference for part-time work than for any other career activity.

Goldberg investigated job satisfaction as a function of autonomy and participative decision making for the two job-status groups.[70]

She found that the relationship between autonomy and job satisfaction was significant and positive for all job-status groups. Regarding participative decision making (PDM), the relationship was significant and positive for the short-hours part-time group and the full-time group. It was significantly less positive for the long-hours part-time group; this finding might be explained by the fact that the long-hours part-time workers were involuntary part-timers who wished to occupy full-time positions. In any case, these results are not surprising, since they really measure the importance of intrinsic aspects of work across job status. One would predict that in holding occupational level constant, there would be few differences based on these aspects given equal opportunity for intrinsic rewards. This would be consistent with the Logan et al. finding that the context facets were more important to part-time employers than were content factors, although overall satisfaction levels were similar.[71]

Katerberg's study was particularly revealing. The full-time employees in his study reported having more variety and autonomy in their jobs than part-time employees did. From this data, one would have predicted higher satisfaction with their work than among part-time employees. Yet despite their regarding their jobs more favorably, their levels of job satisfaction were very similar to those of the part-time group. The researcher explains this finding by theorizing that the social comparison process moderates perceptions of job satisfactions. Choice of peer groups, socialization, and previous experience may create a higher set of expectations for full-time employees than for part-time employees.

Another study found that part-time employees had slightly higher overall job satisfaction than did full-time employees.[72] In breaking down the specific facets of overall satisfaction, these researchers found that part-time employees were more concerned with co-workers and pay, whereas full-time employees were more concerned with promotional opportunities. The work itself was equally important to both groups. These researchers offer an explanation for these findings consistent with the social comparison hypothesis. A lower frame of reference or lower expectations may explain the higher overall job satisfaction reported by part-timers. It may also be that because their expectations about the job itself are low, such extrinsic aspects as pay and relations with co-workers become more important. Pay may also assume additional importance as the primary reason for entering the part-time job market.

The frame of reference notion was used in one study to hypothesize that if organizational factors are the same for all groups of employees at the clerical level, then part-time employees may have more favorable attitudes toward the organization than may full-time employees.[73] These researchers found that their hypothesis was supported as regards satisfaction with pay. When Miller and Terborg examined satisfaction with work itself, they found that full-time workers were more satisfied, contrary to their frame of reference hypothesis. They explain this finding through anecdotal evidence that part-time workers may perform objectively different task activities than full-time employees who hold the same job. Supervisors, viewing the part-timers as "temporary fill ins," may be more inclined to give these workers more tedious and boring work. Thus satisfaction would decline both for the job itself and as a result of comparing one's own work to others' assignments.

Hall and Gordon found that part-time workers were less satisfied than were their full-time counterparts.[74] A sample of part-time employees who were women college students reported greater conflict from home pressures and less satisfaction with career. One's immediate conclusion is that women with families are less satistied during certain life-cycle stages with being in the work force. More studies are needed before making such generalizations, however. These results on attitudes do not yield a clear picture of how part-time scheduling affects overall job satisfaction or satisfaction with specific work-associated facets. Moderating or confounding variables include the frame of reference or social comparisons made by the employees, attitudes of managers toward the employee, the job itself, reasons for working, demographic characteristics, and the employee's life-cycle stage. It appears that difference in attitudes may be a product of the interaction between the type of employee and the work environment itself.

Implications for the Employer

In general, managers who do not employ part-time workers view them negatively, and managers who employ them view part-timers favorably. Both groups of managers believe, however, that part-time employees differ in their behavior and attitude from full-time employees. For permanent part-timers, this view is generally unfounded.

Organizational Effectiveness

Although we do not have systematically measured data, the experience reported in many companies that offer part-time employment has been positive regarding part-timer productivity and effectiveness. An obvious explanation is the notion that shorter hours reduce fatigue, and these employees are thus able to work at a higher level of efficiency while on the job. Two sets of findings from large surveys serve to summarize the advantages of part-time work schedules for the employer.

A survey of government agencies using part-time employees has indicated the following benefits: (1) greater flexibility in meeting work requirements, especially during periods of peak workloads, (2) recruitment of quality personnel who otherwise might not be available, (3) reduced personnel costs, (4) increased interest in permanent employment, 95) positive job attitudes, and (6) better service to the public.[75] Forty-five agency officials indicated that part-timer productivity tended to equal or surpass that of their full-time counterparts. For example, at the Social Security Administration in Los Angeles, some part-time employees handled a workload 27 percent to 59 percent proportionally greater than full-time employees performing similar work.

The second survey, cited by *Alternative in the World of Work* and by Robinson, involved the Massachusetts Mutual Life Insurance Company.[76] This company began using various part-time scheduling alternatives as early as the 1950s and offered full-time permanent employment, part-time permanent employment, full-time temporary employment (for peaks and projects), and "Mothers' Hours" (scheduled to coincide with children's school hours). Massachusetts Mutual found the following benefits:

1. Part-time jobs provided a recruiting resource pool for full-time positions and provided a broader recruiting base from which to meet equal employment opportunity goals for full-time positions.
2. Part-time work facilitated incorporation of advances in computer technology, which reduced many jobs to less than full-time.
3. Part-time workers helped handle peak demands through greater flexibility in staffing.
4. Productivity of permanent part-time workers was high. Among jobs classified as "$6/10$" of full-time positions, employees were doing a full day's work.
5. Personnel training costs were lower.
6. Employee attitudes were positive, and turnover was low.

Perhaps the major benefit associated with part-time employees has been the opportunity (or necessity) for better utilizing the work force to seasonal, weekly, and daily peaks in the workload. Part-time workers also helped provide better service to the public through longer open hours and weekend and holiday operation. This may result in better utilization of plant and equipment.

If full-time employees are willing to reduce their work hours and to share the workload at a reduced level, both management and employees as a group may be able to avoid layoffs during high unemployment periods. This is not a new idea, and many union contracts have been designed to prevent or minimize reduction in work force by allowing for redistribution of work. McNeff et al. report a case at The Washington Post in which work sharing aided the company and employees during financial difficulty.[77] Faced with the possibility of layoffs, union members voted for a shorter work week at less pay for one year. Work sharing avoided unemployment, and at the same time management witnessed improved employee morale and productivity.

At The Washington Post, work sharing was not considered a permanent alternative. However, with present inflation rates and an increasing belief that full employment may not be an achievable goal, it is realistic to consider some form of part-time work as a permanent alternative in order to achieve an increased level of employment.

Recruiting and Training Issues

The availability of part-time positions allows the employer access to a pool of talent otherwise unavailable. For example, the Detroit school system was having difficulty attracting qualified teachers for its inner city. Offering part-time positions quickly resolved the problem.[78] In addition, former employees who are no longer able to work full-time can be recruited into part-time positions, which allows savings in orientation and training costs. Furthermore, part-time employees provide a resource pool from which to recruit for full-time permanent jobs.

Part-time positions are associated with several important benefits for companies trying to meet equal opportunity requirements. In the case of job sharing or pairing, two employees can decide to share one full-time job, thus opening another full-time position and creating an opportunity for affirmative action hiring.

Another affirmative action benefit of part-time work was illustrated by the New York Telephone Company. Rather than laying off 400 employees, the company placed 2,000 telephone operators on a four-day week at four days' pay. Thus newly hired women and minority employees were not dismissed under seniority rules.[79]

Costs

One disadvantage of part-time work is increased administration costs—personnel scheduling, hiring, firing, transferring, and so on. All require additional time. However, companies using part-time positions generally report that the advantages derived more than outweigh problems and costs associated with this expense. This conclusion is consistent with our research.

In addition to administrative costs, some increases in overhead costs result from employee benefit packages, specifically medical and dental programs, which are normally per capita costs. Where these costs cannot be prorated, it may be possible to (1) renegotiate agreements to include part-time employees and/or (2) consider flexible compensation whereby employees have certain options as to the extent of coverage they desire (i.e., cafeteria approach). Concerning compensatory benefits (vacation, sick leave, jury duty, etc.), prorating could be based on hours worked. In fact, savings may result in this area, since part-time employees generally use fewer hours of sick leave and personal days than do full-time workers. Supplementary benefits based on earnings, such as life insurance, travel insurance, and profit sharing, can also be readily prorated. We should emphasize, however, that part-time employees cannot be ignored or overlooked with respect to fringe benefits, as has been the trend in the past. The view that part-time employees represent a saving to the employer because they need not be included in benefit packages is unfair to the employee, and it perpetuates the stereotype of the part-timer as a marginal worker.

In the case of social security payments, an employer may pay less for an employee working full-time all year than for two part-time employees who may not exceed the base maximum taxable level for social security deductions. However, according to lazer the median annual salary of full-time workers is significantly less than this maximum.[80] Consequently, though it is realistic to expect some extra social security costs for part-time workers, many employers will be unaffected.

Unions

A problem employers may face when considering part-time employment programs is possible conflict with union leadership. Labor unions generally express reservations about part-time employment, fearing that it would have a wage-cutting effect, that part-time employees would be hard to organize, and that they would displace full-time workers. In addition, unions may have the following general objections to part-time employment, some of which coincide with disadvantages cited earlier for individual employees:

1. Part-timers receive scaled-down and/or prorated benefits, a situation not necessarily supported by union management.
2. Although in some cases contracts include a provision for yearly salary increases, progression schedules for salary increases are usually extended.
3. Part-time hiring is viewed as a form of discrimination against minorities to impede affirmative action. It maintains underqualification, especially for women.
4. Part-time work encourages moonlighting. According to Owen moonlighters represent 23 percent of all voluntary part-time workers.[81] This situation is unacceptable to union management, since unions are concerned with providing a job for every eligible worker and increasing overall employment levels.
5. Part-time work will generate conflict between part-time and full-time employees, since their objectives are different.

Generally speaking, union management believes that part-time employment will compromise gains that have been made through collective bargaining for full-time workers.

Implications for the Employees

Problems of Stereotyping and Discrimination
One of the most serious problems limiting expanded use of part-time positions is the stereotypic belief that part-time work implies

halfhearted or limited commitment—that part-timers are second-class employees. However, as pointed out earlier, companies using permanent part-time employees in their operations have experienced greater productivity, lower turnover, and decreased absenteeism. According to one group of researchers, part-timers (with the exception of the limited number of professionals) are considered secondary wage earners compared with full-time workers and lacking in commitment to the labor force. Part-time work is viewed as marginal and suitable only for certain job levels and work technologies. Even employers who favor using part-time workers consider part-time and full-time work and workers to be different.[82]

Another misconception associated with part-time work is that it benefits only white, middle-class women—a group supposedly less in need of employment than others. Some critics claim that part-time work is an "elitist concern," since part-time wages cannot provide a living.[83] However, there are serious flaws in such arguments. First, examining wage scales for the part-time labor force should quickly dispell the idea that part-time work benefits *only* middle-class women and students. Moreover, for people whose family responsibilities prevent full-time work, or for handicapped people who can perform part-time work, part-time wages may provide the only possible opportunity for well-being and productivity.

Perhaps what creates these negative stereotypes is the tendency of employers to pay part-time employees lower prorated salaries. Deutermann and Brown found that five years ago, part-timers earned (on the average) less per hour than their full-time counterparts—$2.87 per hour for part-timers compared to $5.04 per hour for full-timers.[84] One reason attributed to this difference is the high number of teenagers in low-paying jobs. In any case, low salaries mean that many people will not be interested in part-time employment. On the other hand, the increased flexibility of part-time hours outweighs this disadvantage for others, as evidenced by the high percentage of people who voluntarily work part-time. The fact remains that low pay is a serious disadvantage of part-time work. Some companies aggravate the problem further by using part-time positions to avoid providing fringe benefits, such as vacation time, sick leave, and pensions.

Availability of Part-Time Employment

Two problems for persons wishing to work part-time schedules have been the unavailability of part-time jobs and the lack of job security. Typically, part-time job opportunities diminish when the labor market becomes tight. Part-timers are often the first to lose their jobs when reductions become necessary, regardless of their skill, training, commitment, or contribution to the company. Lack of part-time job opportunities is especially evident on professional and managerial levels. Fogarty, Rappaport, and Rappaport attribute this problem to four factors:

1. Top job holders require a high level and quantity of up-to-date information for making decisions. The necessary information network is more likely to require working overtime rather than part-time.

2. Successful daily operations in many professions require all members of a specific network to be available simultaneously during regular working hours in order to respond to unforeseeable needs. Only a limited number of network breaks can be tolerated.

3. Part-time workers cannot cope with emergencies which arise outside normal working hours.

4. Filling one full-time position with two part-timers doubles the number of persons to whom and through whom information must be transmitted.[85]

As Fogarty et al. are quick to point out, these arguments must be qualified. After-hours emergencies, regular overtime, and difficulty in finding time for gathering and transmitting information may be curable symptoms of poor work organization. They point out several instances where part-time professional employees handled jobs flexibly by staying in touch with their offices during off hours and by taking work home, as would full-timers holding comparable jobs. As we obtain more information concerning successful part-time professional and managerial employees, such arguments may become less influential in discouraging high-level part-time positions.

Promotability of Part-Time Employees

The opportunity for promotion is also an important consideration for part-timers. The Professional and Executive Corps Program for part-time professional women in the Department of Health, Education and Welfare (HEW) illustrates a disadvantage of part-time employment in this regard. This program was established in 1967 by HEW to use women in civil service jobs at grades GS-7 through GS-15 on a less than full-time basis.[86] Though considered highly successful, this program indicated that part-timers were not as likely to be promoted as full-timers. The government, as well as other organizations throughout the United States, must deal with legal and other requirements for minimum time periods of employment at one job level prior to promotion. Three years at one level for a full-timer, for example, becomes six for an employee working half-time. Promotions for part-timers are therefore retarded.

The Nonwork Domain and Part-Time Work for Women

As with other alternative work schedules, part-time work provides flexibility for combining career and family responsibilities and for reducing role conflict. Shorter working days provide more time to spend with children and to shop during off-peak hours. Recreational and social activities also tend to be simpler to arrange. For these reasons, part-time employment is growing more popular.

For instance, in a study evaluating married women working full-time, part-time, and as full-time homemakers, Hall and Gordon found that more women expressed a preference for part-time work than any other form of activity; only a few would change from part-time.[87] In another study, Hoffman and Nye concluded that part-time working mothers "seem to be physically and psychologically healthy, positive toward their maternal roles, and active in recreational and community activities.[88] Their children compared favorably to the other two groups (full-time housewives and full-time employed mothers) with respect to self-esteem, social adjustment, and attitudes toward their parents."[89] In a third work, Morgenstern and Hamovitch found that child care was far less of an obstacle to women working in part-time occupations than for those having full-time jobs.[90] (In 1974, women with children under age 15 represented 34 percent of single-job part-time workers.[91])

Part-time work is highly advantageous for single parents and for people who have dependents other than children. In addition, part-time work can reduce the number of people on welfare. It can be especially beneficial in assisting women to maintain career continuity during childrearing years. For women who have left the labor force and wish to return, part-time hours may offer the only feasible opportunity to do so. For many re-entry employees, part-time work offers the advantage of adjusting to a work routine before becoming full-time employees; at the same time, it allows them to acquire or regain skills and training.

Despite the obvious advantages of part-time schedules for many women, working women in full-time jobs were somewhat more satisfied with their work than with part-time work. Although few women would change from part-time to full-time, part-time women workers often experienced more role conflicts. These apparent contradictions may be explained by proposing that:

1. Part-time jobs were not especially challenging or interesting for these women.
2. Women part-time workers had pre-existing conflicts, since they viewed part-time work as a compromise between full-time work and full-time homemaking.
3. Women working part-time were reluctant to rearrange or reduce the number of their activities. In some cases, spouse and family may not have adjusted their demands on and expectations of the woman as mother since her return to the work force.

Education and Other Activities

The educational benefits of working part-time are obvious. Employees can more easily return to school without discontinuing employment or greatly extending the time necessary for completing courses of study. This is one of the primary reasons that high percentages of people under age 25 work in the part-time labor force. Students who work part-time generally feel less fear of incurring debts to finance school. Consequently, more individuals can pursue college education under part-time work arrangements.

Under part-time working conditions, men and women also have greater opportunity to split their time between private jobs and political or other community activities. Thus, part-time work offers the best of several worlds: earning money while involved in professional, community, social, recreational, and family activities.

Handicapped Employees

Permanent part-time employment is especially beneficial to handicapped people who cannot bear the strain of a full-time job. Many of these people would like to be independent and self-supporting and make a meaningful contribution to society. Although full-time jobs may be inappropriate for them, they may be able to achieve these goals on a limited basis with part-time employment.

Retiring Employees

With the ranks of retirees increasing because of recent trends toward early retirement, a higher proportion of senior citizens are out of the work force. At the same time, benefits of early retirement have diminished because of inflation's effect on fixed income and because of potential social security cutbacks.[92] In addition, forced retirement may inflict emotional and physical distress, decreasing life expectancy and causing loss of social status within the community, a sense of isolation, and decreased personal satisfaction.[93]

Part-time work conditions provide opportunities for dealing with these problems. Many retirees may wish to work part-time to supplement retirement income. Others may wish simply to remain active on a part-time basis in order to feel useful and to maintain a sense of worth. Older workers can not only gain from employment, but can also contribute their years of experience and training, which are of unquestionable value to our economy and society. Moreover, part-time employment also affords the employee a chance to phase into retirement. During this time, retiring employees can adjust to new lifestyles and increased leisure time, or they can cultivate new interests in their community.

Part-time work also offers some benefits to individuals forced to leave the work force before retirement age (due to ill health, for example). If it becomes possible or necessary to return to work, it is exceedingly difficult for the 55-and-over age group to find full-time employment. Part-time work provides a needed source of income for these individuals; and as with all part-time workers, it gives them an opportunity to prove their skills and abilities to an employer for later consideration in permanent assignments.

Notes

1. Bednarzik, 1975.
2. Flint, 1977.
3. Owen, 1978.
4. Deuermann and Brown, 1981.
5. Eyde, 1975.
6. Deutermann and Brown, 1978.
7. Nollen et al., 1976.
8. Rotchford and Roberts, 1978.
9. Eyde, 1975; Foster, 1977.
10. Robinson, 1976.
11. Nollen, Eddy, and Martin, 1978.
12. Ibid.; Nollen and Martin, 1978.
13. U.S. Comptroller General, 1976.
14. Nollen and Martin, 1978.
15. U.S. Comptroller General, 1976.
16. Nollen and Martin, 1978; Nollen, Eddy, and Martin, 1978; Bureau of National Affairs.
17. Nollen, Eddy, and Martin, 1978.
18. U.S. Comptroller General, 1976.
19. Nollen, Eddy, and Martin, 1978.

20. Gannon and Nothern, 1971.
21. Smith, Kendal, and Hubin, 1969.
22. Logan, O'Reilly, and Roberts, 1973.
23. Hall and Gordon, 1973.
24. Gannon and Nothern, 1971; Katerberg, Hom, and Hulin, 1974.
25. Katerberg, Hom, and Hulin, 1979.
26. Katerberg, 1980; Katerberg, Hom, and Hulin, 1979.
27. Gannon and Nothern, 1971; Katerberg, Hom, and Hulin, 1979.
28. Katerberg, Hom, and Hulin, 1979; Logan, O'Reilly, and Roberts, 1973; Katerberg, 1980; Brief, Van Sell, and Aldag, 1979.
29. Miller and Terborg, 1979.
30. Jackson, Keaveny, and Allen, 1977.
31. Kunin, 1955.
32. Logan, O'Reilly, and Roberts, 1973; Katerberg, 1980; Miller and Terborg, 1979.
33. Gannon and Nothern, 1971.
34. Hall and Gordon, 1973.
35. Gannon and Nothern, 1971.
36. Katerberg, Hom, and Hulin, 1979.
37. Jackson, Keaveny, and Allen, 1977.
38. Brief, Van Sell, and Aldag, 1979.
39. Jackson, Keaveny, and Allen, 1977; Logan, O'Reilly, and Roberts, 1973; Katerberg, 1980; and GOldberg, 1981.
40. Gannon and Nothern, 1971; Miller and Terborg, 1979; Hom, 1979.
41. Brief, Van Sell, and Aldag, 1979; Logan, O'Reilly, and Roberts, 1973.
42. Katerberg, 1980.
43. Hom, 1979; Brief et al., 1979.
44. Katerberg, 1980.
45. Hom, 1979.
46. Ibid.
47. Ibid.
48. Logan, O'Reilly, and Roberts, 1973.
49. Goldberg, 1981.
50. Ibid., Miller and Terborg, 1979; Katerberg, 1980.
51. Hom, 1979.
52. Brief, Van Sell, and Aldag, 1979.
53. Logan et al., 1973.
54. Jackson et al., 1977.
55. Brief et al., 1979; Jackson et al., 1977.
56. Goldberg, 1981.

57. Katerberg et al., 1979.

58. Brief et al., 1979; Hom, 1979; Miller and Terborg, 1979.

59. Logan et al., 1973.

60. Ibid.; Jackson et al., 1977.

61. Brief et al., 1979; Miller and Terborg, 1979.

62. Katerberg, 1980.

63. Ibid.; Miller and Terborg, 1979; Brief et al., 1979; Logan et al., 1973; Jackson et al., 1977.

64. Katerberg, 1980; Jackson et al., 1977; Miller and Terborg, 1979.

65. Hom, 1979.

66. Gannon and Nothern, 1971.

67. Katerberg, 1980

68. Logan et al., 1973.

69. Miller and Terborg, 1979; Hall and Gordon, 1973.

70. Goldberg, 1981.

71. Logan, 1973.

72. Logan et al., 1973.

73. Miller and Terborg, 1979.

74. Hall and Gordon, 1973.

75. U.S. Comptroller General Report, 1976.

76. Alternatives in the World of Work, 1976; Robinson, 1976.

77. McNeff, et al., 1978.

78. U.S. Congress, 1976.

79. Eyde, 1975.

80. Lazer, 1975.

81. Owen, 1978.

82. Rotchford and Roberts, 1978.

83. Discussed in Wilkerson, 1975; and Committee on Alternative Work Patterns, 1976.

84. Deutermann and Brown, 1978.

85. Fogarty, Rappaport, and Rappaport, 1971.

86. Eyde, 1975a.

87. Hall and Gordon, 1973.

88. Hoffman and Nye, 1974.

89. Ibid.

90. Morgenstern and Hamovitch, 1976.

91. Owen, 1978a.

92. Olmsted, 1977.

93. Rosenberg, 1977.

CHAPTER SIX

Job Sharing

Definitions, Variations, and Examples

The previous chapter contained a comprehensive view of part-time employment, of which job sharing is a part. We believe the change in the nature of part-time employment and the anticipated dynamic acceptance of job sharing in the very near future merits an entire chapter on this topic.

Until the concept of job sharing was formulated, part-time employment had been associated with employee groups at low levels within the organization. Likewise, part-time employment had been considered a temporary or stopgap measure. Increasingly, however, professional and technical employees want to work less than full-time. This is where job sharing comes in. Job sharing is a form of permanent, part-time employment that can accommodate career-oriented individuals who traditionally could pursue their careers only in full-time positions. The concept has promising implications for the individual, the organization, and society.

For the individual, job sharing presents an alternative to a grueling 40-hour work week. A flexible work week can give the individual more time for family, personal errands, education, and leisure. Job sharing also provides a way for professional women, older workers, and minorities to join or remain in the work force that was previously unavailable.

For the organization, job sharing offers a potential solution to low productivity, absenteeism, low morale, and turnover. A job-sharing arrangement guarantees the organization continuity of job performance and the ability to retain valued employees.

Advantageous to both the individual and the organization, job sharing also benefits society in general. Like Drucker and Galbraith, we believe that job sharing is not a panacea for the world's employment problems, yet is is an exceedingly useful alternative to full-time employment.[1] Professional women need not make a choice between office and family; older workers can avoid the trauma of sudden unemployment after a lifetime of work; and minority groups can have access to positions previously closed to them—all with the assistance of job sharing.

What follows in this chapter is a summary of all the literature to date on this new concept. Included are profiles of the typical job sharer, a review of early experiments in the public sector, examples of successful applications in the private sector, and a comprehensive list of the pros and cons of this alternate work style.

Job Sharing Defined

Job sharing is typically defined as two people sharing the responsibility of one full-time position, with salary and fringe benefits prorated. It is a form of voluntary, permanent part-time employment.

Under a job-sharing arrangement, both the duties and responsibilities of a single position are divided to provide total job coverage. In some cases the job functions of one individual may be substantially different from those of the other. Each person is accountable for only half the duties and responsibilities of the position.[2] In other cases, two individuals divide the job but have equal responsibility for the total job. The tasks are equally divided between the two individuals, but each individual has the ability to perform the other's duties and may in fact be called upon to do so in the other's absence. From the employer's perspective, one full-time position is being filled.

As a form of permanent part-time employment, job sharing by definition implies a career orientation, a labor force commitment, and a potential for upward mobility heretofore unassociated with part-time work. Increasingly, it also implies the same fringe benefits and job protection as full-time positions.[3]

Differentiation

Specifically, job sharing differs from traditional part-time employment in two ways:

1. Its purpose is to restructure career-oriented, professional positions that cannot be reduced in hours or split between two part-time employees.

2. It often requires a significant degree of cooperation and communication between sharers.

Definitions

Several terms are often associated with job sharing but in fact describe other forms of part-time employment.

Work Sharing. Work sharing is frequently confused with job sharing. Work sharing refers to an organization's short-term response to a particular economic situation. Implemented to retain employees during an economic downturn, it is a method of spreading limited work among current employees. Cutbacks in hours do not generally exceed 20 percent, and the assumption is that workers will return to full-time employment when economic conditions improve.

Job Pairing. In job pairing, two people divide the job but have equal responsibility for the total job. Each works half time, and together they provide full-time coverage. An example of job pairing would be one naturalist position filled by two employees who work at different times to develop a display and program that they will jointly present at a city park.

Job Splitting. Job splitting differs from job pairing in that two people divide the job, but each is independently responsible for only half the work. Two probation officers in one department—each responsible for only half the caseload—is an example of job splitting. One may argue that job splitting is not a pure form of job sharing because such an arrangement does not require communication between sharers. However, in the event that a job-splitting partner covers for the other during illness or some other absence, job splitting may ease its way into the definition of job sharing. Perhaps the level of communication between two people who divide one position can be a qualifying factor in determining whether a position is shared or merely split.

Shared Positions

With these definitions and differentiations in mind, we can see that some positions lend themselves to job sharing more easily than others do. Moreover, as a form of permanent part-time employment, job sharing opens up a variety of positions previously closed to less-than-full-time workers. In the past, part-time positions have been associated with low-level occupations. Job sharing changes that parochial association to include such occupations as administrative assistant, teacher, engineer, researcher, personnel administrator, trainer, project director, comptroller, teller, career counselor, and organizational development specialist.[4]

In general, the types of positions most likely to benefit from job sharing are defined by one or more of the following characteristics:

1. They require a broad range of skills.
2. They have periods of intense peak activity alternating with slack periods.
3. They require a great deal of creativity.
4. They are tedious or monotonous.
5. They result in employee burnout from too much pressure.
6. They need more than eight hours of coverage.[5]

To date, the wide variety of positions that have been shared by two employees indicate that the nature or the requirements of the job are not as critical to the success of job sharing as the two employees' professional and personal abilities and the supervisor's support.

Job-Sharer Profiles

In its early stages of development, job sharing was viewed as a women's issue—an ideal alternative for professional women trapped between family and career. Job sharing can provide these women with a work arrangement that permits them to continue pursuing their careers while spending more time with their families. However, this view of job sharing as a women's issue has recently been changing.

Increasingly, men in professional job categories, seeking more time for family, leisure, and other activities, are finding job sharing a useful alternative. In testimony presented to a subcommittee on Employment, Poverty, and Migratory Labor, Cunningham reported that within a seven-month period, 41 of the 268 people who came through her job-sharing pilot program were males, many of whom were engineers or other technically trained professionals.[6]

In one of the few documented studies of job sharers published, Meier learned that of the 238 job-sharing respondents, 77 percent were working in teams composed of two females; 19 percent were male/female; and 4 percent were male/male. Occupational categories were grouped into six broad categories: teachers, 26 percent; administrators, 25 percent; secretaries, 15 percent; counselors, 13 percent; researchers, 9 percent; and other, 11 percent.[7]

Other interesting findings from the Meier study show that 75 percent of the sharers were less than 40 years old; sharers were predominantly Caucasian (94 percent) and married (81 percent); and almost half of the respondents reported the B.A. as their highest academic degree, with an additional third having an M.S.W., M.A., or nursing degree.

Not only is job sharing relevant to both sexes; it is also relevant to workers of all ages. Job sharing offers an alternative to employers who must release trained, dedicated older workers and replace them with untrained, uncommitted workers. Similarly, this form of permanent part-time employment offers retirement-age workers an opportunity to remain psychologically fit and productive members of society. Mandatory retirement can be a psychological trauma to an unprepared organization or individual.

Organizations frequently make no provisions for the succession of employees; this can result in chaos for the organization and in near-certain chaos for the unfortunate person hired to fill the position. Likewise, mandatory retirement is often a traumatic experience for employees who have devoted their lives to the organization, have no outside interests, and usually are psychologically unprepared for retirement. Used effectively, job sharing can ameliorate both of these situations. Under a job-sharing arrangement, a person who has reached the age of mandatory retirement can work the government-approved number of hours in an advisory or trainer capacity, thus sharing his or her position with a younger employee. Such an arrangement guarantees smooth succession, covers the duties and responsibilities of the job, and provides the organization with a built-in on-the-job trainer. Thus job sharing can act as a transition period and training program.

Structuring the Arrangement

Procedures for restructuring a full-time job into a job-sharing situation involves two basic elements: (1) team formation—that is, how the skills and experience of the sharers related to each other and the job requirements—and (2) the division of time, task, and earnings.[8]

Job sharing may be initiated by either employer or employee. Employer-initiated job sharing may be accomplished with a direct offer to the ranks of the currently employed or through classified advertising. Later in this chapter, we will see examples of companies that offered employees the option of job sharing. It should be noted that the general offers were typically preceded by the employee's decision (usually forced) to leave the organization in order to devote more time to his or her family.

The classified ad by Walgreen Company shown in Figure 6–1 provides an excellent example of an employer's efforts to recruit job sharers. The ad refers to job sharing as "a new and exciting program" that allows workers to arrange their own working schedules and invites applicants to combine their talents and availability in accordance with Walgreen's needs. Notice that the classified ad mentions a benefits program. The ad reportedly drew 60 responses, from which three pairs of sharers were hired.

When job sharing is employee initiated, it is the individual's responsibility to find a partner and to present the team to management. The most persuasive case for job sharing is a team that offers more

Figure 6–1

Advertisement for Job-Sharing Positions

Source: Barney Olmsted and Suzanne Smith, *Job Sharing: Analyzing the Cost* (San Francisco: New Ways to Work, 1981), p. 120.

skills, experience, and talents than would one person alone. It is therefore essential that potential job sharers locate partners who have skills and experience complementary to their own. Finding the right partner is a threefold process: (1) Identifying potential partners within the organization, through professional associations or unions, or through newspaper ads; (2) choosing a partner—they get to know each other; (3) commiting to a partner—synergy develops, and the team begins to plan strategies for the shared job.

Regardless of whether the team is formed through employer or employee efforts, the details of job sharing begin with the following:

1. Dividing the responsibilities.
2. Developing a work schedule.
3. Developing a communication process.
4. Building a good relationship with supervisors.
5. Working out the fringe benefits issue.

A job description is nowhere more important than in job sharing because the first step in dividing responsibilities is defining them and the skills required to do them. This requires an analysis of the job description, including an assessment of the major and minor duties.

The next step is an honest assessment of each person's skills and work experience, covering those skills that relate directly to the job and areas of strength and weakness. Based on this assessment the two workers should divide their job responsibilities. Under the assumption that job sharers are equal partners, responsibilities should be divided so that the work is equal in difficulty, complexity, responsibility, and independence.

When establishing a work schedule, the employer's needs are the primary concern. However, there are variety of ways in which to schedule a shared job and still meet the employer's needs, as shown in Figure 6–2. Some sharers have worked on alternate days. Some rotate their schedule to conform to the work flow or work Monday–Tuesday–Wednesday one week and Thursday–Friday the next. Others overlap every day or once a week to cover peak periods of activity or to ensure sufficient communication. Still other possible schedules provide for every other month on duty or else six months on, six months off.

What we should note here is that job-sharing schedules are flexible and open to redesign as the work flow changes. An example of job sharing that has become a classic in the literature best illustrates this point. State Representative Midge Miller of Wisconsin, a propo-

Figure 6–2

Examples of Job Sharers' Work Schedules

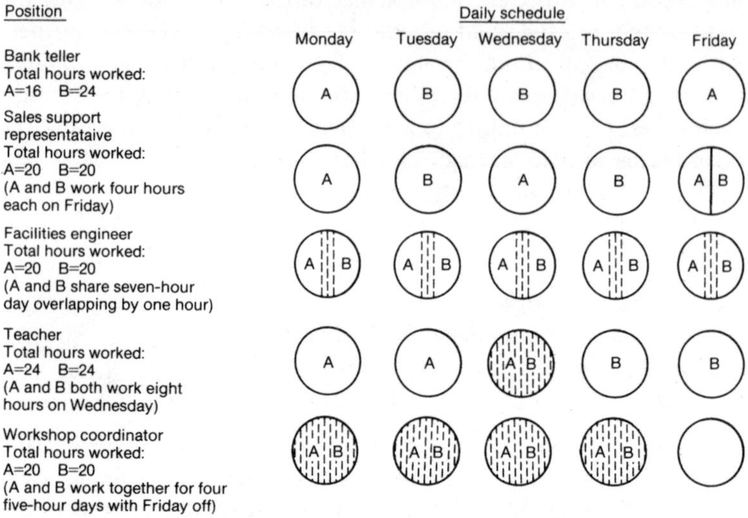

Note: Shading indicates time when both *A* and *B* are working. Although not illustrated here, there are also instances where the working day is extended by incorporating a period during which neither sharer works. Time frames of every other month and six months on, six months off are also popular in some professions.

Source: Barney Olmsted, *Job Sharing* (San Francisco: New Ways to Work, 1980).

nent of job sharing, employs two administrative assistants and boasts that she is the only state representative "who has one administrative assistant in two places at one time." Her job-sharing assistants both work full-time when legislative activity is more hectic and take time off during calmer times.

In addition to the demands of the job, personal needs may dictate the job-sharing schedule. For example, an employee whose child attends nursery school in the morning may prefer to work a morning schedule. Likewise, a parent whose children are in school all day or a semiretired worker may prefer a one-week-on, one-week-off arrangement. Regardless of the arrangement, the key point is that the schedule must meet the organization's needs first, then the individual's needs.

Open and honest communication must exist between job sharers to accomplish this goal. Indeed, communication is one of the elements that differentiates job sharing from other forms of part-time employment. Communication may take place between sharers via weekly or daily meetings, telephone calls, tape recordings, daily logs, and/ or a briefing board. It is the job-sharing team's responsibility to develop an effective communication process, and the communication may or may not take place during work hours.

In order for a job to be successfully shared, it must have the support of the supervisor. Job sharing is probably a new experience for the supervisor; thus job sharers must develop a relationship with their supervisor. Olmsted recommended that job sharers and supervisor agree on a review procedure whereby each individual can assess how well he or she is meeting the other's expectations, both in terms of overall job performance and effectiveness of the team approach.[9] The supervisor should be included in this procedure as a member of three-person team. We also recommend that job sharers assume some of the supervisory function in the job-sharing relationship. In other words, partners should assume some responsibility for motivating each other and for ensuring that the work meets corporate standards for timeliness, quality, and quantity.

Fringe benefits is the issue most commonly used to discourage job sharing by employers and, as such, warrants detailed examination. Fringe benefits typically account for a substantial amount of an employee's earnings; they are largely financed by the employer and include health coverage, unemployment insurance, retirement pensions, annual and sick leave, and social security insurance. As we will see later, some employers have begun to offer permanent, part-time staff the same coverage as their full-time employees under the premise that the extra cost is offset by enhanced commitment to the organization. More often, however, there is a prorated benefits package under which the employer pays half the cost of coverage for the half-time employee, and the employee pays the other half to obtain full coverage.

The "market basket" or "cafeteria" plan is another approach to the fringe benefits issue. Under this approach, employees select the particular benefits that meet their needs; costs vary with the number of hours worked. For example, an employee covered by a spouse's medical plan may opt for a life insurance plan.

A close look at Meier's survey of 238 job sharers reveals that 84 percent of respondents received fringe benefits on the same basis as full-time employees, prorated or specially arranged.[10] Note that 16 percent of the survey group reported receiving fringe benefits, although only 2 percent indicated that benefits were not provided to any employees in the organization.

Entitlement to fringe benefits as related to the six job categories of Meier's study is shown in Figure 6–3. It is interesting that counselors, secretaries, teachers, and researchers were more likely than were administrators to receive the same fringe benefits as full-time employees. This finding may indicate that positions traditionally designated professional are more likely to qualify for full benefits than are nonprofessional jobs. Researchers and teachers were more likely to receive prorated benefits than are counselors, secretaries, or administrators, according to Meier's study. Again, the data indicated that the professional positions are more likely to draw some type of benefits package than are the nonprofessional positions.

Since entitlement to fringe benefits is one element that distinguishes job sharing from traditional part-time work, Meier analyzed the responses to determine what factors related to benefit provision. She learned that some of the usual determinants—salary level, equality of pay, pay increases, and longevity on the job—were found to have little bearing. For example, in terms of salary level, 77 percent of the partners who together earned less than $8,500 did receive benefits, and those in the $16,500–$25,000 salary range showed the greatest disparity in fringe benefits. Nor did equality of pay affect the securing of benefits; 69 percent of those without entitlement to benefits received equal pay with their partners, but 49 percent who received full or prorated benefits also received equal pay. Almost half of the respondents employed less than one year in their shared

Figure 6–3

Percentage of Sharers in Each Job Category According to Entitlement to Fringe Benefits

Job Category	Same as Full-Time Employee	Prorated	Other*	No Benefits
Administrator	24	37	4	35
Teacher	44	46	4	6
Counselor	52	15	11	22
Researcher	42	47	—	11
Secretary	45	26	16	13
Other	41	36	18	5

* Special partial arrangements, such as retirement benefit only, all benefits except medical, or combination of prorata are full fringe benefits.

Source: Gretl Meier, *Job Sharing: A New Pattern for Quality of Work and Life* (Kalamazoo, Mich.: The W. E. Upjohn Institute for Employment Research, 1979), p. 46.

jobs received benefits, whereas only 36 percent of the partners employed for the longer period received these same benefits.

Meier concluded that one important factor in the receipt of fringe benefits seemed to be the nature of the employer (see Figure 6–4). Individuals employed by private, nonprofit organizations were less likely to receive benefits than were those in private profit-making, governmental, or educational organizations. Unionization did have some effect. A person who was neither a union member nor employed in an organization with union representation had a greater chance of not receiving benefits.

The most clear-cut distinction, according to Meier, was in the previous structure of the presently shared job. If the job was originally full-time and held by one person, it was more likely to carry full or prorated benefits. Furthermore, sharers employed in newly created jobs were probably entitled to benefits. (Almost half of those respon-

Figure 6–4

Entitlement to Benefits

Job Situation	Percentage of Sharers in Each Job Situation Who Are Entitled to Fringe Benefits			
	Same as Full-Time	Prorated	Other*	No Benefits
Organization:				
Private nonprofit	19	37	7	37
Private profit	29	24	18	29
Government	44	38	7	11
Public education	53	37	6	4
Unionized organization:				
Yes	47	39	6	8
No	32	35	9	24
Union member:				
Yes	59	36	5	—
No	33	37	8	22
Previous structure of job:				
Full time, one person	46	37	6	11
Part time, one person	19	25	12	44
Newly created	28	45	4	23

* Special partial arrangements, such as retirement benefit only, all benefits except medical, or combination of prorata and full fringe benefits.

Source: Gretl Meier, *Job Sharing: A New Pattern for Quality of Work and Life* (Kalamazoo, Mich.: The W. E. Upjohn Institute for Employment Research, 1979), p. 42.

dents whose shared job was previously considered a part-time, one-person position, received no benefits.)

Background and Field Studies

Overview

The earliest recorded experiments with job sharing occurred in the public sector as far back as 1965. Indeed, the concept has been tested and promoted with the aid of federal and state funds. One of the latter government-funded projects attempted to use state funds to interest private businesses in testing the concept. In 1972 a nonprofit, work resource organization, New Ways to Work (NWW), was founded. NWW's purpose is to explore work/time options for individuals and organizations in today's changing society. The organization has been instrumental in introducing the concept and benefits of job sharing to the private sector. Although job sharing has been quicker to catch on at small- and medium-sized organizations, it is slowly but surely gaining acceptance as an alternate work arrangement at several large organizations, including United Airlines and Pan American Airlines.

The Public Sector

Pilot Programs

Experimentation with permanent part-time employment has been going on for some time. Teaching is one of the first professions in which job sharing proved successful. In 1965 the Women's Educational and Industrial Union established a program in which it consulted with 15 Massachusetts school districts in Framingham and nearby towns and placed 120 carefully paired teams of teachers in their school districts.[11] One year later, the Catalyst Institute, a national research and educational service organization, evaluated the program. Both principals and parents reported enthusiastic reactions to the program, stressing how students benefitted from having two different teachers. Principals and parents cited the advantages of teachers' abilities to concentrate on their own specialty and to maintain a high level of motivation in the classroom. Initial fears about possible lack of communication between the partners, the staff, and parents proved unfounded.

In 1967 John Gardner, then Secretary of the U.S. Department of Health, Education and Welfare (HEW), announced the creation of the Professional and Executive Corps. This was a demonstration program designed to open opportunities for talented, trained employees who could not or did not want to work a regular 40-hour week. Geared largely toward women who had laid aside careers to raise families, the project allowed 22 women from various ethnic and racial backgrounds to work 20 to 35 hours a week in various job categories throughout HEW. Within 17 months, the number in the experiment had grown to 40. Unfortunately, the program was never institutionalized—probably because of the complex personnel ceiling system regulated by the Office of Management and Budget.[12] However, reports based on the program presented a positive view of this form of permanent, part-time employment. The report recommended that agency heads consider the use of job sharing in operational or direct-service jobs. The underlying cause of the recommendation was corps participants' rejection of partnership jobs based on the speculation that matching experience levels might be too difficult in administrative positions.

In another experiment at about the same time, the Massachusetts Department of Public Welfare hired 50 women and converted 25 social worker positions into job-sharing arrangements. Organized by Catalyst, the project was considered successful in terms of productivity and employee satisfaction.[13] Specifically, the project revealed that case workers involved with job sharing used their time more efficiently than did case workers on full-time schedules. Job sharers involved in their project were each carrying an average of 42 family cases, compared with an average 78 cases carried by full-timers. Additionally, job sharers averaged 20 percent more telephone contacts with clients and others involved in their cases.

In 1975 New Ways to Work initiated a job-sharing pilot project funded by the Governor's 4 Percent Discretionary Fund of the Comprehensive Employment and Training Act (CETA). The project was designed to include men and women and to encourage job-sharing experimentation beyond a single employer or a single profession. The project had two main components: (1) workshops to support individuals who were seeking an alternative to the 40-hour work week and (2) job development outreach to convince employers of the feasibility and advantages of job sharing.[14] Seven months after the project was funded, New Ways to Work had contacted more than 40 of the major employers in the San Francisco Bay Area, including electronics firms, hospitals, private manufacturers, school districts, universities, banks, and municipal governments. At the time, most organizations examined the concept in relation to their own employees, as well as experimenting with interviewing processes for New Ways to Work's shared-job teams. New Ways to Work reported that it was beginning to see job-sharing pairs placed, most of them in the public sector, schools, and government, but with a tentative start in private industry.

Favorable Legislation

In addition to these various public sector pilot projects experimenting with job sharing and other forms of permanent part-time employment, there have been several attempts at both the federal and state levels to introduce relevant legislation.

In 1974 Senator John Tunney (D-California) and Representative Yvonne Braithwaite-Burke (D-California) introduced legislation to provide more opportunities for part-time employment to federal employees who cannot or do not want to work full-time. After numerous setbacks, the Federal Employees Part-Time Career Employment Act (PL 95–437) was finally passed on October, 1978.[15] The legislation specifically calls for research and demonstration programs "determining the extent to which part-time career employment may be used in filling positions which have not traditionally been open for such employment on any extensive basis, such as supervisory, managerial and professional positions" and for "determining the extent to which job-sharing arrangements may be established for various occupations and positions." This corresponds with a section in the *Regulatory Requirements of the Office of Personnel Management* that calls for the agency to provide technical assistance that will include "guidance on job sharing and position restructuring."

Several states have also passed legislation or undertaken programs designed to increase opportunities for permanent part-time employment. In 1974 and 1975 Massachusetts and Maryland passed legislation similar to the Tunney-Burke bill, encouraging expansion of part-time employment options for employees of those states.

Also in 1975 a California bill established a pilot project within the Department of Motor Vehicles to test the feasibility of job sharing and other means of voluntarily reducing work hours. In that same year, Wisconsin was awarded a two-year federal grant for Project JOIN (Job Opportunity and Innovation) to put 50 part-time employees, many of them retirees, into 25 full-time jobs. Project JOIN provided some definitive results and therefore merits detailed attention.

Shortly after Project JOIN was initiated, State Representative Midge Miller requested that the Wisconsin legislature create a task force to study job sharing and flexible work hours in that state. The task force had two goals: (1) to determine whether existing statutes had any negative effects of flexible work hours and job sharing, and (2) to determine what additional initiatives were needed to encourage use of flexible hours and shared positions. As a result of the task force investigations and of subsequent testimony at a Fall 1976 hearing, legislation was introduced that mandated Wisconsin state agencies to experiment with flexible hours and to increase the number of permanent part-time opportunities, including job sharing, available in the state civil service system.

The Wisconsin project ultimately developed 56 positions involving 115 job sharers, or more than twice as many as their original objective. A cursory profile of the sharers indicates that 76 percent were female, 24 percent male; five persons were age 55 or older; five were disabled; the average years of education was 16. The Project JOIN staff and research team concluded not only that some employees want job sharing but that it is advantageous to the employer. Project JOIN also determined that job sharing had not been tried more often because it was a new concept and because most supervisors and personnel officers were unfamiliar with the mechanics of dividing one full-time position.[16] The importance of a system for assuring communications and an equitable workload division between job sharers was cited by the Project JOIN staff and research team. Finally, Project JOIN's results showed that a work schedule reflecting the needs of both the sharers and the job was critical to restructure a job successfully. The Wisconsin project concluded that job sharing was another method of recruiting capable employees, increasing job satisfaction and productivity, and lowering turnover and sick leave usage.

Despite the paucity of hard facts on the concept of job sharing, field results in the public sector indicated that it is a positive form of part-time employment for both the employee and the employer. The challenge, however, is widespread implementation of job sharing as an accepted work arrangement at all levels of the organization.

The Private Sector

The dearth of definitive data in the public sector is matched only by that in the private sector. It seems impossible to determine the number of job sharers in the private sector, primarily because job sharing is an individualized work arrangement between employer and employee. It appears that job sharing may in fact be taking place in several organizations without the arrangements being formally labeled as such or included in the organization's tally of part-timers. Despite the lack of systematic research, there are a number of documented examples of job-sharing arrangements in the private sector, including personnel administrators, flight attendants, assembly line workers, lawyers, lab assistants, museum curators, clerical workers, bankers, pharmacists, retail store clerks, and medical technologists. In the three examples described in this chapter, job-sharing arrangements were adopted as a solution to retaining valued employees, meeting an economic downturn, and reducing absenteeism.

TRW-Vidar

One private company that has built a track record (albeit a short one) in job-sharing experience in TRW-Vidar in Sunnyvale, California.[17] In 1977 TRW decided to try job sharing as a way of retaining two employees who didn't want to resume full-time work after maternity leave. A personnel representative and a personnel assistant had approached their supervisors about sharing a job when they both returned from maternity leave. The firm's initial reaction was mixed. However, after managers reviewed their proposal and considered how difficult it would be to replace the 13 years of training and experience the two employees represented, they decided that job sharing was worth a try.[18]

The women initially had to give up their benefit coverage in order to share; TRW-Vidar policy did not cover employees who worked fewer than 30 hours a week. After they had filled one full-time job as a team for 14 months, the company reevaluated its policy and began prorating compensatory benefits (sick leave, holiday, and vacation time) for all employees working 20 or more hours.

Following a cost analysis, TRW-Vidar learned that the job-sharing experiment was a success and decided to expand its use. Furthermore, the company amended its policy and extended full-benefit coverage to employees working 20 or more hours a week. In addition, the firm has publicly stated that job sharing helps to retain employees with valuable experience and training, incorporates a variety of skills in one job, increases productivity, reduces the use of personal time off, and reduces burnout. TRW-Vidar's forthright comments resulted in an unexpected side effect: a great deal of free, favorable publicity. It is not surprising that TRW-Vidar went on to expand job sharing and restructured other positions within the company. The company's Recruitment and Staffing Department incorporated job sharing into its literature and promotion strategies.

Black & Decker

Two major companies that are using job sharing but find it to have limited applications are Black & Decker Mfg. Co. and Hewlett-Packard Co.

Black & Decker had never considered job sharing but decided to give it a try when approached in 1979 by Goucher College in Towson, Maryland, to participate in a job-sharing internship program. Under the Women's Management Development Project, Black & Decker and other area businesses were asked to employ a job-sharing team for 13 weeks in order to provide training and work experience to college-educated women who had been out of the work force, serving in volunteer capacities and/or devoting their time to family activities for a number of years. The team was compensated, but employers were not obligated to hire the women as permanent employees at the end of the internship.

Black & Decker hired two women to share the job of personnel specialist. The job-sharing arrangement worked out so well that the company hired both members on a permanent basis for that position.[19]

Black & Decker had considered several issues in designing the job-sharing position, including:

1. The position(s) identified as appropriate to job sharing (i.e., positions with discrete tasks were found to lend themselves to job sharing).
2. A good relationship between team members.
3. Scheduling.
4. Planned communication between job sharers and supervisor of co-workers.
5. Prorated fringe benefits except for full medical benefits.
6. Productivity—task-oriented, enthusiastic, high energy level.
7. Merit pay increases eligibility—rated separately based on individual effort and groups projects.
8. Increased job satisfaction—time for family and community volunteer work and transition to full-time.

Black & Decker determined job-sharing benefits to the company by bringing the complementary skills of two workers to one position and, at the same time, serving the needs of certain groups of workers in the community.

Hewlett-Packard

A company that has earned a reputation for its employee orientation and one of the first known to experiment with innovative approaches to personnel management is Hewlett-Packard. It instituted a work-sharing plan in 1970 and was one of the first to institute flexitime in 1972.

In 1980 the company's personnel manager estimated there were 300 permanent part-time and 25 job-sharing arrangements within the company. He also reported that job sharing at Hewlett-Packard seems to work effectively in more routine positions that have clearly defined job tasks and that can be split between two people. Hewlett-Packard's experience with job sharing at professional levels indicates that positions having a high degree of responsibility are difficult to share, Hewlet-Packard has had more success when this type of job is restructured into a permanent part-time position.

Although permanent part-time and job-sharing schedules are not extensive at Hewlett-Packard, the personnel manager senses that supervisors are becoming more receptive to these modified work-hour arrangements, and he believes further implementation can be expected.

The Airlines

The airlines represent another industry that began using job sharing in response to an immediate crisis and eventually adopted it as an alternative to full-time employment. During a general downturn in the economy in early 1980, rising fuel costs led to high airline ticket prices. The resulting decrease in passenger traffic forced many airlines to "furlough" flight attendants. United Airlines sought alternatives to layoffs and, in April of that year, responded to a suggestion from the Association of Flight Attendants (AFA) by deciding to experiment with job sharing.

Initially announced as a three-month experiment, the plan allowed flight attendants to pair up and bid as a team. Flight attendants who participated were very satisfied with the program, and United extended the experiment. By the end of the first year, management was able to announce the saving of 365 jobs. As word of the United program spread, other airlines became interested. Members of the Independent Union of Flight Attendants (IUFA), which represents American airways flight attendants, has been trying for several years to negotiate job sharing as an option for its members. In November 1980 Pan American management agreed to test the concept in a six-month pilot project. At the same time, the airline instituted several other programs designed to avert or minimize layoff, which accounts for the comparatively low number of jobs shared in the Pan American program.

Figure 6–5 shows a comparison of the United Airlines and Pan American Airlines job-sharing programs. Note the scheduling and compensation offered by the two airlines. United Airlines offered

Figure 6–5

Comparison of Airline Job-Sharing Programs

	United Airlines	Pan American Airlines
Initiated	April 1, 1980	November 1, 1980
Duration	April through July 1980; extended to April 1, 1981; then again to August, 1981	November through April 1981; to be terminated May 1, 1981
Participants	508	116
Eligibility	At least seven years seniority when program was initiated, later reduced to four years seniority	Minimum five years seniority
Scheduling	Partners arrange own schedule on a monthly or flight-by-flight basis; must keep original partner for duration of pilot program	Three options: 1. One month on, one month off 2. Two months on, two months off; one month on, one month off 3. Three months on, three months off
Compensation	Junior partner paid at senior partner's salary rate; vacation and sick leave accrued at half-time rate for all sharers, regardless of schedule; health and life insurance same as for full timers; all travel benefits retained	Each partner paid at own salary rate; vacation accrual based on time flown; sick leave accrued based on amount of time flown; health and life insurance same as for full timers
Number of positions originally scheduled for furlough	1175	1100
Number of jobs saved	365	58

Source: Barney Olmsted and Suzanne Smith. *Job Sharing: Analyzing the Cost* (San Francisco: New Ways to Work, 1981), p. 15.

its workers the opportunity to arrange their own schedule on a monthly or flight-by-flight basis, with only one constraint: They had to keep their original partner for the duration of the pilot program. Pan American, on the other hand, offered its job-sharing partners three options: one month on, one month off; two months on, two months off; or three months on, three months off. Under United Airlines' program, junior partners received pay at the seniors partners' salary rate; vacation and sick leave were prorated; and health and life insurance benefits were the same for sharers as for full-timers. Pan American's benefits package resembled United's, with the exception that each job-sharing partner was paid at his or her own salary rate.

Another Manufacturer

One of the few examples of job sharing in the private sector that is documented with hard facts and figures is the following. A Midwest manufacturer experimented with a permanent part-time working arrangement in response to a production worker's request.[20] The worker, who had good job skills but a poor attendance record, asked permission to share her job with another employee. Before responding the employer compared the cost of employing one full-time employee against that of two job sharers (as outlined in Figure 6–6).

In making the comparison, the employer decided to include the full cost of health benefits for both partners instead of prorating it. The manufacturer considered the cost of job sharers to be equal to that of full-timers in the following areas: gross straight-time wages, vacation, workers' compensation insurance, life insurance, holidays, bereavement awards, and disability insurance. The firm determined that job sharing would double the cost of health insurance premiums, dental insurance premiums, and unemployment insurance. In contrast, job sharing would slash the cost of attendance awards and absenteeism. The firm looked at the direct costs of restructuring the position, then compared the company's average absence rate with the current absence rate of the employees requesting the new work arrangement. The employees' rates were 14.6 percent and 4.1 percent; the company rate was 1.9 percent.

On the basis of this excessive absentee rate, the employer decided to let the two employees job share for one year and then assess the results at the end of that year. Their conditions of employment as a job-sharing team were:

1. The two partners were responsible for day-to-day coverage. If the schedule sharer was unable to work, the other team member had to work. Partners were responsible for arranging this trade with each other.
2. Each team member was required to work a minimum of 1,000 hours annually.
3. Job sharers were considered permanent part-time employees and were entitled to participate in the fringe benefit program. Health and dental insurance premiums were paid by the company; life insurance, vacation, holidays, bonus and profit sharing plans were prorated.
4. Job sharers had to be willing to work full-time during unusual periods, but exceptions would be allowed if circumstances warranted it.

At the end of the 12-month trial period, the results were staggering. The partners' absenteeism rates had dropped to 1.8 percent and

Figure 6–6

**Per Position Cost Comparison of
Production Workers**

	Full Time	Job Sharers
Gross straight time wages	$14,037	$14,037
Vacation	527	527
Health insurance premiums	638	1,276
Dental insurance premiums	108	216
Unemployment insurance	216	421
Workers' Compensation Insurance	491	491
Life insurance	4	4
Holidays	580	580
Bereavement pay	21	21
Attendance awards	5	—
Disability insurance	190	190
Absenteeism	264	—
Payroll administration (too small to count)	—	—
	$17,081	$17,763
Elimination of overstaffing (program saving)	—	(854)
	$17,081	$16,909

Source: Barney Olmsted and Suzanne Smith. *Job Sharing: Analyzing the Cost* (San Francisco: New Ways to Work, 1981), p. 9.

0 percent. Their performance reviews had gone from satisfactory to high professional in both cases. Recognizing that absenteeism was a problem with other production line employees, the manufacturer set up a process by which employees who wanted to work less time could team up and apply for shared jobs. In 1980, four years after the original experiment, 30 teams were working at this firm. The arrangement had spread from the assembly line to office services to the position of company nurse. The average absenteeism rate of the sharers before they began sharing was 5.8 percent. After sharing, the rate of the same employees dropped to 1.2 percent—a reduction of 4.6 percent and considerably below the company average.

Through job sharing, the company also eliminated some overstaffing. Before it introduced sharing, 31.5 workers were needed to cover 30 positions. The savings in this area amounted to $25,621 (or $854 per position shared) and more than offset the cost per position for extra medical/dental and unemployment insurance. In addition, the company experienced increased scheduling flexibility, higher quality performance, and better employee morale. Supervisor morale improved as well. Job sharers are allowed to design their own work schedules as long as they cover the job, so the responsibility of finding a replacement for an absent employee shifts from the supervisor to the sharer.

Job Sharing in Europe

Job sharing is not a form of part-time employment unique to the United States. It is practiced in Europe with some impressive results and continues to attract a significant following. France's President Francois Mitterand advocated job sharing in his successful election campaign in 1981. In the United Kingdom, General Electric Company recently announced a program to provide half-time jobs to help soak up unemployment around its telecommunications plant in Coventry. In Sweden 34.7 percent of the companies responding to a 1981 *International Management* survey used job sharing; in only 6.1 percent of these cases was the scheme in danger of being dropped.[21] An additional 9.5 percent of the Swedish managers reported that their firms had plans to test job sharing.

The most impressive work documented to date has been conducted in the Netherlands. In the *International Management* survey mentioned above, 11 of the 86 Dutch respondents worked for firms that had tried job sharing. Nine of these programs were continuing; three were being expanded. An additional 14 of the Dutch firms planned to test job sharing.

The Dutch Ministry of Social Affairs has set up a program to promote increased employment by splitting full-time jobs into part-time jobs. The ministry has set a target of 1.5 million people for working part-time in the Netherlands by the end of this decade—about 25 percent of the working population. The Dutch program provides incentives for employers and employees participating in the program. The employer who creates an extra job by splitting a full-time position can claim $960 for the first year. For the first six months, the employee receives a government supplement that restores 60 percent of the money the employee lost by reducing hours. For the second six months, the employee receives 30 percent of the lost wages, and thereafter receives nothing but the part-time pay from the company.

Only 255 organizations took advantage of the program within its first six months. The program administrator says the slow acceptance may result from the fact that only special categories of employees qualify for the program. They must, for example, have worked full-time for at least three years on the job that is to be split. The employee who takes the other half of the job will normally have been unemployed or transferred from somewhere else, and hence does not qualify for the subsidy. Another difficulty is that many jobs that can be easily divided into two jobs pay so little that a half wage is below subsistence level.[22]

Despite its drawbacks there is still a positive outlook for job sharing in the Netherlands. When the experiment ends, the ministry will evaluate whether future policy concerning part-time work should stress compulsion or some continued form of incentive. One clear result that has emerged so far, as the administrator reports, is that "the administrative problems seems mostly to be seen by people who do not have experience with part-time labour."

Clearly, such experiences with job sharing in the private sector, both at home and abroad, indicate a positive outlook for the concept. The biggest challenge facing employees is introducing and familiarizing employers with job-sharing arrangements and convincing them to give the concept a try.

Implications for the Employer

The numerous advantages of job sharing make it an "easy sell" to employers.

Positive Implications

Flexibility

Many positions have periods of peak activity followed by slow spells. Job sharing can provide a more efficient means of using employee time. For example, work schedules can be designed so that both team members work during times of greatest demand and stay home during slump periods. Another alternative is overlapping hours or days during peak periods and arranging gaps during slow spells. The only constraint on job sharer flexibility in work scheduling is the organization's needs.

Retaining Valued Employees

Family responsibilities, the need to complete or continue education, and the desire for more free time are among the chief reasons that employers lose valued personnel. Job sharing offers an attractive option to employees in positions that were previously closed to part-time employment. Retaining valued employees assures job continuity and reduces the employer's need for recruiting, hiring, and training, which are costly to organizations.

Reduced Absenteeism

Employees often call in sick so as to visit the family doctor or accomplish other personal errands. Job sharing provides employees more time for personal chores and sufficient leisure time for meeting other responsibilities. The result is a decrease in absenteeism. Likewise, when some employees in either very tedious or very hectic jobs feel that they cannot face another eight-hour day, many call in sick. There is some evidence to support the hypothesis that job sharing may reduce sick leave and turnover.

Continuity

When one member of a job-sharing team leaves because of accident, extended illness, or personal reasons, the other member may be able to cover full-time until the partner returns or is replaced. The result for employers is continuity of job performance.

Increased Productivity

As mentioned earlier, some employees may have difficulty maintaining high efficiency throughout a 40-hour week, particularly in very tedious or very demanding jobs. By giving employees the option of less-than-full-time positions, employers are accepting the benefits of increased productivity.

Improved Morale

Related to increased productivity but different from it is the new issue of organizational commitment. Employees are aware of how difficult negotiating a job-sharing arrangement can be and are also aware of the scarcity of such arrangements. This knowledge can contribute to employee feelings of well-being toward the organization, which can in turn result in improved morale and commitment to the organization.

Broader Labor Pool

Job sharing may be used in attracting applicants to particular job categories and to particular geographic locations. It may also be used to attract applicants to positions that demand an unusually broad range of skills or that place exceptionally heavy time demands on one individual.

Reduced Recruiting and Training Costs

Retention of valued employees through job-sharing arrangements reduces the need to recruit and train employees for positions left vacant by employees who sought less-than-full-time employment. By teaming experienced employees with new hires, employers may in fact save the cost of training for a large number of positions.

Retaining Older Workers

Older workers who possess a wealth of experience and commitment to the organization are valuable assets. By using job sharing as a type of transition period or phased retirement, the organization can team older workers with younger workers. This arrangement offers two advantages: (1) It matches an experienced, committed employee with a newcomer to the position (if not to the company), which can only instill positive feelings toward the organization in the newcomer; and (2) it serves as an inexpensive form of on-the-job training.

From the organization's perspective, job sharing offers many advantages. A second person can infuse new ideas, energy, and enthusiasm into a job. As any proponent of job sharing might suggest, the organization is getting twice the talent—plus the increased stimulation of each worker on the other, which causes both workers' minds to spark. This in turn can generate industrywide creativity.[23]

Negative Implications

Like most issues, however, job sharing has its negative points. These fall basically into the two categories of accountability and benefits.

Accountability

Due to lack of experience with job sharing, employers sometimes feel concerned that neither member of the team will assume direct responsibility for getting the work done. Employers envision that each member of the team will blame the other for not completing a particular task. The final result, they imagine, will be an unfinished piece of work. New Ways to Work has found that this concern is unfounded in practice. This organization reported that job sharers are often particularly responsible because their morale and commitment to the organization have been enhanced by the opportunity to work hours that better suit their individual needs.

Increased Workload for Supervisors

Employers have voiced concern about doubling the workload for supervisors upon introducing job-sharing programs. Again, these concerns do not seem to materialize in practice, according to New Ways to Work. Performance reviews have proven to be a thorny issue for some organizations. Some supervisors treat sharers separately, some as a team, and some both as individuals and as members of a team. The critical factor appears to be the review method adopted. It should be appropriate to the situation, and it should allow sharers and supervisors to evaluate past performance effectively and to set future goals. On the other hand, an obstacle to the success of implementing job sharing lies in the immediate supervisor's perceptions regarding additional work and coordination.

Recruiting Job Sharers

Although recruiting poses a problem for employers, recent experience suggests that the problem is quickly diminishing. As noted earlier, employers are making job sharing known to employees through in-house announcements and to applicants through classified advertising. Many employers now advertise for one full-time or two part-time applicants. This type of advertising does not commit the employer in advance to a job-sharing arrangement and reduces the possibility that applicants will apply for part-time work even though preferring full-time employment.

Increased Number of Employees

Another factor working against job sharing involves the issue of padded payrolls. Some organizations are clearly against swelling the payroll with additional personnel, citing the increased cost of administration and benefits it would require. In the United States, many private and public employers have limits for the number of people that can be employed in any given budgetary unit.[24]

Increased Benefits Package

The principal disadvantage of job sharing for the employer is the increased cost of benefits. In order to avoid incurring such an inordinate expense, many employes have arranged to prorate benefits; that is, for each half-time employee, the company pays half the costs that it would pay for a full-time employee. Employees can then pay the additional amount for full coverage or not, as their needs demand. Since compensatory benefits (including health coverage) differ widely among organizations, individual companies must consider their own preferences. Although there is obviously some cost increase in extending even prorated fringe benefits to job sharers, those employers who have pioneered in this area seem to believe that the cost can be minimized. There are in fact some employers who believe that extending full coverage to part-time employees justifies its own cost because it reduces absenteeism and turnover. Evidence supports the notion that extending a full or prorated benefits package to permanent part-time employees can also increase productivity and improve employee morale. Olmsted emphasizes the importance of extending benefits to permanent part-time employees to encourage their personal identification as full members of the company's community.[25]

Implications for the Employee

In several instances advantages of job sharing to the employee parallel the advantages to the employer. This is not unusual, considering that a committed employee is typically well motivated and productive.

Advantages

Flexibility

Job sharing gives workers the flexibility to pursue broader, less pressured lives. Part-timers have the opportunity to spend more time with their families, to update their skills and knowledge through further education, and to pursue personal and leisure activities.

Remaining in Job Market

For women in the childbearing years, the option of permanent part-time employment often makes the difference between continuing in their professions or sacrificing their talents for a family. Women who opt for the latter frequently encounter difficulties on reentering the job market several years later. Sometimes the returning worker's limitations are real; often they are perceived. For instance, a woman who has sacrificed her career as a nurse and reenters the profession 10 years later may find herself faced with unfamiliar new equipment and procedures, her skills having become obsolete. Also, male superiors often hesitate to hire women with children because they assume the women are more committed to their families than to the office. Whether the problems are real or perceived, the option of job sharing eliminates employee need to drop out of the work force and face a difficult reentry several years later.

Transition Period for Older Workers

Mandatory retirement forces out many workers who have few interests and hobbies outside of work and who derive their self-esteem and identity from the job. For these workers, mandatory retirement is a traumatic experience. They find themselves a productive member of society one day, an undervalued individual the next. Until society learns how to use these workers' talents and energy, job sharing offers an attractive option. Job sharing provides older workers with a transition period between full-time employment and retirement. Reduced hours at the factory or office made possible through job sharing allows an opportunity for community service work, returning to school, or cultivating other leisure activities that has been impossible while working a 40-hour week.

Improved Job Access

In several instances, job sharing has improved access to jobs otherwise difficult to obtain. In its accepted form as permanent part-time employment, job sharing can give employees entry to positions for which intense competition or inadequate experience would have made hiring improbable. Similarly, job sharing may create job opportunities where none previously existed.[26] As a result of complementarity and specialization possible through teaming two skilled individuals, workers can feel better equipped to handle effectively the various responsibilities required by the job.

On-the-Job Training

The most valuable part of any corporate training program is usually on-site training. Under a job-sharing arrangement, inexperienced personnel may work with experienced personnel who function as on-the-job trainers. This type of personal training makes entry into a new position much smoother for the new employee.

Partner Support

Underlying virtually every advantage of job sharing to the employee is the notion of partner support. That support may be psychological or practical. Partner support means that during a personal crisis one partner can call upon the other to fill in while the other is absent. Partner support also means having someone to learn from, someone to share duties with, someone to brainstorm solutions with, and equally as important, someone to complain to. Working in close contact with another person can be a broadening and enriching experience for both workers and the organization.

Disadvantages

Three issues head the list of disadvantages of job sharing for the employee, any one of which could discourage employees from seeking a shared position.

Time

Although most people enter into job-sharing arrangements in an effort to work halftime, it is not unusual for job sharers to find themselves really working two-thirds time. Even when tasks are clearly delineated, the nature of many jobs is such that work extends to nonwork times. This is particularly true of job sharers who, by definition, require a significant degree of communication between partners; this communication is typically accomplished during non-work times.

Personal Adjustments

Working closely with another individual is bound to cause some problems. Typical comments on this issue range from "You can't run your own show" to "You've got to sit back and compromise." In order to get any amount of work done, there has to be cooperation between partners. The most successful job-sharing arrangements involve a constant give-and-take between the sharers.

Salary Reduction

The most obvious disadvantage of job sharing to the employee is reduction in salary. This reduction limits the number of people willing and able to work under such an arrangement. However, only the worker can decide the issue, based on his or her personal situation.

The cost of salary reduction is minimized by the recent rise in the percentage of two-income families, which enables people to meet financial needs on 1.5 salaries. Significantly, only 6 percent of the job sharers responding to Meier's survey reported that their salary was the sole source of family income.[27] Much evidence supports the hypothesis that the free time and increased flexibility of the job sharing arrangement offset the cost of reduced pay.

Social Consequences

Unemployment, affirmative action, and phased retirement are the key social issues for which job sharing may provide a partial solution. Equally important is job sharing as a partial solution to the professional women's desire to combine family and career.

As unemployment continues to rise in this nation, job sharing provides a means of finding more jobs for unemployed workers and focuses on using people's talents and skills. Job sharing also presents an alternative to affirmative action programs threatened by slowed growth and layoffs. Job-sharing programs initiated as an alternative to layoffs often aim to attract higher-paid senior employees and, consequently, to ease the burden of layoffs on newer staff, who are typically the first to be fired in periods of slowed growth.

The area of phased retirement, however, is where job sharing presents its most outstanding possibilities. Until job sharing emerged as an alternative work schedule, phased retirement was difficult, if not impossible. Job sharing makes phased retirement possible on a large scale, thereby enabling employers to follow Peter F. Drucker's suggestion of "creating full-time jobs that are staffed with part-time people." Drucker believes that phased retirement will be "the central social issue in the United States during the next decade."[28] His concern is that the nation develop policies that "encourage people to stay on the job and remain economically productive," rather than encourage them to retire early and make more room at the top.[29]

Drucker notes the following trends:

1. The ratio of employed workers to retirees and their dependents is growing dangerously narrow. A shift to later retirement would ease the increasing crunch on both private and public pension funds.

2. Demographic trends show that by the 1990s there may well be a labor shortage in certain areas. Encouraging older workers to remain at least partially active in the labor force broadens both the employer and the worker options during economic and social change.

3. Older workers are beginning to express more interest in staying in the workforce longer and in working part-time.

Job sharing may be a partial solution to preretirees who seek part-time work and more flexible hours. This arrangement would also prove beneficial to the organization, since it provides a built-in on-the-job training for younger employees.

As noted earlier, job sharing is also a partial solution for the professional woman making an either/or choice between family and career. Job sharing permits the career woman to continue in her chosen profession while spending more time with her family. This eliminates the trauma of reentry into the workforce in later years. Job sharing thus offers the organization an option for retaining a valued employee, and it provides the working woman with an attractive option for meeting her dual responsibilities.

There are clearly numerous advantages to job sharing as a form of permanent part-time employment. However, before job sharing becomes a widespread, accepted form of employment, two things must happen: (1) It must be adopted by large, private organizations; and (2) the issue of cost efficiency must be resolved.

The literature reveals that small- and medium-size organizations are largely responsible for much of the progress in permanent part-time employment. The large corporations, with a few outstanding examples, are still slow to adopt job sharing.

Much evidence supports the theory that employers resist job sharing because of cost and because of stereotyping of the part-time employees. Employers must solve problems of cost efficiency before job sharing can become widespread. Current fixed cost per employee (particularly including benefits) discourages the use of permanent part-time workers. Although suggestions for the prorating of benefits help to some extent, changes in current tax arrangements (including the introduction of incentives, as offered in some European nations) would encourage more employer interest in job sharing.[30]

Finally, permanent part-time employment must achieve the same status as full-time work if it is to become a realistic option for men and women. Its implied promise of career orientation and upward mobility must in fact be realized if the organization expects its professional staff to choose job sharing as an alternative work schedule.

It seems appropriate to end this chapter with a quotation from Galbraith: "The reasonable goal of an economic system is one that allows all individuals to pursue socially benign personal goals regardless of sex. Only if an individual has a choice as to the length of his or her working week or year, along with the option of taking unpaid leave for longer periods, does he or she have an effective choice between income and leisure."[31]

Notes

1. Drucker, 1978; Galbraith, 1973.
2. R. I. Lazer, 1975.
3. Olmstead, 1980.
4. Ibid.
5. Ibid.
6. Cunningham, 1976.
7. Meier, 1978.
8. Olmsted, 1979.
9. Ibid.
10. Meier, 1978.
11. Moorman, Smith, and Ruggels, 1980.
12. Meier, 1978.
13. Ibid.
14. Cunningham, 1976.
15. Olmsted, et al., 1979.
16. Ibid.
17. We report this case in spite of the fact that the company ceased operation in 1982.
18. Olmsted and Smith, 1981.
19. McCarthy and Rosenberg, 1981.
20. Olmsted, 1981.
21. Clutterbuck, 1981.
22. Ibid.
23. Frease, 1979.
24. Olmsted, 1979.
25. Olmstead, 1977.
26. Nollen and Martin, 1978.
27. Meier, 1978.
28. Drucker, 1978.
29. Olmsted and Smith, 1981.
30. Olmsted, 1979.
31. Galbraith, 1973.

PART THREE

IMPLEMENTATION

CHAPTER SEVEN

Implementing an Alternative Schedule

Organizational Change

Change as a Normative Function

Change is inevitable and therefore unavoidable. Change is necessary for survival; it is part of the maintenance and the growth of organizations. Even in the most static situations, change occurs constantly. Change may lead to greater differentiation and complexity or toward greater integration and stability. The organization's approach, however, will depend upon its priorities and upon the reactive or proactive measures taken to implement them.

The interaction between growth and maintenance functions is complex. Some organizations have long cycles of each; others have quick, alternating cycles. Organizations adapt to information by creating structures that generate new information, thus necessitating new structures. This process of assimilation and accommodation is integral to development and maturation. Like living organisms, organizations are in constant flux as they receive internal and external stimuli, and they must respond accordingly to reestablish homeostasis. This maintenance function results in a higher order of integration.

Since change is omnipresent and inevitable, it seems foolish to try avoiding it by hiding from it or resisting it. Mastering change and its effects on the organization, on the other hand, can only lead to increased competence and consequently to a higher level of functioning. Failure to do so leads to inefficiency, to ineffectiveness, and ultimately to the inability to perform and survive.

Change can occur on a small scale in day-to-day operations, but only the organizational mission can reflect large-scale change. Between these two extremes lies a continuum along which change occurs. Change monitoring is directed to a particular point along this continuum where problems energe. These problems result from difficulties of the system in making changes necessary to the growth/maintenance cycle. However, the point at which a problem emerges should not itself be considered the flaw in the organization. Rather, the symptom (e.g., an underproductive department) indicates problems hidden in other areas. For example, measles produces spots, but the appearance of spots is not the problem but a sign that something is wrong systemically. To cover the spots would be ineffective in treating the illness.

Since organisms are neither omniscient nor omnipotent, problems are just as inevitable as change. Problems and change in fact go hand in hand. Therefore, when problems emerge in organizations, one should explore overall functioning to arrive at a correct diagnosis—the only way to an effective treatment. Immunization is the treatment of choice for measles, but immunization is impossible for organizational problems. However, preventive medicine provides a useful analogy, since a proactive policy to change is the preferred organizational strategy. Managers should plan interventions to increase the organization's ability to respond and adapt. Corrective measures are necessary when self-corrective mechanisms fail.

Whether change is incremental and gradual or radical and abrupt is partly a function of how prepared and how aware the organization is of its part in a larger context. For example, one must regard technological changes not only in the context of technology *within* the organization, but also in terms of technology *throughout* the industry. Just as changing a product line requires understanding the market structure and technological feasibility, so must changes in hiring such specific groups as women, foreign nationals, and minorities also be understood in terms of larger sociocultural issues relevant to those groups. Any change made in one context will thus require changes in others and, without an appreciation of the larger context, changes will not make significant impact or endure.

Change also requires an ability for those involved to tolerate the uncertainties arising throughout the process. Willingness to take risks and flexibility in response to uncertain variables are key elements in the change process. The ability to foresee the need for change and to respond appropriately (even asking for help) is the essence of survival.

Given the normality and pervasiveness of change, it is surprising how many people view it with panic, fear, and other forms of anxiety. Resistance to change is in part a result of these feelings and provides a major impediment to even the best plans for change. Managing change needs to be part of every manager's skills. After all, change is a normal function of every organization, a process in which all personnel levels participate. This process need not be haphazard. Problem solving, conflict resolution, and planned change are all skills organizations can acquire to manage their growth, development, and stability.

Achieving the objectives of a planned change depends on the environment in which the firm operates, organization structure, adequacy of planning and control, type and style of decision-making strategies used by management, and effective management approach and practices consistent with the prevailing organizational climate. The moderating effects of these variables necessitates their consideration in implementing any change. Furthermore, since these variables have different levels of influence within each organization, each change process is always unique and its effect transcends the boundary of the target unit. (See Figure 7–1.)

Figure 7–1

System of Ongoing Evaluation and Organizational Change

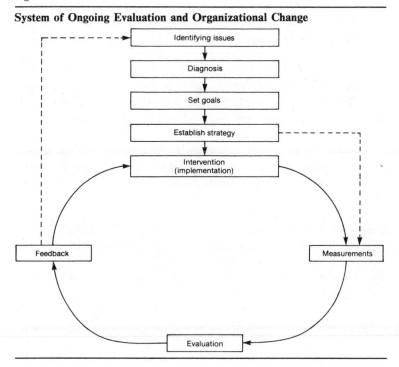

Organizational Change as a Planned Intervention

Organizational change is primarily aimed at improving some aspect of effectiveness, although the process can take different forms. Improving effectiveness can result from attempting to change individual behavior either directly or by changing organizational structure and processes. Implementing alternative working schedules involves both approaches.

Certain aspects of working schedules may be viewed as structural change, and other aspects are intended to change individual employee attitudes and behavior. However, structural change ultimately affects employee behavior and may also cause new attitudes. We are thus differentiating between indirect and direct effects of working schedules on individual behavior and attitudes. It is important that management view the system in this light. Although implementing alternative schedules can improve organizational climate, it is crucial that the prevailing climate be sufficiently conducive to the change. That is, to be receptive to the change a climate must inspire some trust between employer and employee and show potential for allowing to grant more autonomy and control to individual employees. Elements of an appropriate climate include participatory decision making and supportive first-line supervisors. In some organizations, preparing a receptive climate will be the necessary first stage of the change strategy, although organizations with more appropriate climates should also evaluate the implications of the schedules and the reception they will receive from employees at all levels.

Establishing the need for change requires participation by multiple levels of staff. Although the need for change may be recognized at the operations supervisors, middle, or top management level, discussion about the need should be initiated at all levels.

Managers and consultants alike have long been interested in changing organizations to improve their effectiveness. Recently, change agents employing behavioral science principles have systematically engaged in planned organizational change. Many of these professional change practitioners apply techniques known as organizational development (OD), which is basically an educational strategy used to improve the organization's current and long-run problem-solving processes. OD practitioners generally use participative methods to create self-directed change to which organizational members can feel committed.[1] These OD practitioners frequently operate from a humanistic value system. Since these values affect the types of change strategists consider, OD is particularly suitable for implementing alternative work schedules.[2] (See Figure 7–2).

Figure 7–2

Selecting an Alternative Schedule

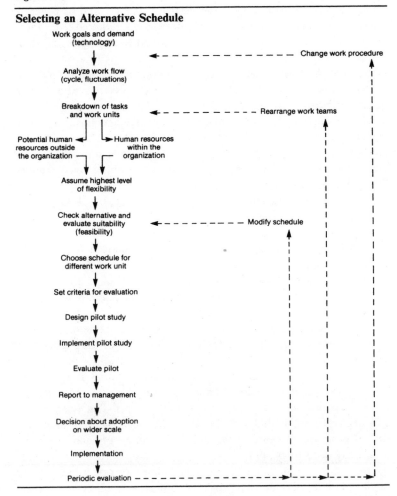

OD may employ different approaches but in general involves the following sequence:

1. Supervisors and managers are interviewed about the problems they perceive and the possible changes that could be implemented. It is important that personnel at these levels recognize and accept the need for change and that they be involved in generating ideas about what changes to implement.

2. Once manager cooperation has been elicited, managers meet

with those people who relate to them to discuss the problems presented, to gain acceptance for the need for change, and to generate ideas about what changes to make. Information gathered from these meetings is compiled and a summary returned to managers and their respective employees.

3. Any decisions reached by that point are communicated to the staff, thus allowing an opportunity for discussion and a chance to air anticipated problems or concerns.

4. This information is related to the change agents so that they can make necessary modifications in the proposed changes; it also alerts them to unanticipated effects and to possible sources of resistance. Teams can address resistance while determining how to implement changes.

5. Evaluation sessions are held once change has been implemented in order to ensure continuity and to address any difficulties arising from the change.

When change is managed in this manner, employees are involved in the process, are more committed to its success, and see the process of change as a challenge rather than a threat. There are times of course when change must be quick and cannot be open to discussion. However, discussions about change need to be encouraged because they will assist staff in making the necessary adjustments and will allow employees to articulate their reactions rather than simply to act resentful.

The purpose of this chapter is to help coordinators and planners cover all important stages and factors necessary to ensure the successful implementation of alternative schedule systems. The assumptions and principles for implementation described are essential for a successful program. Because of the unique character of each organization, there is no single, optimal technique for implementation. Consequently, the checklists and reminders below are presented for the reader to use in developing a program applicable to his or her organizational situation, based on the variables mentioned earlier. The stages of implementation described include: (1) initial consideration of the program, (2) forming a task force, (3) conducting a feasibility study, (4) planning the program itself, (5) defining an evaluation process, (6) conducting a pilot study, and (7) implementing the change companywide.

Consideration for Schedule Selection

The chapters on the various alternative schedules provided a detailed analysis of these schedules and their implications. What determines a schedule's effectiveness, however, is the optimal match of the department's work procedures and available personnel to the alternative schedule itself. Whether the initial idea for changing the schedules comes from the personnel department, a group of employees, or a highly placed executive, it is top management that should initiate the idea, explore it, and weigh its apparent advantages and disadvantages. Managers' evaluations should then be weighed against a list of set goals (usually arranged in some hierarchical order) the organization wishes to achieve. A steering committee headed by an internal or an external consultant should be appointed to carry out this task.

Committee members may include managers, nonmanagement employees, and union representatives. Managers initiating the change should carefully consider the decision to include employees and union members at this stage. On the one hand, these groups should be included early in the planning and implementation process in order to encourage participation and commitment to the change. On the other hand, premature inclusion may raise expectations about the system that may not be met, especially if the organization is equivocal about the program. The decision not to go ahead may affect morale if employees have been actively involved in the initial planning. One guideline for employee involvement is to seek participation at the point the employee's work unit comes under consideration for implementation. If one schedule will be implemented for an entire organization or division, involvement should come earlier in the process. If each department or work unit is to establish its own schedule, then involvement would not be necessary until the decision for the work unit is to be made.

This differentiation also has implications for the level of participation possible. In the former case, participation may be limited to a few employee representatives. For the latter, close to full participation from all employees in the decision-making process may be possible, depending upon the size of the work unit. This will of course require support and coordination from the union if employees are unionized. This steering committee should compile the goals provided by management and employees and present them to top management for approval. We must emphasize that *these goals provide a guideline for both the selection of the appropriate new schedule and the establishment of criteria for later evaluating the implementation's level of success.* What follows is a list of considerations for implementing alternative schedules:

Reduce overtime.

Improve employee attitudes.

Improve quality of work life.

Improve commuting and transportation to and from work.

Improve interpersonal relations.

Decrease withdrawal behavior.

Decrease turnover.

Decrease absenteeism.

Eliminate tardiness.

Increase productivity.

Increase utilization of facilities and equipment.

Increase hours of availability to clients.

Increase ability to attract and recruit presently unavailable segments of work force.

Ease transportation congestion and commuting time.

Reduce congestion during entrance to, and exit from, parking area.

Increase or decrease number of days per week the firm is operating.

Solve peak workload resulting from fluctuation in work demand within day week or month.

From this comprehensive list of possible outcomes, planners should choose those outcomes particularly desirable or feasible for their organization. For instance, if tardiness is a problem for the organization, flexitime may be viewed as a means of diminishing the problem.

Feasibility

The objective of a feasibility study is to determine whether the chosen alternative schedule can be implemented without permanently disrupting organizational functioning. Given the objectives set by the steering committee, a task force must now evaluate how flexitime will affect work flow, technology, and work-unit functioning through arrival and departure times, partial attendance by part-time employees, and so on. The goal should be to examine work conditions in the context of *as flexible a schedule as possible* in order to accommodate individual employee needs and simultaneously fulfill the unit job objectives and work processes.

Note that the purpose of the feasibility study is not to examine employee preferences. We do not recommend the idea of a survey to ask employees if they would prefer an alternative schedule. Not only can this be taken for granted (based on survey data reported in the previous chapters), but it serves only to raise expectations that cannot be met. Surveys are appropriate later in the implementation process—specifically, in evaluating the system for changes in attitudes—but are not appropriate in the beginning. Employee preference can be inferred from such demographic variables as age, sex, and marital and family status (e.g., number and age of children).

The focus of investigating the feasibility of the system should be its effect on work processes. Before continuing, however, we would like to sound a note of caution. Many managers, upon considering flexitime for their organization, reject it out of hand for any type of highly automated, interdependent work unit or assembly line. Although an alternate schedule may present difficulties in implementation, some form of flexibility—even if limited to variations for groups or teams of employees—is usually possible. Managers should give extra consideration to these employees because of the monotonous nature of their jobs. Even a small degree of autonomy in work scheduling may help to improve quality of life through better planned leisure time and reduced or more convenient commuting. With this in mind, the following issues should be addressed in the feasibility study:

1. Identity and description of work force—total number of employees to be affected (workers and supervisors); personnel characteristics.

2. The need for additional employees and the available resources among the different segments of the work force locally.

3. Task functions and workload characteristics for each functional department, including the following:

a. Interdependence of work flow within and between departments.
b. Amount and times of contact with public and customers.
c. Peak workload periods—within a day, within a week, within a month.
d. Size of work force necessary in peak periods.
e. Frequency of meetings and their timing.
f. Schedule of incoming supplies, materials, telephone calls.
g. Schedule of outgoing products.
h. Interdepartmental communications.
i. Administrative function.
j. Need for supervisory coverage and presence.

4. Legal or contractual constraints.
5. For those organizations in which a high level of openness is

the norm, investigation of employee preferences for a new schedule and its variation (e.g., preferred arrival and departure times, present mode of transportation, and possible changes). However, please keep in mind our caution about raised expectations.

6. Environmental conditions and support services. Support services staff should be consulted about potential change in their operations resulting from flexible schedules, including:

a. Cafeteria hours.
b. Safety and security services.
c. Medical services.
d. Switchboard hours.
e. Elevators.
f. Maintenance.
g. Power—electricity, gas, coal.
h. Heating or air conditioning.
i. Cleaning and janitorial services.

7. Identifying those who will be limited in or prevented from participating in the program. Define possible resulting problems and consider solutions.

a. Consulting with supervisors of those potentially restricted from joining the group.
b. Exploring possible alternatives in work processes, including group instead of individual determination of schedule. This may be effective in assembly line situation—especially if sufficient "in process" inventory can be provided between groups of workers to allow some degree of independent functioning.

8. Writing a report with conclusions and recommendations and presenting it to management (steering committee) for evaluation and approval.

Pilot Study—Trial Period

Assuming that presenting the feasibility study to the steering committee has resulted in approval for a pilot study, management should then begin carefully designing and planning the study. The original committee that conducted the feasibility study may continue with the pilot, although it may be necessary to expand the committee because of the additional workload. In planning the pilot study, consider the following.

The purpose of the pilot study is to test the suitability of the suggested work schedules in the organization. The study should provide statistical information on the behavioral and attitudinal criteria defined in the evaluation stage and should enable the organization to decide whether or not to adopt a system on a departmental or companywide basis. Once these decisions are made, the pilot study helps to determine the most suitable system through the experience already obtained and to identify potential problems.

The pilot program includes three major stages: planning phase, implementation phase, and evaluation phase. We will describe evaluation in detail as part of the planning stage to emphasize the importance of defining criteria and determining how they will be measured ahead of time. The actual evaluation is conducted at the end of the pilot, when all data have been collected. In addition to the items delineated in the planning sections, the following list presents considerations for trial-period implementation.

Set goals for the pilot study.

Select a department for the pilot in which the criteria for evaluation can be identified.

Set a period for the trial (three to six months is typical).

Consult with the supervisors and managers in the proposed departments in order to solicit full cooperation.

Obtain approval and support from union representatives.

Appoint a coordinator, and possibly a departmental committee, from the pilot department who will participate in subsequent phases of implementation.

Choose an appropriate schedule for this department and its subunits, considering obstacles and variations.

Choose time-recording systems and records procedures.

Review policies for absenteeism, leave, and overtime usage.

Review the decisions made thus far and obtain final approval from the department head and top management.

Inform the rest of the company (usually via memo) of the pilot study, its purpose, and the requirements for a successful outcome.

Prepare guidelines and information sessions for participants. Review the following:

a. Company policy.

b. Definitions and general system description.

c. The actual schedule to be implemented.

Conduct supervisor orientation sessions addressed to the special needs of this group, including monitoring and control issues.

Conduct a review (in detail) of the evaluation procedure and data collection.

Plan a system for handling complaints or disputes.

Meet with employees and iron out details.

Start pilot.

Making a Decision

At the conclusion of the pilot study and evaluation process, an extensive report should be made to the steering committee and to top management, presenting the findings according to the criteria originally determined. The process of decision making may include the following steps:

Report results and recommendations to top management and union officials.

Reevaluate features and consider alternatives.

Decide on organizationwide implementation—go ahead or drop the program.

Obtain approval and commitment from union officials.

Decide on level of departmental autonomy in determining schedules.

Communicate decisions with department heads.

Companywide Implementation

At this stage enough information has been collected to ensure effective policy guidelines by top management. Decisions regarding the system itself, time recording, absenteeism and overtime policies, grievance procedures, and record-keeping should have been made. Once these aspects are determined, the task of companywide implementation is reduced to two key processes, *coordination and communication.* Certain actions may facilitate these processes:

1. Name a central coordinator.
2. Name a local coordinator for each independent subunit participating in the program.
3. Inform all employees about the implementation. Usually, written documents precede group meeting at local levels. Endorsement of top management and the union, if relevant, should be made clear.
4. Prepare separate educational programs for employees, supervisors, and managers on the schedule's implications for job performance.

Union representatives (stewards) should also have a special educational session if a union is involved.
5. Once the program has been implemented—
   a. Monitor and evaluate progress.
   b. Periodically report and evaluate.
   c. Give periodic feedback to management and supervisors.

Summary and Conclusions

Implementing an organizational change should be considered a continuous process within the organization, not just a one-time intervention. Once goals have been set and criteria for their measurements determined, measurement and evaluation should be an on-going process. If the resulting feedback does not meet the criteria for organizational effectiveness, the goals of the program must be redefined, or else the process effecting the change must be reconsidered.

We have attempted to present, in an abbreviated form, an exhaustive list of considerations for implementing an alternative work schedule. Not all of these considerations will apply for every organization. Furthermore, in terms of the steps described in the process of implementation, some firms will skip stages, and others will repeat the same stage several times.

Each organization must determine its own criteria for effectiveness and the means of measuring these criteria. However, as emphasized earlier, it is imperative to plan the measurement and evaluation process *before* beginning the pilot study. Finally, this process should be modified and incorporated into the permanent evaluation systems of the organization.

Notes

1. Beer, 1980.
2. Alderfer, 1977.

CHAPTER EIGHT

Evaluation

The following section discusses the subject of evaluation in detail, since it is critical to the decision-making process. The considerations described here also apply to the ultimate evaluation of the new schedule after companywide implementation. We include evaluation as part of planning the pilot study because managers should decide upon the method for gathering and analyzing results *before implementation.*

The effects of any planned organizational change must be carefully measured and monitored (1) to evaluate whether the goals set in planning the change have been achieved; (2) to provide feedback for any alterations or improvements in the implemented change; and (3) to identify unexpected effects, either positive or negative, that may result from the change.

In field research about organizational change, however, measurement of effects may not be so straightforward. Compared with laboratory experimentation, which allows control of variables and isolation of causal relationships, field research is less "scientific." Because no change can operate in isolation in the field, investigating planned change and measuring its effects are difficult. They require a rigorous plan of study and evaluation utilizing the knowledge available in the fields of organizational behavior and research methodology. We urge organizations considering alternative work schedules to employ the skills of an expert, even if it is necessary to obtain an objective outside consultant. The results of any objective research evaluation should be divorced, wherever possible, from the subjective impressions and sometimes unwarranted conclusions of managers or participants. The research design should optimally employ "before and after" data and experimental and control groups.

Determining specific data-collection processes is better left to the individual organization, with its unique attributes, technology, and structure. However, we shall delineate the important criteria for evaluating the new working schedule's effects. These criteria closely follow those listed earlier for describing field results (Chapters 3, 4, 5, and 6). We have seen that alternative schedules may improve organizational effectiveness as well as the individual's quality of work life. The objectives of the study should therefore be to research and evaluate variables in both of these broader categories. Organizations should investigate measures of performance and withdrawal behavior.

Relevant in terms of the individual employee are behavioral patterns after the change (such as departure, arrival, and commuting patterns), attitudes toward the organization, and the particular working-time system. Within these broader categories, the organization should also evaluate the success of monitoring systems used under the new working schedules, such as time-recording devices and the maintenance of attendance information.

We emphasize that managers can base measurement of these variables on either objective or subjective measures, or both. Certain variables, such as job attitudes, are by definition based on the subjective reports of individuals. Other variables, such as productivity, should include as categories both evaluation of objectively measured criteria for productivity and subjective reports from supervisors and employees. Absenteeism offers opportunities for accurate, objective measures; and since most organizations keep absenteeism information for a long while, changes should be relatively easy to evaluate. Although both objective and subjective measures offer valuable and needed information, the organization should make the utmost effort to collect objective information whenever and wherever possible.

One important aspect of the research methodology that requires special attention is the reliability of the information offered through questionnaires and subjective reports. Questionnaires are particularly useful for obtaining attitudes toward (1) the organization, (2) members of the organization, and (3) the planned change itself. Guaranteed anonymity of respondents is usually a necessary condition for the assurance of an accurate and honest response to questionnaires or surveys, although any identifying information that does not jeopardize anonymity should be included. Such information as biographical data (e.g., sex, age, marital status, family composition, salary, and work experience) is valuable in order to compare changes in behavior and attitude among different subgroups. The chosen alternative schedule may not affect all groups equally. In general, the more accurately an employee can be described demographically, the more conclusive can be an analysis of results for comparative and longitudinal studies.

Organizational Effectiveness (Performance)

Because any changes in organizational effectiveness are critical to the evaluation, all possible resources should be utilized to detect such changes—including objective data, evaluations by supervisors, and employee reports. Although membership behavior is one component of the overall evaluation of the organization effectiveness, we will present this category separately. Criteria for evaluating changes in effectiveness include:

Productivity

Output volume, quantity.
Quality of work performed.
Utilization of equipment (time span).
Machine downtime.
Unit productivity—that is, labor cost per unit output.
Service to public—deliveries, telephone availability, etc.
Necessary attendance levels during peak work periods.
Overtime wages.
Increases in hours of availability to customers.

Additional Responsibilities of Supervisors

Work scheduling and planning.
Maintaining work flow.
Problems in monitoring, controlling, and supervising performance.
Customer complaints.
Supervisor—worker relations.

Communications

Interdepartmental communication.
Intradepartmental communication.
External communications.

Costs

Implementation of system including a time-recording system.

Physical plant and energy consumption—gas, coal, electricity.

Support personnel—elevators, maintenance, security, cafeteria.

Attitudes

Most organizations are well acquainted with employee attitude surveys. Many of the variables usually included in such surveys are applicable here as well. In addition to changes in job attitudes (such as satisfaction), the attitudes toward different aspects of the new systems should be surveyed. There are many questionnaires in the field suitable for tapping these attitudes.

Job Satisfaction Components

Supervisor.

Organization and management policy.

Physical condition.

Co-workers as a supportive group.

Effectiveness of teamwork.

Recognition and feedback from peers and supervisors.

Satisfaction with work itself.

Autonomy and responsibility.

Overall job satisfaction.

Satisfaction with the Alternative System

This section requires different criteria, depending on the implemented alternative schedule and its variation. The specific elements of the variation should be included in the questionnaire (e.g., bandwidth, core time flexbands, and lunch break are all aspects of flexitime). Part time may have completely different aspects to be investigated, depending on the variation used. For example, a part-day may have different implications than a part-week system. A detailed questionnaire should be composed inquiring all aspects of the particular time schedule adopted. In addition to these items, the questionnaire may include the following criteria:

Time-recording system.

Commuting-style changes.

Overtime availability.

Grievances.

Attitude of employees not included in system.

Attitude toward the implementation process itself.

Membership Behavior (Withdrawal)

Membership behavior should be assessed by objectively measuring changes in leave usage, absenteeism, and tardiness. The one area limited to measurement by opinion is the amount of abuse of the system, since abuses are not usually recorded. Questions regarding abuse should always be asked in terms of comparing abuses to those under the old work schedule because in some companies lax attitudes toward work hours may be an organization problem that predates implementation of the new system. Aside from abuse, other criteria for evaluating membership behavior can be measured objectively. These include the following:

Turnover.

Ease of recruiting and hiring new employees.

Absenteeism.

Leave usage.

Tardiness.

Time and attendance records.

Administration of records.

Injuries and accidents.

Credit/debit accumulation.

Attendance during work peak periods.

Cooperation with peers and supervisors in attendance record-
keeping.

Time Management

Changes in the individual's use of time are at the heart of any alternative work schedule concept. There is an almost endless list of possible criteria for measuring changes in this area. These are a few of the basic categories to consider:

Ability to plan and use leisure time.

Ability to use recreational facilities.

Ability to make use of educational opportunities or facilities.

Ability to conduct personal business and schedule medical/dental
appointments without conflict.

Easing of child care responsibilities.

Ability to spend more time with family.

Ability to participate in community and social events.

Easing of commuting stress.

Changes in mode of transportation and length of commute.

Changes in gasoline consumption if driving to work.

Changes in congestion at parking lots, elevators, lockers, etc.

Implications for the Community

Depending on the size of the work force adopting new schedules and its percentage of the local community, changes in the following may be possible:

Highway utilization and traffic congestion.

Mass transportation availability and scheduling.

Participation in carpools.

Availability of recreational facilities.

Availability of health and social services.

Final Considerations*

The preceding chapters have attempted to show the variety and adaptability of alternative work schedules to both employer and employee needs. The compressed work week, flexible working hours, part-time employment, and job sharing can all serve to make the workplace a more congenial and creative environment. Which of these schedules will suit a particular organization is of course a question that managers in that organization must answer. But if the experience of hundreds of European and American firms gives any indication, alternative work schedules will prove themselves worthwhile.

However, successful implementation depends not just on the innovative aspects of these schedules, but also upon their adaptation to a variety of external circumstances. One such circumstance is the legal context within which a firm can schedule its employees' work. Another is the contractual context in which the firm negotiates with unions and other collective bargaining groups. Then there is the logistical context of transportation. For alternative work schedules to succeed, managers must give some thought to these circumstances and how they will affect planning and implementation. This final chapter provides an overview of these three contexts and then examines a recent phenomenon that is not only an innovative work sched-

---

* The legal and contractual discussion in this chapter is an abbreviated version adapted from a draft prepared by Gerald Schilian, Esq., and Deborah Watarz, Esq., two attorneys specializing in employment law. I am thankful to them for their advice throughout the preparation of this book.

ule in its own right, but that may also influence other alternative schedules.

Legal Aspects of Alternative Schedules

A vast and complex set of federal, state, and local laws and regulations govern the American worker. These laws and regulations will most likely affect a company's design and implementation of an alternative working schedule.

In previous chapters, we have discussed many possible variations in the structure of working schedules, ranging from a limited flexible workday to almost unlimited flexibility. Although organizational and operational needs dictate the choice of a particular schedule, laws also affect certain aspects of the choice. Even after choosing a model, one must be ready to deal with the laws that regulate the method of implementing it.

Most of the laws affecting the operation of working schedules establish a maximum work period and mandate the payment of wage premiums for work in excess of those maximum work periods. On the federal level, these overtime laws include the Fair Labor Standards Act (FLSA), the Contract Work Hours Act, the Walsh-Healy Act, and U.S. Code Title 5. Other laws affect the implementation. For example, the National Labor Relations Act imposes certain restrictions upon employers who implement substantial changes in terms and conditions of employment where a union is involved.

Each of the laws has a limited application. Which law, if any, applies to a particular schedule is a function of various elements of the employment relationship. Is a person employed in the public or private sector? If in the private sector, is he or she engaged in work on a public job or contract? If in the public sector, is he or she employed by the federal government, a state government, a city or town government, or some other public or quasi-public entity? What is the employee's level of responsibility? Salary level? Regarding the employer: What industry is involved? What is the employer's gross volume of business? Are the employees unionized? Is there a collective bargaining agreement in effect? Is there a union organizing drive? The answers to each of these questions will clarify which laws are likely to affect a particular choice of alternative work schedules.

Background

Traditionally, most organizations have resolved the problem of work schedules by assigning fixed hours. Although the current, standard five-day work week (between 35 and 40 hours) represents a substantial reduction from the six-day, 72-hour week that prevailed at the turn of the century, the concept of fixed scheduling has remained. The law reflects this tradition. The various laws regulating hours of work have institutionalized fixed scheduling by mandating the payment of wage premiums for work in excess of 40 hours in a week and, in some cases, 8 hours in a day.

Although some maximum-hours laws date from the late 19th century, the principal elements of the maximum-hours laws existing today derive from the antidepression legislation of the 1930s. These laws were adopted for reasons that were sound at the time of their enactment. They served to curb the exploitative practice of some employers, who demanded 10 to 12 hours of work for 8 hours pay. Moreover, during times of recession and depression, the maximum-hours laws encouraged employers to spread the limited available work among a greater number of workers.

In 1937 President Roosevelt launched a major attempt to secure broad federal wage and hour legislation. In a message to Congress, he stated that "to conserve our primary resource of manpower, government must have some control over maximum hours, minimum wages, the evil of child labor and the exploitation of unorganized labor." Out of that message grew the Fair Labor Standards Act of 1938 (FLSA). As originally passed, the FLSA mandated a maximum work week of 44 hours, a minimum wage of 25 cents per hour, and severe restrictions on the use of child labor in covered employment in the private sector. Many jobs and industries were excluded or exempted. This law still exists. It is the cornerstone of wage-and-hour regulation. Coverage has been broadened, although there are still certain exclusions and exemptions.

Of course the minimum wage has been substantially increased, but the 40-hour work week, which became effective shortly after passage of the original act, remains and with it the requirement of time and one half of the worker's wage payable after 40 hours work per week.

Current Status of Maximum-Hours Legislation

During the 1930s the principal focus of protective legislation was private sector employment. For the most part, employees of federal, state, and local governmental entities were not yet covered by laws regulating hours of work. Today, in its regulation of wages and hours of private sector employees, the FLSA continues to have an impact on more workers than does any other law controlling hours of work. Moreover, there is now a proliferation of legislation regulating wages and hours of public employees as well.

Those provisions of the FLSA relating to maximum hours and overtime, which are of interest to us here, have been applied primarily to the private sector. However, 1961 amendments to the FLSA extended its coverage to persons employed in enterprises having a traditionally private character, *even though such enterprises were governmentally owned and operated.* In 1966 amendments further extended coverage to certain federal employees and to employees of state and local hospitals and educational institutions. The Supreme Court of the United States affirmed the validity of this extension.[1]

In 1974 the FLSA was again amended to extend its coverage to other federal, state, and local employees; there was, in response, another court challenge. This time, however, the Supreme Court held unconstitutional the congressional application of minimum-wage and maximum-hour rules to state and local government employees.[2] Therefore, only federal employees and a very limited number of state and local employees engaged in operations having a traditionally private character remain covered by the FLSA. Other public employees are not covered.

Since the FLSA wage and hour rules are not generally applied to employees of state and local government, these entities have full authority to make their own rules without federal interference. This means that state and local governments have greater latitude to take advantage of the full range of alternative work schedules. (Unless, of course, state or local laws or union contracts otherwise restrict them.)

Summary of Specific Laws

Since this discussion cannot explore in detail the legal aspects of alternative work schedules, the following summary serves to alert managers to laws that may affect programs of implementation. Please note that the summary refers only to federal law; analysis of state and local law is far beyond the scope of this chapter.

Fair Labor Standards Act

The FLSA provides that its overtime regulations apply to any employee who "in any work week is engaged in commerce or in the production of goods for commerce."[3] In addition to determining whether or not a business is by this definition engaged in commerce, its managers must ascertain whether or not the business meets certain monetary requirements. The FLSA also sets forth for certain classifications of employee exemptions that will affect an organization's standing. Some of the classifications are executive, administrative, and professional. There are some industrywide and specialized exclusions as well—for railroads, air carriers, and other transportation industries; for various small retail or service establishments; and for a variety of other businesses.

Walsh-Healy Act

The Walsh-Healy Act requires payment of overtime premiums to covered employees for hours worked in excess of 40 hours in one week or 8 hours in one day. This act is far more restrictive than is the FLSA, which only requires the payment of an overtime premium after an employee works 40 hours in a week. Under the FLSA an employer may utilize a flexible week by which employees can work more than 8 hours on any day so long as they work no more than 40 hours in the week. The Walsh-Healy Act restricts work hours more rigidly, with consequences on the kinds of alternative work schedules an organization could implement. It applies to businesses engaged in various activities in behalf of the federal government.

Other Laws Affecting Employees of Private Employers
Engaged in Work for the Federal Government

There are a number of federal laws that establish employment standards for private employees engaged in various activities on behalf of the federal government. In addition to the Walsh-Healy Act, these include the Davis-Bacon Act, the Copeland Antikickback Act, the Contract Work-Hours and Safety Standards Act, and the Service Contract Act. These laws set minimum standards for wages, overtime, and other terms and conditions of employment for specified employees.

Public Employment Laws

The basic terms of employment for most federal employees—including salary schedules and overtime and weekend, holiday, and shift premiums—are governed by federal law (specifically, Title 5 of the U.S. Code). Nonfederal public employees are not covered. Each state has its own version of a civil service law setting forth in varying degrees of detail the employment conditions for its employees. In some states the civil service law applies to municipalities and other political and state subdivisions. Elsewhere, each locality sets its own rules. There are literally hundreds of state and local statutes governing employment conditions for employees of those entities. Understandably, the number and variety of these regulations will affect the implementation of alternative work schedules, yet federal agencies have successfully introduced such schedules, and the trend seems likely to continue within the framework provided.

National Labor Relations Act

The National Labor Relations Act is the principal law covering labor relations in private industry in America.[4] Insofar as alternative work schedules are concerned, our interest in the NLRA is limited to the *employer's duty to bargain.* The NLRA makes it an unfair labor practice for any employer to refuse to bargain collectively with its employees' representatives. Where employees are represented by a labor union or a union is in the process of organizing, the employer is obligated to bargain over the proposed changes in work schedules. Although *the duty to bargain does not imply that the parties must reach an agreement,* a union's firsthand knowledge of employee needs and attitudes could well result in its making positive contributions that would increase the changes of success and productivity upon implementing an alternative work schedule.

New Promise for Alternative Work Schedules
in Legislation

It is clear that requiring wage premiums to be paid for overtime work imposes severe financial limitations on the design of alternative schedules. Most employers would not want to grant employees the authority to schedule overtime for themselves, given current overtime compensation rates. The laws regulating work schedules have deep roots in America's industrial history. Despite increasingly favorable interest in the new work scheduling techniques, a long time may have to pass before Americans modify their laws to accommodate such innovations.

But there are signs of change. Since 1974 a number of bills authorizing alternative work schedules for federal employees have reached Congressional vote. These efforts culminated in the Federal Employees Flexible and Compressed Work Schedules Act of 1978, which passed Congress in 1978. At the signing ceremony, Jimmy Carter, who was then president, said the introduction of more flexible work alternatives would "benefit, among others, persons with children, students and the older or handicapped worker." He also expressed hope that "flexible work schedules will increase government productivity and responsiveness to public needs, and provide a new pool of talent for government services."

This recent legislation facilitated three years of further experimentation with alternative schedules within the public sector. As a result, further modifications to existing law by federal, state, and local governments seem likely, although there was no immediate change proposed.

Labor Contracts and Negotiations

Another central consideration in designing an alternative work schedule is the impact the new system will have on existing personnel policies. Virtually every employer has some formal, informal, loose, or rigid policy defining the structure of the work relationship. Where a union represents employees, the personnel policies will usually be embodied in a written collective bargaining agreement. These personnel policies often provide for benefits greater than the minimum available by law. They create restrictions upon an employer's freedom in addition to those found in statutes.

The personnel policy changes necessary to implement an alternative work schedule will probably be the subject of negotiations. Any new policy contrary to a provision in an existing labor contract may of course be implemented only if the union agrees to change the contract. On the other hand, where there are no applicable provisions, changes may be made without union agreement after management has offered to negotiate with the union and an impasse is reached. (See previous section.) Even where there is no union, management should understand that the existing terms and conditions of employment constitute an informal contract with employees; management should make every effort to involve employees in planning the alternative schedule.

The following sections summarize a number of the specific terms and conditions of employment that, in one form or another, prevail in most organizations and are affected by alternative schedules. The analysis must necessarily be limited to a general identification of problem areas. However, each individual organization must create a system to fit its own unique circumstances.

Full-Time Work

Implementing some alternative work schedules will not require changes in existing policies regarding hours of work. In flexitime, for instance, the number of hours worked in a given period can remain the same, although starting, quitting, and break time may vary. An organization that currently works a 40-hour week can continue to work a 40-hour week; an organization that works 35 hours per week or 37½ hours per week can continue with those hours. However, where a collective bargaining agreement specifies that hours of work commence at a particular time and end at a particular time, or where shifts with specific hours are set forth, the language will have to be revised to accommodate the alternative work schedule. Many collective bargaining agreements likewise specify the standard to be a 40-hour work week or 8-hour days. Such provisions would not require modification for a flexitime model in which the employee worked an eight-hour day and that offered flexibility only for the times of arrival and departure. However, other schedules involve more complex forms of accommodation.

Part-Time Work

In general, contract provisions specifying hours of work refer to hours for full-time employees. The increasing numbers of employers utilizing part-time and job-sharing procedures, however, will require additional adjustment. The nature and structure of part-time work vary from organization to organization, and even within a given organization. The attitudes of unions toward part-time work vary from acceptance to rejection. As with full-time work, contract provisions covering part-time work range from loose to restrictive. Part-time arrangements include working less than 8 hours for five or fewer days a week, working less than five 8-hour days per week, working 40 or more hours per week for only a portion of the year, or any combination of the above. These arrangements constitute what could be called *regular part-time,* as distinguished from casual employment.

By their nature, part-time arrangements within an organization tend to be far more flexible than full-time ones. One reason for this is the fact that employees don't have to worry about payment of overtime premiums, which normally are not legally mandated until the employee works in excess of 40 hours in any particular week; and labor contracts often allow payment of reduced benefits for part-timers. Consequently, employers may have fewer adjustments to make for part-time employees within an alternative system.

Many unions oppose the use of part-time labor because it reduces the number of full-time employees. Consequently, part-time labor should be of particular concern to any union if there is a possibility that the introduction of an alternative schedule could undermine the rights, privileges, or benefits of full-time workers. Adequate definitions and realistic restrictions ensuring a reasonable degree of mobility among part-timers and full-timers are essential to prevent friction and to increase the possibility of success when implementing an innovative schedule.

Limitation of Employer's Freedom to Make Changes

Where organizations have employees on a variety of work schedules, applicable collective bargaining agreements frequently contain provisions restricting the employer's ability to effect unilateral changes in scheduling. Some agreements require an employer to give advance notice of any scheduling change; others mandate that the employer consult with the union; still others require that the union give prior approval to such changes. A few agreements even provide for wage premiums as penalties where scheduling changes are made without proper notice. Among these provisions are:

Notification prior to change of schedule.

No scheduling change unless agreed to by the union.

Limitation on the number of hours by which a schedule can be changed.

Penalty of pay premium for employer violation of notification provision.

Obviously, many contractual restrictions on scheduling of work would have to be modified to accommodate alternative systems, since maintaining rigid schedules of days off and hours of work is incompatible with flexible scheduling. Unions may strongly resist such changes for historical reasons, however. Many contractual scheduling restrictions evolved because unions wanted to counteract employer abuse of the right to schedule work time. When the employer unilaterally changed schedules without prior notice, the employees believed their personal time was being infringed upon. Unions therefore fear that employers will use alternative work schedules—which should be, and are, looked upon by employees as a benefit—as an excuse to return to old habits.

Premium Pay Rules

Contractual overtime provisions tend to be somewhat more complex than the simple statutory mandates. Overtime practices vary from employer to employer; the complexities often derive from union and management attention to particular labor relations problems within their organizations. Consequently, of the collective bargaining agreements that provide for overtime, many have specific provisions. These include: doubletime pay premiums; overtime premiums of time and a half for an initial period of overtime work in a given day, with one or more higher premiums paid on a graduated scale thereafter; graduated overtime premiums for work in excess of a certain specified number of weekly hours; premium pay for working through lunch periods; and a great variety of others.

In most instances, there will have to be some modification of contractual overtime provisions to accommodate alternative work schedules. How much modification is required will be determined by the scope of the model and by the needs of the organization and the desires of the workers involved.

In some cases, introducing an alternative schedule may result in a reduction of the need for traditional overtime work. Reduced need results from many factors, including the availability of some portion of the work force for more hours during the workday than previously; moreover, employees will be at work when they are most productive.

Premium Pay for Weekend Work

Most employees work the traditional five-day week from Monday through Friday; but in many industries work on Saturdays, Sundays, or both is necessary. Even where weekend work is not a standard practice, there may be an occasional need for someone to work a Saturday or a Sunday. Since weekend time off is of great importance to American workers, premium pay for weekend work provides a necessary inducement and/or compensation for requiring employees to work those days.

Where weekend work is overtime, an employee may have a contractual right to refuse work. Distinctions may be made between Saturday and Sunday work—Sunday work generally carrying a higher premium. Where the weekend work is part of the work week, however, a different provision may apply. Weekend work may be deemed a benefit to be offered to senior employees, or it may be considered a burden that workers can refuse.

The extent to which the introduction of alternative work schedules has impact upon weekend premiums is directly related to the employer's personnel requirements and the level of flexibility offered. In an organization that normally operates on weekends, such as a department store, rules regulating weekend work should be very few. However, where an employer wishes to give weekend flexibility to employees who normally work only Monday through Friday, a number of systems-design and implementation problems arise. How do you ensure adequate staffing on weekends under these circumstances? It is not difficult to design rules to resolve possible problems, but what is most urgent is that these questions be identified and satisfactory solutions be devised in advance of implementing an alternative schedule.

Miscellaneous Contract Provisions

Most collective bargaining agreements provide for such benefits as holidays, vacations, sick leave, and shift differential. In addition, some require compensation for time off for such an event as jury duty or the death of a family member. Lunch and other breaks are also incorporated into labor agreements. Such benefits are not limited to unionized employees. Nonunion employers usually provide at least some of these benefits.

The alternative schedule should not alter such benefits. The general rule to follow is to design a system that will cause the least possible change to existing employee benefits.

Conclusions

The aim here has been to alert the parties concerned to the many issues that arise in personnel policies upon implementing alternative work schedules. The difference between how unionized employees and nonunionized employees are handled is a matter of form. Unionized employers will have to negotiate solutions with their unions. All employers will have to deal with potential or organized employee opposition to innovation. In any case, the terms and conditions of employment previously discussed will have to be dealt with—whether inside or outside the negotiating forum.

Transportation

We should also consider an aspect of the contemporary work environment that both affects the implementing of alternative work schedules and is affected by them. This aspect is transportation.

Since one European firm invented flexitime to solve a transportation problem, other European firms have experimented with alternative work schedules, many of them because of the same initial issues. A survey of 300 European companies published in 1976 shows the concern about transportation: Respondents noted improvement in transportation as the fourth most frequently noted benefit of the new schedules, but it was the *most* frequent response given for what prompted experimentation in the first place. The rapid acceptance of alternative work schedules in Europe reflects the acknowledgement of transportation as a major employee concern.

Certainly the problems are no less acute in the United States. The accompanying photographs graphically illustrate the situation. What these photographs show is the phenomenon known as peaking in the transportation sector—the sudden increase in demand for transportation for short periods in the morning and evening. A similar situation affects our system of roads and highways. This phenomenon is most commonly known as the rush hour—even though everyone knows that rushing anywhere is the last thing possible at these times. During the recent past, transit authorities responded to the problem by attempting to expand the system to accommodate peak hours. However, in light of urban fiscal problems and limits on space and other resources, further expansion now seems unlikely.

Accordingly, one of the benefits of alternative work schedules is their effects on transportation. The citywide adoption of variable schedules tends to flatten the peak demand curve over a wider period of time. Passengers depart and arrive during a span of several hours, rather than just during the rush hour. The most obvious result is diminished crowding on trains, buses, and highways. There are other benefits as well. One is decreased overloading of equipment—hence producing less wear and tear. Another benefit is less strain on the commuters themselves; employees arrive at work more relaxed and energetic. Moreover, the improved efficiency and comfort of a system used in this manner may eventually increase ridership of mass transit and decrease reliance on private automobiles. Alternative work schedules, if widely adopted, might therefore benefit not just individual employees but the urban population as a whole.

Local transportation authorities must become involved in any widespread alternative schedules project, since transit schedules must accommodate the transformed levels of demand. Otherwise, employees may find service inadequate, thus producing frustration not only with the transit system, but perhaps with their new schedules as well. Parking lots may also require special attention during the early phases of changing schedules, since their patterns of traffic flow will probably change.

Another significant effect of alternative work schedules involves car pools. These schedules frequently increase employees' willingness to use car pools, although such changes are limited to situations of fully flexible working schedules rather than staggered hours or a compressed work week. Under flexible working schedules, workers

A subway platform on a working day.

At 4:30 P.M.

At 5:12 P.M.

At 5:45 P.M.

are free to form car pools with neighbors or family members—even if they work for different organizations. Some people might argue that car pools tend to defeat the purpose of flexible hours, since the employee is then tied to the car pool schedule. However, the important fact is that employees using car pools do so of their own choice, and most people using flexible working hours tend to choose a regular schedule that they like. The circumstances involved with a compressed work week and part-time work or job sharing are similar. Organizations may wish to facilitate car pool forming through some form of rider/driver matching service.

In conclusion, the need for a solution to transit problems is obvious to anyone who lives or works in a congested urban area. Survey results indicate that the problems are widespread, and that alternative work schedules can provide a simple and inexpensive improvement in peak load demand. Organizations that have implemented alternative schedules have experienced improvements even on a local level; this suggests great promise for improvements through coordinated citywide efforts. Meanwhile, individual employees most often find that their new schedules ease their own transportation woes.

Telecommunications—"Remote Work"

Last, a remarkable but still uncertain development within the American work environment deserves our attention. This is what has come to be called *remote work*. Sometimes termed *telecommuting* or *flexiplace*, remote work is work employees perform in their own homes. Clerical workers with specific skills, for instance, may perform their usual tasks at video display terminals linked to an office rather than at the office itself. Such work is feasible especially for word processors, insurance claim processors, computer programmers, and other employees trained in electronic skills. Given the rapidly increasing flexibility and distribution of computer technology, employees in several fields now find themselves potentially freed from the confines of organizational space (the office) or time (company hours). They can work at home just as easily as they could at the office. At least in theory, remote work therefore offers the ultimate flexible work schedule.

Remote work caught the public's attention most noticeably during the mid- and late 1970s, when Alvin Toffler touted it as the "Electronic Cottage" in his book *The Third Wave*. [5] According to Toffler's vision of the future, sophisticated computers will allow employees of many different professions to work without the inconvenience and exertion of commuting to another location; communications net-

works will replace a geographical site. Toffler's prediction struck
many observers as farfetched—or at least as premature. Still, more
cautious voices have nonetheless agreed that remote work might
prove an important trend. Dr. Tora Bikson of the Rand Corporation,
for instance, has estimated that within 10 years, 10 percent of the
office work force could be doing all or a significant part of its work
from home via computer.[6] Both employers and employees have expressed enthusiasm for the possibilities of remote work. For employees, the most attractive prospect has been the chance to eliminate
commuting and other consequences of working away from home.
For employers, the advantages include financial savings from lowered
overhead, increased production, and at times the retention of otherwise unavailable workers. Pilot programs at a variety of companies
suggest that initially, at least, most participants found remote work
to their advantage. Remote work has even allowed some disabled
or otherwise homebound persons to find employment in the absence
of other alternatives.

However, what first appeared to be the wave of the future has
turned out considerably less dramatic. Although such companies
as Control Data, Aetna Life & Casualty Company, and Continental
Illinois Bank have experimented with remote work in considerable
earnest, the arrangement has not spread nearly as far or as fast as
Toffler and others have predicted.[7] One reason is simply economic,
since establishing a remote work program requires a high initial
investment. The sluggish U.S. economy has made managers hesitant
to gamble on untried schemes. Other reasons touch on more general
issues, and some of them cast doubt on the whole enterprise. At
their darkest, these doubts concern the possibility that remote work
could result in exploitation of employees. Precisely what makes remote work flexible—the absence of restrictive hours—could make
it burdensome to workers under certain circumstances. Managers
would have to exercise extreme caution to avoid overextending employees in an essentially free-form schedule. Some critics have objected that remote work threatens to become a kind of high-tech
sweatshop: "Electronic home work is a curious amalgam of late
20th-century technology and what in some instances amounts to
early 19th-century working conditions."[8] Not all companies have
avoided the risks inherent in such an arrangement.

Yet some of the risks are of a less sinister sort. Even employees
who choose to do remote work and generally like it may still suffer
unexpected consequences. For instance, two Israeli social scientists

studying the phenomenon discovered that despite the common complaints American workers express about commuting to work, many of them found their daily trips to serve the important purpose of marking off work from the nonwork domain. Remote work tended to blur the line between the domains. At times the consequences were startling and negative, such as when family members found that they now had too much time together. Other employees complained that they missed human interactions at the office—interactions that served to provide professional stimuli as well as social relaxation.[9] Another study suggested that some workers who accept remote work do so not because they like the arrangement, but because all other arrangements seem worse. (For example, a single mother might accept remote work because it allows her to attend to a young child at home; yet remote work is often difficult while attempting to provide child care, and a child's presence in the "workplace" in turn disrupts the employee's work.[10]) In short, remote work seems less and less like the panacea many observers first considered it to be.

Does remote work have any legitimate place among current alternative work schedules? Despite the reservations expressed above, the answer is unquestionably yes. The appropriate time and place for it, however, is more specific than early proponents suggested. Remote work can serve legitimate purposes in providing work for certain employees who cannot maintain a more traditional schedule, such as disabled or otherwise homebound workers; it can allow a helpful degree of flexibility to parents whose child care responsibilities restrict them to the home; and it can extend considerable freedom to certain professionals (writers, scientists, engineers, computer programmers, etc.) who thrive on a self-defined schedule. Moreover, several theorists have proposed arrangements that might diminish the risks of isolation in remote work. One such arrangement is the neighborhood work center; there employees could perform their tasks at computer terminals distant from the central office, yet closer to home. Neighborhood work centers would allow a separation of work and nonwork domains, yet without the stresses inherent in a long commute. If properly organized, such centers might provide sufficient child care facilities to take the burden of constant attention off working parents. These arrangements are promising but as yet undeveloped.

In short, the entire concept of remote work remains full of possibility. What will come of it remains uncertain. Remote work has probably suffered from the exaggerated claims of its early proponents. Its limited but genuine promise—now that the Utopian visions have faded—is still unexplored.

Notes

1. *Maryland* v. *Wirtz,* 392 U.S. 183 (1968).
2. *National League of Cities* v. *Usery,* 426 U.S. 833 (1976), which overruled *Maryland* v. *Wirtz.*
3. Section 7(a)(1) 29 USC 207 (a)(1).
4. 29 USC 151 *et seq.*
5. Toffler, 1980.
6. Romero, 1983.
7. Mattera, 1983, p. 390.
8. Ibid.
9. Nilles et al., 1980.
10. Olson and Tasley, 1983.

Epilogue

The compressed work week, flexitime, part-time work, job sharing—these innovations can markedly improve and even transform the American workplace today. Are they right for all organizations? Probably not. Some industries and services unquestionably thrive on the traditional arrangements. But in an age of economic uncertainty, alternative work schedules offer access to one of America's most underutilized resources: time.

Admittedly, the trend toward alternative work schedules is complex and uncertain. The options are numerous; organizational policies are in a state of flux; even employee attitudes vary as they learn more about possible changes in their work life. No wonder some managers tend to consider the situation before them to be needlessly intricate. Perhaps (they sometimes tell themselves) alternative work schedules are little more than a fad. Perhaps the old nine-to-five is better in the long run. Why bother?

The fact remains that alternative work schedules are vastly more than a fad. The task of choosing and implementing one is not the source of societal complexity but rather a method of addressing the complexity. No longer can a manager rely on old motivations and old methods of structuring employee efforts. No longer will employees respond to the mere exchange of dollars paid for hours worked. American society now demands complex efforts and provides complex rewards. Accordingly, managers must respond imaginatively to the circumstances in the workplace and elsewhere that face all members of an organization. Alternative work schedules provide a flexible, varied means for addressing these circumstances.

The question is more than simply whether or not a company will respond to the future. There is little alternative there. The question is how imaginative the response will be.

References and Selected Readings

ALDERFER, C. P. Group and intergroup relations. In J. R. Hackman and J. L. Suttle (eds.), *Improving Life at Work: Behavioral Science Approach to Organizational Change.* Santa Monica, Calif.: Goodyear, 1977.

ANSCHELL, S. A place for part-timers in your organization. Seattle: University of Washington Institute of Government Research, 1978.

_____. Part-time careers in public service: Feasibility and implications. *Intergovernmental Personnel Act Grant Final Report,* 1978. (Available from Institute of Governmental Research, University of Washington, 3935 University Way, N.E., Seattle, WA 98105).

BACON, A. W. Leisure and the alienated worker: A critical reassessment of three radical theories of work and leisure. *Journal of Leisure Research,* 1975, *7,* 179–90.

BAUM, S. F., and YOUNG, W. M. *A Practical Guide to Flexible Working Hours,* Park Ridge, N.J.: Noyes Data Corporation, 1974.

BEACH, D. S. *Personnel.* New York: Macmillan, 1980.

BEDNARZIK, R. W. Involuntary part-time work: A cyclical analysis. *Monthly Labor Review,* 1975, *98,* 12–18.

_____. Part-time work and public policy. Ph.D. dissertation, University of Missouri, 1978.

_____. How many hours of work do the unemployed want? *Monthly Labor Review,* 1978, *101,* 70–72.

_____. Worksharing in the U.S.: Its prevalence and duration. *Monthly Labor Review,* July 1980, pp. 3–12.

BEER, M. *Organizational Change and Development: A System View.* Santa Monica, Calif.: Goodyear, 1980.

BERRY, J.; McCARTHY, E.; BATER, J. M.; and TERRILL, H. J. *Development of Permanent Part-Time Employment Opportunities for Girls and Women.* Kansas City: University of Missouri, 1969.

BEST, F. Recycling people: Work-sharing through flexible life scheduling. *The Futurist,* 1978, *12,* 5–16.

BLAUNER, R. *Alienated and Freedom: The Factory Worker and His Industry.* Chicago: University of Chicago Press, 1964.

BRIEF, A. P.; VAN SELL, M.; and ALDAG, R. J. Affective reactions of full and part-time employees. Unpublished manuscript, University of Idaho, 1979.

BUREAU OF NATIONAL AFFAIRS. *ASPA-BNA Survey: The Changing Workweek.* Washington, D.C.: Bureau of National Affairs, January 6, 1972.

_____. Bulletin to Management No. 1295, *ASPA-BNA Survey No. 25—Part-Time and Temporary Employees.* Washington, D.C.: Bureau of National Affairs, 1974.

BURRACK, E. H., and SMITH, R. D. *Personnel Management.* New York: John Wiley & Sons, 1982.

CAMPBELL, J. P. Personnel training and development. *Annual Review of Psychology,* 1971, *22,* 565–602.

CASCIO, W. F., and AWAD, E. M. *Human Resource Management,* Reston, Va.: Reston Publishing, 1981.

CALVASINA, E. J., and BOXX, W. R. Efficiency of workers on the four-day work week. *Academy of Management Journal,* 1975, *18,* 604–10.

CHEEK, L. M. Cost effectiveness comes to the personnel function. *Harvard Business Review,* 1973, *51,* 96–105.

CLUTTERBUCK, D. Work sharing takes off in the Netherlands. *International Management,* September 1981, pp. 55–58.

COHEN, A. R., and GADON, H. *Alternative Work Schedules: Integrating Individual and Organizational Needs.* Reading, Mass.: Addison-Wesley, 1978.

COMMITTEE ON ALTERNATIVE WORK PATTERNS AND NATIONAL CENTER FOR PRODUCTIVITY AND QUALITY OF WORKING LIFE. Alternatives in working time. *Alternatives in the World of Work,* Winter 1976, pp. 1–30.

CONFERENCE BOARD OF CANADA. The altered work week. A symposium held in Ottawa by the Conference Board in Canada, November, 1973.

COWLEY, T. F., and FISS, B. Federal employees see increase in productivity. *Monthly Labor Review,* 1977, *100,* 66.

CUNNINGHAM, A. *Job Sharing Project of New Ways to Work, Palo Alto, Calif:* Testimony in the U.S. Senate. Hearings before the Subcommittee on Employment, Poverty and Migratory Labor, April 8, 1976.

DARROW, S. T., and STOKES, S. L. Part-time professional and administrative employment at the University of Michigan, part I. Ann Arbor: University of Michigan, Center for Continuing Education of Women, 1973.

_____. Part-time professional employment in three settings at the University of Michigan, part II. Ann Arbor: University of Michigan, Center for Continuing Education of Women, August 1973.

DASKI, R. S. Area wage survey test focuses on part-timers. *Monthly Labor Review,* 1974, *97,* 60–62.

DAVIS, L. E., and CHERNS, A. B. (eds.). *Quality of Working Life.* New York: Free Press, 1975.

DENNIS, N.; HENRIQUES, F.; and SLAUGHTER, C. *Coal is Our Life. An Analysis of a Yorkshire Mining Community.* London: Eyre & Spottiswoode, 1956.

DEUTERMANN, W. V., JR., and BROWN, S. C. Voluntary part-time workers: A growing part of the labor force. *Monthly Labor Review,* 1978, *101,* 3–10.

DICKENSON, T. L., and WIJTING, J. P. An analysis of workers' attitudes towards the four-day, 40-hour workweek. *Psychological Reports,* 1975, *37,* 383–90.

DILLIN, D. A new look at part-time employment. *Civil Service Journal,* July–September 1977, pp. 34–37.

DOWELL, B. E., and WEXLEY, K. Development of a work behavior toxonomy for first-line supervisers. *Journal of Applied Psychology,* 1973, *63,* 563–72.

DRUCKER, P. F. Flexible age retirement: Social issue of the decade. *Industry Week,* April 1978.

DUBIN, R. Industrial workers' worlds: A study in the central interests of industrial workers. *Social Problems,* 1956, *4,* 131–42.

DUNHAM, R. B., and HAWK, D. L. The four-day/40-hour week: Who wants it? *Academy of Management Journal,* 1977, *20,* 644–55.

EASTERLIN, R. A. Population. In L. G. Reynolds, S. H. Masters, and C. H. Moser (eds.), *Readings in Labor Economics and Labor Relations.* Englewood Cliffs, N.J.: Prentice-Hall, 1978, pp. 15–21.

Effects of "baby buts" are shrinking ranks of younger workers. *The Wall Street Journal,* September 19, 1981.

Examination of alternative working hours and arrangements. Hearings before the Subcommittee on Employment, Poverty and Migratory Labor, April 7 and 8, 1976.

Ex-Travelers Insurance employees work out problems of retirement. *The Wall Street Journal,* July 22, 1981, p. 31.

EYDE, L. D. *Flexibility through Part-Time Employment of Career Women in the Public Service.* Washington, D.C.: U.S. Civil Service Commission, Personnel Research and Development Center, June 1975*(a),* pp. 1–17.

_____. *Flexibility through Part-Time Employment of Career Workers in the Public Service.* Professional Services 75–3. Washington, D.C.: U.S. Civil Service Commission, Personnel Research and Development Center, June 1975*(b),* Government Printing Office No. 066–000–00930–1.

_____. Permanent part-time employment in the public sector. Paper presented at Annual Convention for the American Psychological Association's Division Fourteen, "For Whom the Whistle Blows: Alternative Work Schedules," New York, September 1979.

Federal Employees Part-Time Career Employment Act of 1978. Public Law 95–437, (95th Congress), October 10, 1978.

FIELDS, C. Variable work hours—the experience. *Personnel Journal,* 1974, *13,* 675–78.

FINKLE, A. L. The four-day work week. *International Personnel Management Association* (IPMA) *News,* August 1979.

FISS, B. L., and MARTIN, V. H. Definitions. Alternate work schedule, undated, pp. 4–5.

FLINT, J. Growing part-time work force has major impact on economy. *New York Times,* April 12, 1977.

FOGARTY, M. P.; RAPPAPORT, R.; and RAPPAPORT, R. N. *Sex, Career and Family.* London: Allen and Unwin, 1971.

FOSTER, L. W.; LATACK, J. C.; and REINDL; L. J. Effects and promises of the shortened work week. Paper presented at the 39th Annual Meeting of the Academy of Management, Atlanta, Ga., 1979.

FOSTER, P., Part-time work patterns. *New Ways of Working Faire.* Los Angeles: Center for Quality of Working Life, UCLA, March 1977, pp. 122–27.

FOTTLER, M. D. Employee acceptance of a four-day work week. *Academy of Management Journal,* 1977, *20,* 656–68.

FREASE, M., and ZAWACKI, R. A. Job sharing: An answer to productivity problems? *The Personnel Administrator,* 1979, *24* (October), 35–38.

GALBRAITH, J. K. The economics of an American housewife. *Atlantic Monthly,* October 1973.

GANNON, M. J., and NOTHERN, J. C. A comparison of short-term and long-term part-time employees. *Personnel Psychology,* 1971, *24,* 687–96.

GANNON, M. J. The management of peripheral employers. *Personnel Journal,* 1975, *54.*

_____. An analysis of the temporary help industry. In Labor Market Intermediaries, Special Report No. 22: 195–225. Washington, D.C.: National Commission for Manpower Policy, March 1978.

GLICKMAN, A. S., and BROWN, Z. H. *Changing schedules of work: Patterns and implications.* Washington, D.C.: Upjohn Institute for Employment Research, 1974.

GOLDBERG, A. S. A comparison of attitudes and job factors of part-time and full-time employees. Ph.D. dissertation, Psychology Department, New York University, 1981.

GOLEMBIEWSKI, R. T.; HILLES, R.; and KAGNO, M. S. A longitudinal study of flexitime effects: Some consequences of an OD structural intervention. *Journal of Applied Behavioral Science,* 1974, *4,* 503–32.

GOLEMBIEWSKI, R. T.; FOX, R. G.; and PROEHL, C. W., JR. Flexitime: The supervisor's verdict. *The Wharton Magazine,* 1980, *4,* 42–48.

GOLEMBIEWSKI, R. T., and PROEHL, C. W., JR. A survey of the empirical literature on flexible work hours: Characteristics and consequences of a major innovation. *Academy of Management Review,* 1978, *3,* 837–53.

GOLEMBIEWSKI, R. T.; YEAGER, S.; and HILLES, R. Some attitudinal and behavior consequences of a flexitime installation: One avenue for expressing central organization design values. In R. H. Kilmann, L. R. Pondy, and D. P. Slevin (eds.), *Management of Organization Design,* Vol. 2. New York: North-Holland, 1976.

GOMEZ-MEJIA, L. R.; HOPP, M. A.; and SOMMERSTAD, C. R. Implementation and evaluation of flexible work hours: A case study. *Personnel Administrator,* 1978, *23,* 39–41.

GOODALE, J. G., and AAGARD, A. K. Factors relating to varying reactions to the four-day workweek. *Journal of Applied Psychology,* 1975, *60,* 33–38.

GRAF, L. A. The impact of flexitime on the first-line supervisor's job: A preliminary investigation. Paper presented at the 38th Annual Meeting of the Academy of Management, San Francisco, Calif., 1978.

GRAHAM, R. In permanent part-time work, you can't beat the hours. *Nation's Business,* 1979, *67* (January), 65–67.

GREENWALD, C. S. Part-time work: When less is more. *MS,* March 1980, pp. 41–42.

GREENWALD, C. S., and LISS, J. Part-time workers can bring higher productivity. *Harvard Business Review,* 1973, *51,* 20–21.

GREENBERG, P. D., and GLASER, E. M. *Quality of Work Life.* Kalamazoo, Mich.: W. E. Upjohn Institute for Employment Research, 1980.

HAGEDORN, R., and LABOVITZ, S. Participation in community associations by occupation: A test of three theories. *American Sociological Review,* 1968, *33,* 272–83.

HALL, D. T., and GORDON, F. E. Career choices of married women: Effects on conflict role behavior and satisfaction. *Journal of Applied Psychology,* 1973, *58,* 42–48.

HALLAIRE, J. *Part-Time Employment: Its Extent and Problems.* Paris: Organization for Economic Cooperation and Development, 1968.

HARRY, J. Work and leisure—situational attitudes. *Pacific Sociological Review,* 1971, *14,* 301–9.

HAVIGHURST, R. J. Alternative work schedules: Implications for older workers. *Journal of the College and University Personnel Association,* 1977, 28, 60–65.

HEDGES, J. N. How many days make a workweek? *Monthly Labor Review, 1975, 98,* 29–36.

HEDGES, J. N., and GALLOGLY, S. J. Full and part-time—a review of definitions. *Monthly Labor Review,* 1977, *100,* 21–28.

HELLRIEGEL, D. The four-day work week: A review and assessment. *MSU Business Topics,* Spring 1972, pp. 39–48.

HERRICK, N. O., and MACCOBY, M. Humanizing work: A priority goal of the 1970s. In L. E. Davis and A. B. Cherns (eds.) *The Quality of Working Life.* New York: Free Press, 1975.

HICKS, W. D., and KLIMOSKI, R. J. The impact of flexitime on employee attitude. *Academy of Management Journal,* 1981, *24,* 333–41.

HODGE, B. J., and TELLIER, R. D. Employee reactions to the four-day week. *California Management Review,* 1975, *18,* 25–30.

HOFFMAN, L. W., and NYE, F. I. *Working Mothers,* San Francisco: Jossey-Dass, 1974.

HOM, P. W. Effects of job peripherality and personal characteristics on the job satisfaction of part-time workers. *Academy of Management Journal,* 1979, *22,* 551–65.

HOWELL, M. A., and GINSBURG, M. G. Evaluation of the professional and executive corps of the Department of Health, Education, and Welfare. *Public Personnel Management,* 1973, *2,* 37–42.

INSTITUTE FOR SOCIAL RESEARCH. Job satisfaction has decreased, study shows. *ISR Newsletter,* 1979, *7,* 10–11.

INTERNATIONAL LABOUR OFFICE. Part-time employment: An international survey. Geneva, Switzerland: International Labour Office, 1973.

INTERNATIONAL MANAGEMENT. Putting 9 to 5 on the shelf. *International Management,* October 1981, pp. 16–19.

IRIS, B., and BARRETT, G. V. Some relations between job and life satisfaction and job importance. *Journal of Applied Psychology,* 1972, *56,* 301–4.

IVANCEVICH, J. M. Effects of the shorter workweek on selected satisfactions and performance measures. *Journal of Applied Psychology,* 1974, *59,* 717–21.

IVANCEVICH, J. M., and LYON, H. The shortened workweek: A field experiment. *Journal of Applied Psychology,* 1977, *62,* 34–37.

JACKSON, J. H., KEAVENY, T. J., and ALLEN, R. E. An examination of preferred job characteristic differences in part-time and full-time workers. Paper delivered at the 37th Annual National Meeting of the Academy of Management, Orlando, Florida, August 1977.

JACOBSON, B. *Young Programs for Older Workers: Case Studies in Progressive Personnel.* New York: Van Nostrand, Reinhold, 1980.

JAEGER, J. B., and GROUSHKO, M. A., *Flexible Working Hours in Europe.* Brussels, Belgium: Management Centre Europe, 1976.

JOHNSTON, D. F. The U.S. labor force: Projections to 1990. *Monthly Labor Review,* July 1973, pp. 3–13.

JONES, E. B. *Women and Part-Week Work.* Springfield, Va.: National Technical Information Service, 1978.

JONES, E. B., and LONG, J. E. Part-week work and human capital investment by married women. *Journal of Human Resources,* in press.

KABANOFF, B. Work and Nonwork: A review of models, methods, and findings. *Psychology Bulletin*, 1980, *88*, 60–77.

KABANOFF, B., and O'BRIEN, G. E. Work and leisure: A task attributes analysis. *Journal of Applied Psychology*, 1980, *65*, 596–609.

KATERBERG, R. Affective responses of full- and part-time employees: What one does versus how much one does it. Unpublished manuscript, University of Cincinnati, 1980.

KATERBERG, R., JR., HOM, P. W., and HULIN, C. L. Effects of job complexity on reactions of part-time employees. *Organizational Behavior and Human Performance*, 1979, *24*, 317–32.

KATZ, D., and KAHN, R. L. *The Social Psychology of Organizations*, New York: John Wiley & Sons, 1978.

KATZELL, R. A. Changing attitudes toward work. In C. Kerr and J. M. Rosow (eds.), *Work in America: The Decade Ahead.* New York: Van Nostrand, Reinhold, 1979.

KERR, CLARK, and ROSOW, J. M. (eds.). *Work in America: The Decade Ahead*, New York: Van Nostrand, Reinhold, 1979.

KIM, J. S., and CAMPAGNA, A. F. Effects of flexitime on employee attendance and performance: A field experiment. *Academy of Management Journal*, 1981, *24*, 729–41.

KORNHAUSER, A. W. *Mental Health of the Industrial Worker*. New York: John Wiley & Sons, 1965.

KUNIN, T. The construction of a new type of attitude measurer. *Personnel Psychology*, 1955, *8*, 65–78.

LAZER, E. A. Constructing an employee benefit package for part-time workers. A Catalyst Position Paper, New York, 1975.

LAZER, R. I. Job sharing as a pattern for permanent part-time work. *Conference Board Record XII*, October 1975, pp. 57–61.

LEON, C., and BEDNARZIK, R. W. A profile of women on part-time schedules. *Monthly Labor Review*, 1978, *101*, 57–61.

LEVINSON, D. J.; DARROW, C.; KLIEN, E.; LEVINSON, M.; and MCKEE, B. *The Seasons of a Man's Life.* New York: Alfred A. Knopf, 1978.

LEVITAN, S. A., and BELOUS, R. S. Initiative at home and abroad. *Monthly Labor Review*, 1977, *100*, 16–20.

LITWIN, G., and STRINGER, R. *Motivation and Organizational Climate*, Cambridge, Mass.: Harvard University Press, 1968.

LOEB, M. Three *R*s of productivity. *Time Magazine*, September 25, 1978, p. 69.

LOGAN, N.; O'REILLY, C. A.; and ROBERTS, K. H. Job satisfaction among part-time and full-time employees. *Journal of Vocational Behavior*, 1973, *3*, 33–41.

LONDON, M.; CRANDALL, R.; and FITZGIBBONS, D. The psychological structure of leisure: Activities, needs, and people. *Journal of Leisure Research*, 1977, *9*, 252–63.

LONDON, M.; CRANDALL, R.; and SEALS, G. W. The contribution of job and leisure satisfaction to the quality of life. *Journal of Applied Psychology*, 1977, *62*, 328–34.

LONG, M. C., and POST, S. W. *State Alternative Work Schedule Manual.* Washington, D.C.: National Council for Alternative Work Patterns, 1981.

MABERT, V. A., and RAEDELS, A. R. The detail scheduling of part-time work force: A case study of teller staffing. In M. W. Hopfe and H. C. Schneider (eds.), *American Institute of Decision Sciences Proceedings*, Cincinnati, 1975.

MAHONEY, T. A.; NEWMAN, J. M.; and FROST, P. J. Workers' perceptions of the four-day week. *California Management Review,* 1975, *18,* 31–35.

MAKLAN, D. M. *The Four-Day Workweek: Blue-Collar Adjustment to a Nonconventional Arrangement of Work and Leisure Time.* New York: Praeger, 1977.

MANSFIELD, R., and EVANS, M. G. Work and nonwork in two occupational groups. *Industrial Relations,* 1975, *6,* 48–54.

MATTERA, P. Home computer sweatshops. *The Nation,* April 2, 1983, pp. 390–92.

MCCARTHY, M. E., and ROSENBERG, G. F. *Work Sharing Case Studies.* Kalamazoo, Mich.: W. E. Upjohn Institute for Employment Research, 1981.

MCNEFF, N. H.; MCNEFF, M. R.; O'CONNELL, M. M.; and O'CONNELL, G. E. Alternatives to employee layoffs: Work sharing and prelayoff consultation. *Personnel,* 1978, *55,* 60–64.

MEIER, G. S. Job sharing: A new pattern for quality of work and life. *W. E. Upjohn Institute for Employment Research,* 1978.

MEISSNER, M. The long arm of the job: A study of work and leisure. *Industrial Relations,* 1971, *10,* 239–60.

MEIVES, S. F. Part-time work: A multiperspective analysis. Ph.D. dissertation, University of Wisconsin, Madison, 1979.

MILLER, H. E., and TERBORG, J. R. Job attitudes of part-time and full-time employees. *Journal of Applied Psychology,* 1979, *64,* 380–86.

MOORMAN, B.; SMITH, S.; and RUGGELS, S. *Job sharing in the schools.* San Francisco: New Ways to Work, 1980.

MORGENSTERN, R. D., and HAMOVITCH, W. Labor supply of married women in part-time and full-time occupations. *Industrial and Labor Relations Review,* 1976, *30,* 59–67.

NARAYANAN, V. K., and NATH, R. A field test of some attitudinal and behavior consequences of flexitime. *Journal of Applied Psychology,* 1982, *67,* 214–18.

National League of Cities v. *Usery,* 426 U.S. 833 (1976), which overruled *Maryland* v. *Wirtz.*

NEFF, W. S., *Work and Human Behavior,* New York: Atherton, 1968.

NILLES, J. M.; CARLSON, F. R.; GRAY, P.; and HANNEMAN, G. J. *The Telecommunication-Transportation Trade Off: Options for Tomorrow.* New York: John Wiley & Sons, 1980.

NOLLEN, S. D. Permanent part-time and job sharing. In D. Robinson, *Alternate Work Patterns—Changing Approaches to Work Scheduling,* report of a conference cosponsored by National Center for Productivity and Quality of Working Life and Work in America Institute, Inc., New York, June 2, 1976, pp. 17–19.

_____. Does flexitime improve productivity? *Harvard Business Review,* 1979 *(a), 57,* 16–18.

_____. *New Patterns of Work.* Work in America Institute Studies in Productivity. Scarsdale, N.Y.: Work in America Institute, Inc. 1979 *(b).*

_____. *New Work Schedules in Practice.* New York: Van Nostrand, Reinhold, 1982.

NOLLEN, S. D.; EDDY, B. B.; MARTIN, V. H.; and MONROE, D. *Permanent Part-Time Employment: An Interpretive Review.* Springfield, Va.: National Technical Information Service, 1977.

_____. *Permanent Part-Time Employment: The Manager's Perspective.* New York: Praeger, 1978.

NOLLEN, S. D., and MARTIN, V. H. *Alternative Work Schedules, Part 1: Flexitime. An AMA Survey Report; Part 2: Permanent Part-Time Employment; Part 3: The*

Compressed Workweek. New York: AMACOM (a division of American Management Association), 1978.

NORD, W. R., and COSTIGAN, R. Worker adjustment to the four-day week: A longitudinal study. *Journal of Applied Psychology,* 1973, *58,* 60–66.

OLMSTED, B. Job sharing—a new way to work. *Personnel Journal,* 1977, *56,* 80.

_____. Job sharing: An emerging work style. *International Labor Review,* 1979, *118,* 283–395.

_____. *Job Sharing.* San Francisco: New Ways to Work, 1980.

OLMSTED, B.; HELLER, W.; RUGGELS, S.; and SMITH S. *Job Sharing in the Public Sector.* San Francisco: New Ways to Work, 1979.

OLMSTED, B., and SMITH, S. *Job Sharing: Analyzing the Cost.* San Francisco: New Ways to Work, 1981.

OLSON, M. H., and TASLEY, R. Telecommunications and the changing definition of the workplace. Unpublished paper at the Telecommunications Policy Research Conference, New York University, April 26, 1983, p. 3.

ORPEN, C. Work and nonwork satisfaction: A causal-correlational analysis. *Journal of Applied Psychology,* 1978, *63,* 530–32.

_____. Effect of flexible working hours on employee satisfaction and performance: A field experiment. *Journal of Applied Psychology,* 1981, *66,* 113–15.

O'TOOLE, J. *Work, Learning and the American Future.* San Francisco: Jossey-Bass, 1977.

OWEN, J. D. *An Empirical Analysis of the Voluntary Part-Time Labor Market,* Springfield, Va.: National Technical Information Service, 1977.

_____ *(a).* Why part-time workers tend to be in low-wage jobs. *Monthly Labor Review,* 1978, *101,* 11–14.

_____ *(b). Working Hours.* Lexington, Mass.: Lexington Books, 1978.

Part-time social workers in public welfare. New York: Catalyst, 1971.

Part-time teachers and how they work. New York: Catalyst, 1968.

PATTEN, T. H., JR. *Pay.* New York: Free Press, 1977.

PAVLOU, S. B. *Metro's Experience with Part-Time Operators: 1978–1979.* Available from S. B. Pavlou, Metro Municipality of Metropolitan Seattle, 821–2nd Avenue, Seattle, WA 98104.

Phone company's idea is better. *New York Times,* May 18, 1975, Section E, p. 8.

POLICY AND STANDARDS DIVISION. *Final Report on Shared Positions.* Sacramento: California State Personnel Board, 1978.

POOR, R., and STEELE, J. L. Work and leisure: The reactions of people at four-day firms. In R. Poor (ed.), *4 Days, 40 Hours.* Cambridge, Mass.: Bursk and Poor, 1970.

PORT AUTHORITY OF NEW YORK AND NEW JERSEY. *Flexible Work Hours Experiment.* New York: Port Authority, 1975.

RICE, R. W.; NEAR, J. P.; and HUNT, R. G. The job-satisfaction/life-satisfaction relationship: A review of empirical research. *Basic and Applied Social Psychology,* 1980 *1,* 37–64.

RICH, L. Job sharing: Another way to work. *Worklife,* May 1978.

ROBINSON, D. *Alternative Work Patterns—Changing Approaches to Work Scheduling.* Report of Conference cosponsored by National Center for Productivity and Quality of Working Life and the Work in America Institute, Inc., New York, June 2, 1976, pp. 1–40.

ROBINSON, J. P. *How Americans Use Time: A Social-Psychological Analysis of Everyday Behavior.* New York: Praeger, 1977.

ROBINSON, O. Part-time employment in the European community. *International Labour Review,* 1979, *18.*

ROMERO, D. The invisible employee: Can you meet the challenge? *Hardcopy,* January 1983, p. 39.

RONEN, S. Arrival and departure patterns of public sector employees before and after implementation of flexitime. *Personnel Psychology,* 1981*(a), 34,* 817–22.

_____. *Flexible Working Hours: An Innovation in the Quality of Work Life.* New York: McGraw-Hill, 1981*(b).*

RONEN, S., and PRIMPS, S. B. The impact of flexitime on performance and attitudes in 25 public agencies. *Public Personnel Management,* 1980, *9,* 201–7.

_____. The compressed work week as organizational change: Behavioral and attitudinal outcomes. *Academy of Management Review,* 1981, *6,* 61–74.

ROSENBERG, G. S. Statement of the National Council for Alternate Work Patterns—before House Subcommittee on Employee Ethnics and Utilization, of the Committee on Post Office and Civil Service, July 8, 1977, pp. 3–6.

ROSOW, J. M. Quality-of-work-life issues for the 1980s. In C. Kerr and J. M. Rosow (eds.), *Work in America: The Decade Ahead.* New York: Van Nostrand, Reinhold, 1979.

ROTCHFORD, N. L., and ROBERTS, K. H. Part-time workers as missing persons in psychological research. Unpublished paper, University of California at Berkeley, 1978.

ROUSSEAU, D. M. Relationship of work to nonwork. *Journal of Applied Psychology,* 1978, *63,* 513–17.

SARASON, S. *Work, Aging and Social Changes.* New York: Free Press, 1977.

SAYLES, L. R., and STRAUSS, G. *Managing Human Resources.* Englewood Cliffs, N.J.: Prentice-Hall, 1977.

SCHEIN, E. H. *Career Dynamics: Matching Individual and Organizational Needs.* Reading, Mass.: Addison-Wesley, 1978.

SCHEIN, V. E.; MAURER, E. H.; and NOVAK, J. F. Impact of flexible working hours on productivity. *Journal of Applied Psychology,* 1977, *62,* 463–65.

SCHONBERGER, R. J. Inflexible working conditions keep women unliberated. *Personnel Journal,* 1971, *50* (November), 834–45.

SCHWARTZ, F. New work patterns for better use of womanpower. *Management Review,* 1974, *63* (May), 4–12.

SEEMAN, M. On the personal consequences of alienation in work. *American Sociological Review,* 1967, *32,* 273–85.

SELTZER, J., and WILSON, J. A. Leisure patterns among four-day workers. Working Paper 307. Graduate School of Business, University of Pittsburgh.

SHAMIR, B. A note on individual difference in the subjective evaluation of flexitime. *Personnel Psychology,* 1980, *53,* 215–17.

SILVERBERG, M. M. Part-time careers in the federal government. *The Bureaucrat,* 1972, *1,* 247–51.

SILVERBERG, M. M., and EYDE, L. D. Career part-time employment: Personnel implications of the NEW professional and executive corps. *Good Government,* 1971, 11–19.

SMITH, P. C.; KENDALL, L.; and HULIN, C. *The Measurement and Satisfaction in Work and Retirement.* Skokie, Ill.: Rand McNally, 1969.

STEERS, R. M. *Organizational Effectiveness: A Behavioral View.* Santa Monica, Calif.: Goodyear, 1977.

STEERS, R. M., and PORTER, L. W. *Motivation and Working Behavior,* McGraw-Hill, 1979.

STEIN, R. L., and MEREDITH, J. L. Growth and characteristics of the part-time work force. *Monthly Labor Review,* 1960, *83,* 66–75.

STEWART, C. A. Job sharing in municipal government: A case study in the city of Palo Alto. Stanford, Calif.: Stanford University Action Research Liaison Office, 1975.

SWART, J. C. *A Flexible Approach to Working Hours.* New York: AMACOM, 1978.

SUTTLE, J. L. Improving life at work—problems and prospects. In J. R. Hackman and J. L. Suttle (eds.), *Improving Life at Work.* Santa Monica, Calif.: Goodyear, 1978.

SWERDLOFF, S. The Revised Workweek: Results of a Pilot Study of 16 Firms. U.S. Department of Labor, Bureau of Labor Statistics, Bulletin No. 1846, 1975.

TELLIER, R. D. The four-day workweek and the elderly: A cross-sectional study. *Journal of Gerontology,* July 1974, 430–33.

TERIET, B. Flexiyear schedules—only a matter of time. *Monthly Labor Review,* December 1977, 62–65.

The army of the party employer. *Forbes,* March 2, 1977.

The workplace is changing . . . . . . but not too fast. *Daily News,* March 10, 1981, pp. 25 and 28.

TOFFLER, A. *The Third Wave* (New York: Bantam Books, 1980).

TUCKMAN, H. P., and VOGLER, W. D. Research summaries: The fringes of fringe group part-timers in academics. *Monthly Labor Review,* 1979, *102,* 46–49.

TUNSTALL, J. *The Fisherman.* London: McGibbon and Kee, 1962.

Two views of the four-day workweek. *U.S. News and World Report,* May 3 1971, p. 57.

U.S. COMPTROLLER GENERAL. Report to the Congress. "Part-Time Employment in Federal Agencies." FPCD–75–156. Washington, D.C.: U.S. General Accounting Office, January 2, 1976. Published in U.S. Congress Senate Subcommittee on Employment, Poverty and Migratory Labor of the Committee on Labor and Public Welfare. "Changing Patterns of Work in America," 1976. Hearings, 94th Congress, 2nd Session, April 7 & 8, 1976.

U.S. CONGRESS, SENATE SUBCOMMITTEE ON EMPLOYMENT, POVERTY AND MIGRATORY LABOR OF THE COMMITTEE ON LABOR AND PUBLIC WELFARE. Changing patterns of work in America. Hearings, 94th Congress, 2nd Session, April 7 & 8, 1976.

VAN MAANEN, J., and SCHEIN, E. H. Improving the quality of work life: Career development. In J. R. Hackman and J. L. Suttle (eds.), *Improving Life at Work: Behavioral Science Approach to Organizational Change.* Los Angeles: Goodyear, 1977.

Vanishing vigor: Worker output slackens around the world. *Time,* June 26, 1978.

WALTON, R. E. How to counter alienation in the plant. *Harvard Business Review,* November–December 1972, 70–81.

————. Work innovations in the United States. *Harvard Business Review,* 1979, *57,* 88–98.

WEICK, K. E. *The Social Psychology of Organizing.* Reading, Mass.: Addison-Wesley, 1979.

WERTHER, W. B., JR. Part-timers: Overlooked and undervalued. *Business Horizons,* 1975, *18* (February), 13–20.

_____. Minishifts: An alternative to overtime. *Personnel Journal,* 1976, *55,* 130–33.

WHEELER, K.; GORMAN, R.; and TARNOWIESKI, D. Four-day week: An AMA research report. New York: American Management Association, 1972.

WILENSKY, H. Work, careers, and social integration. *International Social Science Journal,* 1960, *12,* 543–60.

WILKERSON, M. B. Flexible Scheduling. Annual Meeting of the Federation of Organizations for Professional Women, Washington, D.C., 1975, pp. 1–4.

YANKELOVICH, D. Work, values and the new breed. In C. Kerr and J. M. Rosow (eds.), *Work in America: The Decade Ahead.* New York: Van Nostrand, Reinhold, 1979.

YUCHTMAN (YAAR), E., and SEASHORE, S. E. A system resource approach to organizational effectiveness. *American Sociological Review,* 1967, *32,* 891–903.

ZALUSKI, J. L. Research Department AFL–CIO. Remarks before the National Conference on Alternative Work Schedules, Chicago, March 20–22, 1977.

Index